Latin American
Diplomatic History

Latin American Diplomatic History

An Introduction

HAROLD EUGENE DAVIS

JOHN J. FINAN

F. TAYLOR PECK

Louisiana State University Press

Baton Rouge and London

1980 printing

LIBRARY OF CONGRESS CATALOGING IN PUBLICATION DATA

Davis, Harold Eugene, 1902-
    Latin American diplomatic history.

    Bibliography: p.
    Includes index.
    1.   Latin America—Foreign relations.
I.   Finan, John J., 1925-   joint author.
II.   Peck, Frederic Taylor, 1920-   joint
author.   III.   Title.
F1415.D335   327.8   76-58901
ISBN 0-8071-0260-1
ISBN 0-8071-0286-5 pbk.

Contents

Preface

In this modest volume the authors have attempted to give a comprehensive view of Latin American international history in an approach that is new, at least as far as the literature in English is concerned. Stated in simplest terms, our object is to present this history both from a general Latin American viewpoint and from the national viewpoints of the several nations, rather than from the outside, as has so often been done. This ambitious project prompts an immediate word of caution to the reader, however, warning him not to expect a definitive history of this broad scope. Such a definitive work would best be written by a Latin American scholar having a broad acquaintance with the history of all the countries, or by a group of scholars from several countries. Even so, it would be a next-to-impossible task at the present time because of great gaps in the monographic materials. What the authors of this volume have attempted, therefore, is something much more modest—merely to provide an introductory and interpretative guide for the serious reader and student.

Although the monographic literature upon which this volume is based is scanty and uneven, it is currently growing. The diplomatic background of independence, the international relations of several of the major post-independence wars, and the history of the more serious boundary disputes, have been studied extensively by scholars, though all too often tendentiously. Latin American authors have also produced a notable literature on international law, some of which bears directly on the history of the international relations. The relatively abundant research of scholars in the United States, Great Britain, France, Germany, Japan, the USSR, and other countries, tends to treat specific problems or to study policy aspects of the relations of their several nations with Latin America. These studies are eminently useful, but they do not provide anything like the general synthesis needed. Nor do they bring out the persistent tensions and conflicts among the nations—border conflicts, economic rivalries, population pressures, and ethnic clashes. The most important work of a Latin American author treating diplomatic history as such on a hemispheric basis is the three-volume *Historia Diplomática Hispanoamericana* by Vicente G. Quesada, published half a century ago (1918–1920) in Buenos Aires. An excellent work of its kind, and still very useful, the Quesada study is limited to the nineteenth century; it also lacks the advantage of access to the products of twentieth-century scholarship. A number of countries, of course, have good national diplomatic histories. These include Brazil, Argentina, Mexico, Chile, and Colombia. Others have a scanty literature.

This book is intended chiefly as a guide to open up the subject to students who intend to go further in study and interpretation; but it should also be useful in a general way in the study of Latin American history or politics, correcting the biased impressions generated by books and courses oriented narrowly toward an analysis of the Latin American policy of the United States or other countries.

Footnotes have been kept to a minimum; they are used for the most part to refer the reader to major monographic works and to published documents. A select bibliography at the end of the book will guide the student to a wider range of sources.

The authors are indebted to Professor John P. Soder of George Mason University for assistance on Chapters 6 and 7. For some of the material in the section of Chapter 9 entitled "Chile" acknowledgment is made to an unpublished paper written at The American University by Christel Converse: "Chile's Break of Diplomatic Relations with Germany in WW II and the Influence of the Germans and Chilean-Germans." For help in the laborious task of typing we thank Phyllis Levine, Jeanne Finan, and Patricia Goldberg. Charles Traub helped to prepare the bibliography.

Latin American
Diplomatic History

1 The Origins and Nature of Latin American Foreign Policies

HAROLD EUGENE DAVIS

The external relations of nations, and the policies they follow in these relationships, move within limits set by their geography, their history, and the power structures they have erected. But the effect of these factors in setting limits for the formulation of policy and conduct of relations in accordance with them is not automatic. The decision-making process in policy formulation involves rational choices among concrete alternatives, as well as the acts of will to carry out the necessary measures. The individuals and groups who make these decisions confront problems, both long range and immediate, in deciding how they will direct the power they control toward achieving certain objectives conceived to be in the national interest or in deciding that it is wiser not to act. Certain limits to freedom in these decisions are obvious. Since many of the forces and considerations involved are the same as in the domestic sphere, it follows that decisions on domestic policy matters may well influence, even control, decisions on international policy and vice versa. Moreover, geographic, economic, ethnic, and cultural conditions, while producing the popular aspirations that politicians mobilize to create political power, also set limits to the freedom of these leaders to act.

The Heritage of the Past

Historical experience, through shaping the nations, their nationalisms, and indeed their very will to act, also plays a fundamental and in some respects a limiting role in this policy making, both domestic and foreign. Thus the foreign policies of the Latin American nations are a product of all the conflicts and rivalries of the European nations in their centuries-long fight with each other for the possession of America. The foreign policies also reflect the conflicts and rivalries involved in the national struggles for independence and the many different experiences of the international relations of the new nations since achieving nationhood. Since most of these countries got their independence in the same era of modern history—the American and French Revolutionary-Napoleonic-Metternich era—they have had many comparable if not identical experiences in their histories as nations. Hence their policy aims and the principles they follow in their international relations also show many similarities.

This similarity is particularly true in the case of the Spanish American nations. Their attitudes toward Britain, for example, were shaped by the long struggle of Spain to resist the British invasion and annexation of parts of the American empire. They were modified by the British economic and military aid to Spain in the Peninsular War, by Britain's expanding trade with Spanish America during the Napoleonic era, and especially by British aid to the Spanish American republics in the last stages of their wars for independence.

Spanish American attitudes toward France differed from those toward Britain because Spain's relations with France during the colonial era were different and because France had a quite different relationship to the Spanish American struggle for independence. Spanish America inherited the effects of the crisis in the eighteenth-century French-Spanish alliance and the tragedies for the Spanish world of the Napoleonic period. One major political focus of these critical years was the Spanish national uprising against France's forcing the abdication of King Charles and Prince Ferdinand in 1808 and the imposition of Napoleon's brother Joseph as king of Spain. This revolt, ironically, gave Spain an independence movement of her own during part of the period in which her colonies were seeking their independence. But an equally critical focus was the breakup of the Spanish empire, begun during the Napoleonic years and completed during the Metternich era. Indirectly, the crisis also involved the loss, first to Spain, and subsequently to Mexico, of Louisiana and the Spanish borderlands, including Florida, New Mexico, Texas, and California, ceded to the United States. It also included the unsuccessful intrigues of Queen Carlota of Portugal-Brazil (sister of the deposed Ferdinand VII of Spain) to claim the loyalty of the Rio de la Plata region in the name of the Bourbon crown, following the imprisonment of Ferdinand in France—an intrigue that had some of its roots in the centuries-old rivalry of Portugal and Spain for the possession of South America.

Brazil inherited the Portuguese hostility to the Netherlands and France, dating from the sixteenth- and seventeenth-century intrusions of these powers into Brazil. This heritage was modified only slightly by the French cultural currents of the Enlightenment. A more basic element in Brazil's heritage from Portugal was the latter's longstanding alliance with Great Britain. This alliance had led to the transfer of the Portuguese court to Brazil, in the face of the Napoleonic invasion of 1807 (supported by Spain), and to the subsequent restoration of the Braganzas to the throne in Portugal, with the support of British arms. As we shall see, Brazil profited from this British alliance in a number of ways during her early years of independence, despite her resistance to British efforts to suppress the African slave trade. Indirectly, this British support, after independence, as during the colonial period, aided Brazilian territorial expansion into Spanish South America. Brazil also inherited the expansionism of Portugal in South America, to the expense of Spanish America.

Haiti has a notably different foreign policy heritage. She was a product of the French Revolution and of a successful slave insurrection during the radical phase of that revolutionary movement. But she was also a product of the British-directed defeat of Napoleon. Unfortunately the nature of the Haitian independence movement left her a heritage of hostility both to Britain and to Restoration France, as well as to proslavery forces in the United States. The difficulties of her international position after independence, and during much of the nineteenth century, stemmed in considerable measure from this contradictory heritage.

This mixed Latin American heritage from the past, including certain similar, though not always shared colonial experiences, as well as those shared in the achievement of independence, created the bases for a kind of hemispheric regionalism, the most important segment of which was the feeling of commonality among the Spanish American nations based on their common background and historical experiences. The ties of British, French, and Portuguese America to Spanish America were in many ways those of rivals, in the psychological sense that rivalry may be called a tie. That is to say, these non-Spanish Americans were united to Spanish America chiefly by a common interest in preventing the colonizing powers of Europe from reestablishing or increasing their control of the destinies of the new American nations. But the historical experiences of the Latin American nations contributed not only to their regionalism but also to the forming of their distinctive national characteristics, including inner contradictions arising from conflicting values and forces; they also set limits to the regional ties.

Two Axes of Relationships

André Siegfried once pointed out what he called two axes of force running through the history of Canada—one geographic, running north and south, the other historical, running east and west.[1] Latin American history may also be understood in terms of two such axes. The first, the cultural axis, is horizontal, extending in a general east-west direction. All the nations of America have cultural, political, and economic ties to their European countries of origin. Thus, the Spanish American nations are linked to Spain, while Haiti and other former French territories have ties to France, Brazil to Portugal, Surinam to the Netherlands, and Trinidad, Jamaica, the other islands of the British West Indies, Guyana, and Belize to Great Britain. These links are important lines of force in the political sense. Ties of another character link these American nations to Italy, Germany, India, Japan, China, the Slavic countries, and the Middle East, these latter ties arising from the national origins of many nineteenth- and twentieth-century immigrants. The ethnic and racial links of the American Negro populations with the new nations of Africa, though

1. André Siegfried, *Canada* (New York: Harcourt Brace, 1937).

metamorphosed by centuries of slavery, are also potential power links of increasing importance in the twentieth century, stimulated by a sense of common ethnic origin.[2]

The second axis is the center of a variety of forces that run north-south, drawing the nations of Latin America toward each other and toward the United States and Canada. This axis has special significance as the basis of the regionalism behind the various movements for hemispheric unity of some kind. The north-south ties are geographic in origin, but they are also historical, economic, and political. In some respects they are ethnic and sociological. The geographic bonds arise from the configuration of the continent, its common coast lines, its mountain chains, plains and table lands, and its international river systems. But the separation of America from the Eurasian-African land mass by great oceans is also a factor of importance that has tended to give America a history of its own.

However, the land masses of Europe, Africa, and America are in a certain sense grouped *around*, and thus united by, the North Atlantic Ocean, rather than separated by it. The communication routes across this ocean, therefore, add strength to the east-west axis, linking America with Europe and North Africa. The Caribbean Sea and the Gulf of Mexico, on the other hand, strengthen the north-south axis. These two bodies of water constitute an American sea comparable in its unifying effect to that of the Mediterranean on the relations of Europe and Africa.[3]

Historical and cultural ties of the north-south axis derive from the common American historical experiences, those of discovery, exploration, conquest, colonization. They derive from the Christianization of the natives, the achievement of national independence, and the movement for regional political unity in various forms. In certain respects, the expansion and conflict of the British, French, Dutch, Spanish, and Portuguese peoples in America were also a part of this common experience. As we shall note in the next chapter, the Latin

2. See, for example, Roy A. Glasgow, "Recent Observations on the Developing Southern Strategy of Brazil, Portugal and Africa," *Issue*, II (Fall, 1972).

3. On geopolitical factors, see Lewis A. Tambs, "Geopolitical Factors in Latin America," Chap. 2 in Norman A. Bailey (ed.), *Latin America: Politics, Economics, and Hemisphere Security* (New York, Washington, London: Frederick A. Praeger, 1965).

American nations likewise inherited the conflicts of their colonial era. Common roots of the indigenous cultures, in fact the very presence of indigenous peoples in all of the countries (preponderant in some), and the common experiences of all of the nations in dealing with them, both in the past and in modern times, constitute another element in this north-south axis. The historical experience of the large Afro-American population distributed throughout the continent, but with important concentrations in the southern part of the United States, the Caribbean area, and northern Brazil is a comparable element. This black experience is American, despite the ethnic links of Afro-America with Africa. In all the American nations the blacks are a product of the same slave trade; they share the experience of slavery in similar plantation economies, emancipation, and the bitter post-liberation experience of adaptation to a still-alien environment.

The economic ties of the Americas along this north-south axis are even more complicated than the historical and cultural ones. Historically, the markets for most American products were in Europe. For several centuries Europe supplied the necessary capital and the new technologies, as well as the requisite inflow of skilled labor. Yet even during colonial times economic contacts developed along the north-south axis. Expanding in the nineteenth century, these north-south ties grew to become a major aspect of the economic life of the twentieth century, as the United States came to be preponderantly the source of new capital and a major market for the exports of the other Americas. Economic bonds among the nations of Latin America have had lesser significance, on the whole, since independence, though these bonds had increased notably by the second half of the twentieth century.

The Reality of Latin American Regionalism

The Spanish scholar Félix Fernández Shaw opens his discussion of the history of the Organization of American States (OAS) by calling attention, in another fashion, to this double and paradoxical character of American reality.[4] From their independence movements, he points

4. Félix G. Fernández-Shaw, *La Organización de los Estados Americanos* (2nd ed.; Madrid: Ediciones Cultura Hispánica, 1963).

out, the American nations derived many basic policy aims, principles, and attitudes that were inconsistent with their European heritage. These principles include the revolutionary right of self-determination of peoples, the principle of freer international trade, that of the free movement of persons (including the right to change citizenship), and the right of opposition to slavery and to the international slave trade. They also include belief in the possibility of extending the application of international law to achieve a peaceful world within an order of self-governing nations, the commitment to prudent neutrality in European quarrels, and a dedication to achieving continental union of some sort.

Even before independence, the concept of the New World as something apart from the Old had appeared. Thus the Anglo-French treaty of 1713 defined the New World as a sphere separate from the Old and insulated from Old World controversies. The Spanish-Portuguese Treaty of Madrid (1750), fixing the boundaries of the two powers in South America, included a similar concept, as did the Commercial Treaty of the United States with France in 1778. Alberto Miramón has written that the American states initiated a new era of diplomacy, in which secret diplomacy and *raison d'etat* gave way to considerations of national and popular interests.[5]

The preceding analysis assumes the existence, in at least some respects, of a regional identity in Latin America as one of the bases of policy. The historical fact of regionalism has been discussed earlier as one of the two axes of American reality. Aspects of regionalism will be noted in subsequent chapters, especially in connection with the evolution of the Organization of American States; but the subject requires at least a brief additional mention at this point as an aspect of foreign policy. It is often asked whether foreign policy may be examined historically on a regional basis—whether regional policy is a proper subject of history. The question is by no means simple; rather it embraces several distinct questions. Is it logical, for example, to assume that nations will have similar diplomatic histories because they form a geographical region? Is it valid, in any sense, and is it true

5. Alberto Miramón, *Diplomáticos de la Libertad* (Bogotá: Empresa Nacional de Publicaciones, 1956), 9.

historically, that nations pursue different aims and follow different principles of action in respect to different regions of the world? Even this latter, seemingly simple, question is really two separate questions. The first of these questions is this: may the national interest have different objectives in various regions? This is, in effect, to ask whether certain definable regional characteristics require a differentiation in policy objectives. The second question is raised by some critics in a quite different sense. The real question to be asked, they say, is this: do regional international organizations, such as the OAS, have a valid place within an international order of peace? Or are they, rather, obstacles to attaining a world order of peace? Or, again, in a more pragmatic sense, they may ask: are regional structures valid, or even useful, instruments through which national interests may be pursued?

Even among those who assume the historical validity of a regional examination of policy, a further question arises, that of the uses of this regionalism. One school of thought, largely for historical reasons, would have the member states use the inter-American organization as much as possible in their relations with each other. Others, however, disregarding the historical implications, see the OAS as merely one of several useful channels for diplomacy, perhaps one of the least useful. Many Latin Americans in the 1970s are talking again of a Latin American regionalism apart from the union with the United States. We also have the regionalisms of the Caribbean, of the Andean group, and of Central America. The issue of regionalism has been defined even more narrowly by the expression of different attitudes in the realm of international economic relations and in hemispheric defense and military relations.

A variation of this question of the validity and usefulness of regional organization reaches to the very nature of such an organization. Some students urge the importance of strengthening the OAS, not so much in the immediate national interest, as to make it an instrument for peace in the hemisphere, strengthening the basis of world peace. Others view the OAS as largely an evil "sphere of interest," a bloc of power in world politics, a collection of satellites clustered around a great power. Still another school of thought deems the OAS fictional, illusory at best, and at worst a hindrance to building a stronger United Nations. Arthur Whitaker, in his *The Western Hemisphere Idea*, assumed that a regional consensus for the OAS existed for a time, but that after World War II it was broken up.[6] A recent study by James Vivian questions whether such a consensus existed at the time the First Inter-American Conference was planned in the 1880s.[7] Behind all three positions lies the further question: how far, if at all, is it feasible (some would say conceivable) to subordinate the national interest to the larger interest of world order?

The significance of such questions as these will appear much clearer as we follow the history of Latin American relations. For the present we should note that regionalism, so vital to a study of inter-American relations, must have a theoretical basis and that views of regionalism differ in accordance with the theories of politics that underlie them. The political realist who regards regionalism as essentially a power phenomenon rejects the idea of hemispheric unity as "Utopian," insisting that the reality of inter-American regionalism since independence is quite different from its appearance, and especially from its verbalizations. For him the history of Latin American international relations since independence is a continuation of the colonial struggle for power—the expansion of British influence at the expense of the Spanish and French empires in America. Thus he would say that the United States, albeit with a new initiative born of independence, has followed in the path already carved out by Britain. Entering upon the world scene just as the Napoleonic wars were precipitating the end of the Spanish empire, the United States shared with the British empire the benefits of this Spanish imperial collapse.

In a more philosophical mood, the "realist" will admit the influence of the national myth—its effects on the ideals and objectives which the nations have created out of their history. But he will tend to see

6. Arthur P. Whitaker, *The Western Hemisphere Idea* (Ithaca, New York: Cornell University Press, 1954).

7. James F. Vivian, "The Politics of Pan-Americanism, 1884–1890" (Ph.D. dissertation, The American University, 1971).

these "ideals" as illusory and fictional. Thus, for the British scholar Gordon Connell-Smith, regionalism, in its stark reality, is merely a structure or sphere of power or influence.[8] From this standpoint, Latin American foreign policy must in general be interpreted in a negative sense—as resistance or submission to outside power.

The philosophical idealist, on the other hand, may insist that the "principles" of inter-Americanism are truer definitions, both of national objectives and of national power. He sees their particular importance in the fact that they not only define the directions toward which power moves but that they also *are* power *because* they have direction. For him this concept is the meaning or direction of history, and it expresses the values in accordance with which the nation has the capacity to commit the national will in action. This is the concept represented in S. G. Inman's *Problems of Pan-Americanism* and in his *History of Inter-American Conferences* (1826–1954); it also appears in the writing of the Chilean international lawyer Alejandro Alvarez.[9]

Whatever theory or philosophy it may rest upon, regionalism has two quite distinct aspects in the pragmatic sense. The first is the national aspect, the regional character which the policy of nations may acquire, as expressed in treaties or other agreements defining common objectives and establishing rules or principles of conduct in their relations with each other. The second aspect is the international, that of the policies adopted and pursued by regional international bodies. In America, this aspect of regionalism became increasingly important after World War II through the growth of the OAS.

Obviously, national policies seek similar objectives in the various

8. Gordon Connell Smith, *The Inter-American System* (London and New York: Oxford University Press, 1966).

9. S. G. Inman, *Inter-American Conferences, 1826–1954: History and Problems* (Washington: University Press of Washington, D.C., 1965), Chap. 15; Alejandro Alvarez, *The Monroe Doctrine: Its Importance in the International Life of the States of the New World* (New York: Oxford University Press, 1924). On regionalism as a basis for international organization see Pitman B. Potter, "Universalism versus Regionalism in International Organization," *American Political Science Review*, XXXVII (October, 1943), 850–62, and "Regional Organization Today," *World Affairs*, CXXIV (1961), 45–46, in which he changed his view. See also Whitaker, *The Western Hemisphere Idea*, Antonio Gómez Robledo, *Idea y Experiencia de América* (Mexico: Fondo de Cultura Económica, 1958), Chaps. 1 and 11, and Luis Quintanilla, *Pan Americanism and Democracy* (Boston: Boston University Press, 1952).

parts of the world and hence cannot differ in certain fundamentals for the various areas, however much they may have regionally oriented aims and principles. In this connection, it is interesting to note the frequently expressed USSR view that policy must be universal. The Soviet Union reconciles this view with great flexibility in the strategy and tactics it may be using, including its ties under the Warsaw Pact and the regionalism expressed in the Brezhnev "doctrine." Universality of basic objectives also characterizes the policies of the Latin American nations, especially as all of them have insisted upon making international law an objective and a basis of international policy. In their public commitments, as we shall see, the nations of Latin America have seen no basic conflict between this tendency to seek universality and the regionalism arising from historical and geographical factors peculiar to the Americas. Rather, they have reconciled their regionalism with universalism, as in the Declaration of Mexico adopted at Chapultepec in 1945, by insisting that they stand ready to extend to other nations the application of the regional principles which they accept among themselves. They have also reconciled the subregionalisms of the Caribbean, of Central America, and of the Andean group with that of the Inter-American System. In general, they also tend to think of a Latin American economic union of some kind as not inconsistent with the larger continental system.

International Law in Latin American Foreign Policies

The new nations of Latin America gained independence and faced the necessity of defining the bases of their independence in an era in which international law seemed to be taking on added importance. It is not surprising, therefore, that they came to attach special significance to certain principles such as the rights of neutrals, freedom of the high seas, the recognition of de facto (rather than "legitimate") governments, the right to emigrate and change nationality, and the peaceful settlement of international disputes by arbitration and in accordance with principles of law.

Like the United States, in whose footsteps they followed in this matter, the nations of Latin America tended to make such principles the bases of their foreign policies, both in relations with each other and with the nations of Europe. An illustration of this role of international law may be seen in the fact that a great Spanish American scholar, Andrés Bello, who acted as an advisor in the Chilean foreign office, also produced the first significant treatise of international law in Spanish America.[10] These nations also developed certain principles of public law more characteristically their own. Thus, the Spanish American countries followed the recommendation of Simón Bolívar in adopting the principle *uti possidetis juris*, in accordance with which they followed the provincial lines as of 1810 in settling their national boundaries. Brazil followed a similar, but more pragmatic principle of *uti possidetis actual*, that of adverse possession as of the date on which a boundary settlement was made.

The Spanish Americans often extended certain rights of citizenship to each others' nationals, and to those of Spain. They established, and later incorporated in treaties, the right of diplomatic asylum in their embassies for political refugees within host countries. They developed the Calvo principle, named for Carlos Calvo, a noted Argentine diplomat and jurist. This principle, which came to be incorporated in international agreements for foreign investment, provided that the foreign capitalist should accept as final the jurisdiction of the laws of the host country and should not appeal to his own government for any special intervention. Another Argentine principle, the Drago Doctrine (also originating with Calvo) went further, rejecting the traditional right of intervention and declaring that economic claims should never give rise to a legal right to intervene by force in another country.

The nineteenth-century movement for Spanish American union, once the need for a strong negotiating position against Spain had passed (roughly by the time of the Panama Congress of 1826), tended to evolve into a movement for codification or development of international law on a hemispheric (basically Spanish American) basis. This trend or movement continued under the Pan American Union (after 1890) and under the Organization of American States (after 1948). One of its unique achievements is the incorporation of the Bus-

10. Andrés Bello, *Derecho Internacional*, ed. Miguel Luis Amunátegui (Santiago: Impreso de Pedro G. Ramírez, 1886), Vol. X of *Obras Completas*.

tamente code of *private* international law in a treaty ratified by most of the Latin American nations.

In the late nineteenth century, as we shall see, the United States adopted an interventionist policy developed under the Roosevelt Corollary of the Monroe Doctrine. At Montevideo, in 1933, the United States, with the other nations of America, abandoned this policy and accepted the Drago principle as rule of law. The principle of nonintervention, incorporated in the Montevideo Treaty on the Rights and Duties of States, was carried even further in the Buenos Aires (1936) Protocol to the Montevideo Treaty. These two documents became a fundamental basis of the newly evolving Inter-American System.

In this connection it may be noted that certain principles underlying the Inter-American System (the structure of treaties, institutions, and agencies of which the OAS is the political arm) are better understood when viewed from the Latin American standpoint, however interiorly contradictory the Latin American positions may seem. These principles fall into two categories: (1) those derived from the common origins of a family of nations having common problems, such as the principle of *uti possidetis* applied to boundary questions and the principles applied in dealing with the rights of foreigners, both Spanish American and other, and (2) those best understood as reactions of defense against the expansionism and interventionism of the United States (as well as against interventionism by other Latin American states) and also as exemplified in the Drago and Estrada doctrines.

The Latin American nations have evolved several new principles relating to the recognition of new governments, as distinct from the recognition of newly independent nations. These principles have an obvious origin in the Latin American experience of revolutionary change in governments. The most distinctive of these principles is that connected with the name of the Mexican foreign minister, Genaro Estrada. The Estrada Doctrine denies the right to withhold recognition of any new revolutionary government. This principle is presented as the complete recognition of the right of popular (revolutionary) sovereignty.

A second principle relating to recognition, one which evolved with the beginning of this century, is quite different. The Ecuadorian diplomat-jurist Carlos R. Tobar proposed a principle of policy that subsequently found expression in treaties and in practice. It was the principle followed by President Woodrow Wilson and the ABC countries (Argentina, Brazil, Chile) in dealing with the problem of recognition of one of the competing revolutionary regimes in Mexico after the overthrow of President Francisco Madero in 1913. In accordance with the Tobar principle, nations should agree to withhold recognition from any government that came into existence by violent rebellion against its predecessor, in order to strengthen the structure of constitutional democracy. A post–World War II version of the Tobar principle, as we shall see, was expressed by President Rómulo Betancourt of Venezuela in the 1960s.

A third principle of recognition was proposed by an Uruguayan minister of foreign relations, Alberto Guani, during World War II. Guani, then chairman of the Emergency Committee on Political Defense with headquarters in Montevideo, proposed that during the wartime crisis the American nations consult before recognizing a new government that came into existence by revolution. This policy was followed in dealing with the revolutionary regime in Bolivia in 1944. A related principle for dealing with revolutionary regimes that threatened the democratic process was subsequently advanced by another Uruguayan foreign minister, Eduardo Rodríguez Larreta, who proposed resort to multilateral collective action in such cases, said that such action should not be considered intervention within the terms of the 1933 Treaty on the Rights and Duties of States. In a much attenuated form, this proposal ultimately found a place in the Rio de Janeiro Treaty of Reciprocal Assistance (1947).[11]

A number of other principles of public law have emerged in the experience of the Latin American nations, as we shall see. Among these must be recognized the important American Declaration of the

11. On international law in Latin America consult H. B. Jacobini, *A Study of the Philosophy of International Law as Seen in the Works of Latin American Writers* (The Hague: Martinus Nijhoff, 1954), and A. V. W. and A. J. Thomas, *The Organization of American States* (Dallas: Southern Methodist University, 1963). On the Estrada, Tobar, Brum, and Rodríguez Larreta principles see John L. Mecham, *The United States and Inter-American Security* (Austin: University of Texas Press, 1961), 116, 232–33, 287–88.

Rights of Man adopted at Bogotá in 1948, a document that influenced the development of the comparable United Nations Declaration of Human Rights and that later produced the Organization of American States Commission on Human Rights.[12]

Four Facets of Latin American International Relations

In the following chapters the reader will see that the historical international relations of Latin America have four distinguishable facets. The one most familiar is that of the relations of the Latin American nations with the United States. The role of the United States as a world power in the twentieth century has given special and at times seemingly overwhelming significance to this aspect of Latin American politics. A second facet is that of the relations and policies of Latin America with non-American states. The chief nations involved until the present century have been Britain, France, Spain, and Portugal. In recent decades, however, the relations with Communist Russia and China, with Japan, and with the "Third World" have achieved great importance. The third facet is that of the relations of the Latin American nations with each other. The fourth facet, the most truly international, is that of the Organization of American States as the regional international organization of the Americas, and the subregional organizations. This facet includes the policies of the various nations towards the OAS and the policies of both the OAS and of the several nations toward the United Nations and other universal international organizations. All four of these facets, as the reader will see, figure in the history of Latin American international relations.

The Historical Periods

The first period to be examined in this history of Latin American relations is the prenational era. Colonial conflicts and rivalries in the exploration, conquest, and colonization of America will be treated as the basis of subsequent problems of the independent nations. An argument might well be made at this point for studying the relations of the European conquerors with the native Americans and with the king-

12. Mecham, *The United States and Inter-American Security*.

doms of Africa from which millions of slave workers were taken for the plantations and mines of America. Indigenous linguistic, ethnic, and political ties also complicated international boundary problems in various ways, before and after independence. But, in the main, the conflicts that will be traced here are those of the European powers, especially Spain, Portugal, France, Britain, and the Netherlands during the colonial years.

The second period, and the earliest national phase, is that of the relations of the movements for independence (1791–1825). These movements are linked historically with the North American and French revolutions and with the developments of the Napoleonic and Metternich eras. The successful movements for independence in Spanish and Portuguese America came during the last half of the period: Spanish America from 1808 to 1825 and Brazil in 1821. The independence of Haiti (1791–1804) came during the first half of this era, although the movement had earlier beginnings. The culmination of these movements was among the new problems to be confronted in Europe and America after the end of the Napoleonic conflicts. This second period came to an end with a series of significant events, including the withdrawal of Britain from the Quadruple Alliance, the United States' treaty of 1819 with Spain (providing for the acquisition of Florida and defining a transcontinental boundary separating the possessions of Spain and the United States from the Atlantic to the Pacific coasts), and the recognition of the independence of Spanish and Portuguese America, first by the United States and Britain, and soon by others.

The events that marked the end of this second period also initiated the third phase (1825–1860). The three and a half decades after 1825 were a "time of troubles." They saw an often frustrating search for the basis of national stability in Latin America as well as a search for national foreign policies. During these years, the United States, now in possession of Florida and Louisiana, expanded its activity to dominate the Gulf of Mexico. Texas acquired independence (1836) and later was annexed to the United States. A war between the United States and Mexico (1846–1848) brought the cession to the United States of the southwest territories, including California. The United States expansionism of these years also included an unsuccessful effort to purchase Cuba from Spain during the 1850s. These were also years of bitter rivalry between the United States and Britain in respect to the routes across the Isthmus of Central America, routes which had become crucially important to the United States after the expansion of her territory to the Pacific coast.

During the years of this third phase the Latin American nations confronted problems of establishing political and commercial relations with the nations of Europe and with each other, as well as the difficulties of reaching agreements with the Vatican on Church-state relationships. Internal factional strife which prevented agreement upon national political structure, uncertain national boundaries, and unstable finances produced conditions of anarchy that invited intervention by European powers as well as by Latin American states in each other's political lives. Civil wars occurred in most countries. The National War of Central America drove out the filibuster William Walker. The first war of Chile against Peru and Bolivia took place, and Brazil joined with Uruguay and the Argentine provinces of Corrientes and Entre Rios to drive Juan Manuel Rosas from power in Buenos Aires. Armed interventions by Britain and France troubled the relations of Mexico and of the Río de la Plata countries. The movement for Spanish American union, although revived from time to time, went no further than the abortive congress assembled by Bolívar at Panama in 1826.

The fourth period (1860–1870) is what we have called in Chapter 5 a period of transition, of conflicts and challenges that introduced a new era of power politics. The period began with a series of wars in various parts of the hemisphere and was characterized in general by a new form of power struggle within America. It was a time of testing the survival ability of the newly acquired national stability in Spanish America. The period paralleled the Civil War in the United States (1861–1865) and embraced the European intervention in Mexico leading to the short-lived empire of Maximilian. It included the unsuccessful Ten Years' War (1868–1878) for Cuban independence and such power struggles in Latin America as the reestablishment of Spanish authority in the Dominican Republic, the war of Spain against Peru and Chile that grew out of Spanish seizure of the Chincha Islands, and the war of Brazil, Uruguay, and Argentina against the Paraguay of Francisco Solano López (1865–1870).

A fifth period (1870–1900) reveals the new power politics as having some connections with the European "economic imperialism." During this period, also, the movement for Spanish American union was transformed into a movement seeking agreement upon a body of rules and principles of international law. The War of the Pacific (1879–1882), in the course of which Chile occupied and annexed the Bolivian and Peruvian territories of Atacama, Tarapacá, Tacna, and Arica, brought the period to a close. No major part of Latin America was untouched by these struggles.

During the sixth historical period (1900–1930) United States interventionism under the Roosevelt Corollary became a major issue in the relations of many of the nations, producing a wave of anti-Americanism and efforts to unite the Latin Americans in an anti-interventionist stand. U.S. encouragement of the independence of Panama brought a rift with Colombia, healed only by the treaty of 1921. The opening of the Panama Canal revolutionized the transportation for west-coast South America. The revolution in Mexico troubled the relations of that country after 1910, especially those with Great Britain and the United States; but it also involved the good offices of several of the Latin American nations to deal with the issues raised. World War I produced a crisis in Latin American foreign trade; it led in general to a troubled neutrality, in some cases favoring the cause of the central powers, in others that of the allies and the United States. Regulation of the boom industry of petroleum involved Mexico in serious controversies with the United States and Britain. After 1920 a second petroleum boom in Venezuela and Colombia raised similar questions.

Britain, which had been the major source of foreign capital for Latin America, yielded first place to the United States after World War I. This change accompanied the growth of a new expansionism in the United States, earlier expressed in U.S. intervention in the war for Cuban independence in 1898. This United States expansionism was part of the larger spread of the so-called economic imperialism of the era and was connected with the increasingly close identification on the part of the United States with the world interests of Britain and her allies of the World War I era. Britain continued, of course, to play a major role in Latin American relations during the interwar years, although her influence was declining.

Surprisingly enough, the Inter-American System expanded, though slowly, during the years 1889–1928 in a series of conferences, although almost falling apart in the Santiago conference (1923). The ambivalence of the United States, which simultaneously pursued contradictory policies of inter-Americanism and expansionist-interventionism, was matched by a Latin American ambivalence of repulsion against and attraction toward the increasingly powerful northern neighbor.

Several decades were to pass before this ambivalence in inter-American relations and the policy dilemmas it presented to both Latin and North America were understood sufficiently to effect, even to a small degree, a hemispheric understanding. Unfortunately, the resolution achieved in the 1930s was to be essentially a negative one, based largely upon the principle of nonintervention. This resolution of the dilemma made possible some effective collaboration during World War II; but it postponed to the postwar period the more difficult problems of constructive political and economic cooperation.

The years 1930–1945, treated in Chapters 8 and 9, included the collapse of world trade and credit structures (the Great Depression) and the Second World War; they constitute a seventh period in inter-American relations. The 1930s are often referred to as the years of the Good Neighbor policy, although some scholars see this Good Neighbor phase running through World War II.[13] From the standpoint of relations with the United States, the essential changes were two: acceptance of the principle of nonintervention and adoption of the policy of reciprocal trade (import tarriff) agreements. German, Italian, and Japanese trade drives made headway during the

13. Bryce Wood, *The Making of the Good Neighbor Policy* (New York and London: Columbia University Press, 1961) and Donald Marquand Dozer, *Are We Good Neighbors? Three Decades of Inter-American Relations, 1930–1960* (Gainesville: University of Florida Press, 1959).

1930s and the propaganda accompanying them evoked some political support. But in the final analysis Latin America accepted the Hull program of reciprocal trade treaties as a preferable alternative to the German barter agreements. As the European crisis evolved into World War II, the Latin American nations participated in creating, out of the previously weak Pan-American Union, the structure of a regional organization of great potential strength by the time of the Chapultepec Conference of 1945.

When President Franklin D. Roosevelt announced the Good Neighbor policy in 1933, shortly after assuming office, the United States had for some time, under the Hoover administration, been reassessing its interventions in Haiti, the Dominican Republic, and Nicaragua, and had begun to consider revision of the treaty with Panama and of the Platt Amendment provisions in the treaty with Cuba. In 1929 the Department of State had published Reuben J. Clark's *Memorandum on the Monroe Doctrine*, which pointed out that the original statement of President Monroe did not include any of the interventionist doctrines subsequently added to it. When a wave of Latin American revolutions occurred in 1930, the United States had announced it was returning to the older principle of recognition of de facto governments.

The effect of this new policy on Latin American relations appeared in a more positive sense when the United States avoided direct military intervention in Cuba at the time of the revolution of 1933/34, and soon thereafter revised her treaty with Cuba to eliminate the Platt Amendment. In the seventh Inter-American Conference, at Montevideo (1933), the United States yielded to the Latin American demand and solemnly pledged nonintervention. The principle of hemisphere consultation in the event of an international crisis was established at Buenos Aires (1936) and Lima (1938). During the years of World War II, the United States at first acted in very close partnership with the nations of the Americas in hemispheric defense.[14] After the Allies regained control of the Atlantic shipping lanes, and the war scene shifted to the African and European theaters, inter-American

14. See Stetson Conn and Byron Fairchild, *The Western Hemisphere: The Framework of Hemisphere Defense* (Washington: Office of the Chief of Military History, Department of the Army, 1960).

collaboration became relatively less significant. Yet, as the war neared its end, the Chapultepec Conference (1945) was able to chalk up substantial gains in strengthening inter-American relationships, with corresponding changes in national policies.[15]

An eighth and contemporary phase in inter-American relations, treated in Chapter 10, began about 1947. Anticommunism came to be an important domestic political issue in Latin American countries about this time, bringing the "cold war" to Latin America. But many of the nations, particularly the large countries, tended to resist the efforts of the United States to draw them into the cold war in a close alignment against Soviet Communist power; they rightly felt that their interests were being neglected by the United States because of her preoccupation with the economic and defense problems of Europe and Asia. This attitude expressed itself especially in response to the reluctance of the United States to hold a conference on hemisphere economic policy agreed upon at Chapultepec in 1945, including implicit arrangements for an inter-American bank and for commodity price supports.

During these years an enlarged and more vigorous OAS, under the leadership of Latin American secretaries-general, gave several demonstrations of how such an organization could deal effectively with threats to the peace in the hemisphere. But application of the provisions of the OAS charter and of the Rio de Janeiro Treaty of Reciprocal Assistance introduced new conflicts centered in relations of the governments of Guatemala, Cuba, and the Dominican Republic. Economic multilateral cooperation lagged until the Buenos Aires Economic Conference of 1957 produced a sufficient Latin American consensus on such basic measures as an inter-American bank, commodity agreements, and regional economic cooperation—the measures essential to the Alliance for Progress launched three years later. Political relationships with the nations of Europe slowly revived; those with the Soviet Union were mainly clandestine, through the Communist parties, until the Cuban Revolutionary government entered an entente with the USSR.

---

15. See my Chapter 17 in Floyd Cave (ed.), *Origins and Consequences of World War II* (New York: Dryden, 1948).

A ninth period may well be distinguished, as suggested in Chapter 11. This is a period following the cold war—the years since the Cuban Revolution—including the years of the Alliance for Progress and the consequent movements toward Latin American integration.

2 Colonial Backgrounds

HAROLD EUGENE DAVIS

Much as they may have wished to do so, the new nations of Latin America were unable to escape their colonial heritage as part of the European power struggle for empire in America. These centuries-long struggles had profound continuing influence on the independence movements, as we shall see. In fact, in an important sense, the independence movements were an outgrowth and continuation of these struggles of the French Revolutionary, Napoleonic, and Metternich eras. After independence, these rivalries continued to affect the economic and political foreign relations of the new nations; they found that their foreign policies had ineradicable roots in their past. Particularly, they found themselves continuing, in some form, the old colonial territorial rivalries.

The most significant elements in these colonial backgrounds are: the conflict between England and Spain, the struggle for empire and European hegemony between Britain and France into which the Anglo-Spanish struggle merged in the eighteenth century, the Portuguese-British alliance, and the emerging economic and political power (especially after their independence) of the British North American colonies.

Bases of European Claims to America

European claims to territory in America had several bases, all assuming that Christian Europeans had rights superior to those of the natives. The Spanish and Portuguese claims rested fundamentally on

23

the right of discovery, exploration, and conquest, plus a papal sanction based upon the undertaking of the Spanish and Portuguese monarchs to Christianize the natives. All of America was awarded to the two Iberian nations on these principles; a papal bull of Alexander VI (1493) then drew a line of demarcation separating the claims of the two nations, leaving only the eastern tip of Brazil to Portugal. The following year (1494) the Treaty of Tordesillas moved this line westward to a point 370 leagues west of the Cape Verde Islands, giving Portugal about a fourth of present-day Brazil and Spain all of the interior of the South American continent, including the valleys of the Orinoco, the Amazon, and the Plata. Subsequently, of course, the Portuguese greatly expanded this territory at the expense of Spanish claims.

The other nations of Europe challenged this Iberian legal monopoly, claiming that territorial rights were valid only when exploration was followed by actual settlement. Thus both France and England established rival claims in both North and South America in the sixteenth and seventeenth centuries. The Portuguese drove the French from Brazil in the sixteenth century, and the effort of Sir Walter Raleigh to establish a British colony in Guiana failed at that time. But eventually France and Great Britain established claims to much of North America (originally all Spanish under the papal bull of 1493) as well as to islands in the Caribbean (Haiti, Jamaica, and others), to Belize in Central America, and to parts of Guiana in South America. For roughly a century (1689–1783) they fought a series of wars in which they vied for power in Europe, but also fought over their territories in Asia and America. France was expelled from North America as a result of these wars, but retained such important island possessions in the Caribbean as Haiti, Martinique, Guadeloupe, and her portion of Guiana (Cayenne) in South America.

In the course of Portugal's war for independence from Spain (1580–1640), the Dutch made use of this advantage to expropriate much of the Portuguese trading empire in the Far East; they also moved into New York, Guiana, and parts of northern Brazil. From Brazil they were dislodged only after Portugal acquired independence from Spain, and then largely by Brazilian colonial forces. This action of the Brazilians is an obvious parallel to the action of the British colonists in North America in the Seven Years' War, in which the French were driven from Canada (except that the French were not the intruders). The Dutch remained in Guiana, displaced only temporarily during the Napoleonic wars and ultimately dividing their lands there with the British at the conclusion of the wars.

The British-Portuguese Alliance

One of the oldest and most significant alliances in modern European history is that of Great Britain and Portugal. The alliance has historical roots reaching as far back as a treaty of 1373 signed by Edward III of England and Fernando of Portugal, but in the most significant sense it dates from the independence of Portugal from Spain in 1640. Britain supported Portugal in gaining this independence from Spain and entered into the treaties of 1642, 1654, and 1661, under which she exploited both the advantages of trade with Portugal and Brazil, as well as the opportunities to utilize the strategic position of Portugal in her own rivalry with the power of France and in controversies relating to overseas trade and possessions. By the eighteenth century, after the treaties of Methuen (1703) and Utrecht (1713), the Portuguese was the most advantageous trade the British merchants conducted. It was basically the exchange of British woolens for Portuguese wines, largely free of duties; it was enlarged by a substantial contraband trade with the British American colonies and in Brazilian gold and diamonds.[1] Despite the predominance achieved by the British (and North American) traders in the slave trade of the eighteenth century, the British seem to have largely respected the Portuguese monopoly of this trade between Angola and Brazil, although some contraband seems to have occurred.

Dutch in America

The Dutch intrusions in Ibero-America lessened after Portugal and the Netherlands both gained their independence from Spain, more particularly after the expulsion of the Dutch from northern Brazil (by

1. See Alan K. Manchester, *British Pre-eminence in Brazil* (Chapel Hill: University of North Carolina Press, 1933), Chaps. 1 and 2.

1654) and Cromwell's defeat of the Dutch in the trade wars of the mid–seventeenth century. The Dutch contraband trade in America decreased thereafter, and Dutch interests were largely confined to Guiana and a few islands in the Caribbean. After 1689 the Dutch overseas interests and Dutch foreign policy coincided in large degree with those of Great Britain, at least until the end of the Seven Years' War. In the War of the American Revolution, however, the Netherlands exhibited friendship for the cause of the North American colonies, and during the French Revolutionary-Napoleonic era the Netherlands came under French dominance. Thus she became the object of British attacks upon her possessions (*e.g.*, Cape of Good Hope and Guiana). In this way the Dutch continued to be a significant factor (not always recognized) in the background of the diplomacy of Latin American independence.

Franco-Spanish Relations

France has played an important role in Latin American foreign relations since independence. It is therefore important to note the relations of France with Spain and Portugal during the colonial years. Until the end of the Thirty Years' War (1648) the basic power struggle in Europe was that between Spain and France. It was in the last stages of this conflict that the Anglo-Portuguese alliance was born. Thereafter, Spain came increasingly under French influence, especially after the accession of a Bourbon prince (Philip V) to the Spanish throne at the beginning of the eighteenth century. This Franco-Spanish tie increased in importance during the century, explaining the cession of French Louisiana to Spain at the end of the Seven Years' War (as compensation for the loss of Florida), rather than allowing it to fall into British hands. Within this context the alliance with Portugal took on added political significance for Britain, as a useful means of counteracting this Bourbon family compact. After the American Revolution Britain had some success in establishing better relations with Spain, to the extent of getting British-Spanish cooperation against the French. But this process was interrupted by the French Revolution, especially after Thermidor, when the policy of the Directorate and Talleyrand succeeded in winning back the loyalty of Spain to France.

This temporary Franco-Spanish realignment was broken again, of course, when in 1810 Britain came to the support of the Spanish rebellion against Napoleon's imposition of his brother Joseph on the Spanish throne.

Spanish-Portuguese Relations

The relations of Spain and Portugal in the eighteenth century have a special importance as elements in the background of the foreign relations of the nations of South America, if for no other reason than that Brazil is contiguous to all of the other nations in the continent except Chile and Ecuador (unless the Ecuadorian *irredenta* claim is accepted). In a more general sense, they are important also for the nations of the middle of the continent, since, as suggested above, Portugal was caught up in the British-led struggle against the predominant power position of France and her ally Spain in Europe. Whether on this account, or because of the restlessness and expansionism of the Brazilian colonists, the Portuguese territorial claims in South America had begun to expand well beyond the lines of the 1494 treaty by the time (1750) the two powers addressed themselves to drawing a new boundary line. One of the key points of controversy at this time was the Portuguese colony and trading center, Colonia do Sacramento, established in 1680 on the Río de la Plata, well within Spanish territory under the Treaty of Tordesillas. The new line as drawn in 1750 more than doubled Portuguese (Brazilian) territory. Consistent with the Spanish policy of neutrality at that time, the treaty included the "two spheres" theory that European conflicts would not affect colonial relationships. The approval of this treaty proved less difficult than securing its acceptance and its execution in America.[2]

The execution of the treaty encountered serious opposition, especially from the Jesuit missionaries in Paraguay among the Guarani Indians. They viewed the transfer of their mission's territory to Por-

2. The standard work on the treaty of 1750 is Jaime Cortesão (ed.), *Alexandre de Gusmão e o Tratado de Madrid (1750)* (8 vols.; Rio de Janeiro: Ministerio de Relacões Exteriores, Instituto Rio Branco, 1950–1960). See also João Pandiá Calogeras, *A Política Exterior do Imperio* (2 vols; Rio de Janeiro: Impresa Nacional, 1927), I, Chaps. 7 and 8.

tuguese sovereignty as a direct threat of enslavement of their Indian wards, and they were so successful in organizing opposition to the transfer that the two countries agreed to set aside the treaty (1761). By a later treaty, adopted in 1777, the Portuguese yielded on their claims to the Jesuit missions (from which the Jesuits had meanwhile been expelled, from the Portuguese empire in 1759 and from the Spanish empire in 1767),[3] as well as to Colonia do Sacramento. But the treaty confirmed Portuguese possession of lands from Rio Grande do Sul to the banks of the Guaporé, as well as to most of the vast Amazon basin. The boundaries were never surveyed and marked, however, so that after independence Brazil inherited unsettled boundaries with all her Spanish American neighbors, as well as with the European-controlled Guianas to the north. Rival claims to much of Paraguay and Uruguay were to be especially troublesome, as Portugal pushed her territorial claims further during the troubled Napoleonic years, reclaiming the Banda Oriental and pushing northward into the Guianas. The fact that the seat of the Portuguese empire moved to Brazil in 1807–08 gave a special importance to the Portuguese rivalry with Spain, even to the point that the Princess Carlota, wife of the Portuguese prince regent (later King João VI) and sister of the imprisoned Ferdinand, assumed the authority to represent the Bourbon royal claims in South America.

Franco-British Relations

British-French colonial relations also furnished a basic element in the Latin American heritage, in the sense that the series of armed conflicts sometimes called the Second Hundred Years' War[4] established a new balance of colonial power in America, increasingly tilted toward Great Britain. Vicente Palacio Atard has pointed out that possession of America was the great preoccupation in the negotiations leading to the Peace of Utrecht (1713), the settlement which began the process of replacing France as the first power in North America.

3. See Magnus Mörner, *The Expulsion of the Jesuits from Latin America* (New York: Alfred A. Knopf, 1965), 117–172.
4. Arthur H. Buffington, *The Second Hundred Years War, 1689–1815* (New York: Henry Holt and Company, 1929).

By this settlement Britain got an opening wedge in the trade with the Spanish colonies, including a right of deposit in the Río de la Plata, while Portugal, as we have seen, recovered the Colonia do Sacramento and increased her territory in Guiana. French opinion accepting the desirability of a balance in America was expressed by the Marquis de Mirabeau, writing in *L'Ami des Hommes* (1758) that a balance in America was necessary to the tranquility of Europe.[5]

Spanish-British Relations

The changing character of Spanish-British relations in the eighteenth century had special significance in the independence and post-independence relations of the Spanish American nations. In general the history of those relations was one of continued expansion of British settlements and commerce around the periphery of the Spanish empire, accompanied by a growing British trade that included trade in African slaves with the Spanish colonies, partly legal but largely contraband.

At the end of the War of the Spanish Succession (1713), as noted, Britain acquired the right to send one ship of merchandise annually to the Spanish colonies. She also acquired a monopoly (for a time) of the trade in slaves from Africa. The volume of this trade grew during the century, especially in the Caribbean, where the British were established in Jamaica and other islands of the Antilles, and where they had lumbering rights in Belize. But this growth of British commerce was not without difficulties. The War of Jenkins' Ear (1739) was one such difficulty, resulting from the Spanish capture of British traders. It initiated a trade war that gradually merged with the general European and colonial power struggle.

Defeated in the War of Jenkins' Ear, Spain adopted a policy of isolation and neutrality in the power struggle under Ferdinand VI ("El Sabio"). In a certain sense this neutrality was reflected in the provision of "the two spheres" in the Spanish-Portuguese treaty of 1750, separating the issues of the European power struggle from New

5. Vicente Palacio Atard, "El Equilibrio de América en la Diplomacia del Siglo XVIII," *Estudios Americanos* (Sevilla), I (May, 1949), 461–79, quoting Mirabeau.

World colonial matters. Lawrence Henry Gipson has called our attention to the nearly successful effort of Great Britain to establish
friendly relations with Spain by settling all the trade and other problems of the two nations in the Caribbean, including those of logging,
in the years just before the "enlightened monarch" Charles III, Ferdinand's successor, allowed Spain to be drawn by France into the
Seven Years' War in time to share defeat with her ally.[6] In this war
the British captured Manila and Havana, but returned them to Spain
under the Treaty of Paris (1765) in exchange for Florida. As previously
noted, France ceded Louisiana to Spain in compensation for this loss
of Florida and to prevent it from falling into British hands. During
this war Spain drove the British log-cutters out of Belize, but after the
war she allowed them to return.

The British policy after the Seven Years' War of seeking peace with
Spain and increasing trade with her and her American colonies was
not as successful as the policy toward Portugal, either commercially or
politically. In part this was because Spain was vigorously restructuring her empire for more effective administration and promoting imperial trade. Texas and California were at this time occupied by Christian missions (Franciscan) protected by garrisons of troops. The
Spanish organized an effective colonial militia; new vice-royalties
were established in Río de la Plata and New Granada; and Buenos
Aires was opened for direct trade with Spain. A system of intendants
was established throughout the empire, following the recommendations of the *visitador* and later colonial minister, José de Gálvez, to promote trade and administer colonial finances.

Spain reluctantly followed France into the War of the American
Revolution, though not coming to any political agreement with the
new republic. Again she drove British log-cutters out of Belize, and
again allowed them to return. A Spanish expedition captured Florida
and penetrated into the lower eastern Mississippi valley, reestablishing trading relations with the Indians of that area. Spain's recovery of
the Banda Oriental, by the treaty of 1777, was also a product of this
new power situation. Britain returned Florida to Spain, although she

6. "Anglo-Spanish New World Issues," *American Historical Review*, LI (July, 1946), 627–
48.

had half promised it to the U.S. Her loss of the North American colonies with French and Spanish support had shown the bankruptcy of
Britain's foreign policy that produced her virtual isolation in the war.
After the war, therefore, she sought again to establish a Spanish
commercial and political understanding, as well as to gain back the
friendship of the Netherlands, Prussia, and Russia, all of whom had
supported the cause of United States independence. The result was a
short-lived alliance (as noted) against the French Revolutionary regime, an alliance that lasted until Talleyrand renewed the French-
Spanish alliance under the Directory.

After this renewal of the Franco-Spanish alliance, Britain again
treated Spain in some ways as an enemy, while courting the trade of
the Spanish American colonies. Her control of the seas gave her a
virtual monopoly of this colonial trade after Trafalgar, except as it was
shared with the Portuguese in Brazil and with the newly independent
United States. The British annexed Trinidad (1797), occupied Dutch
Guiana, and sent two unsuccessful military expeditions into Buenos
Aires (1806 and 1807). She blew hot and cold on Francisco Miranda's
plans for liberating Spanish America as she did on the claims of the
Bourbon Princess Carlota to the loyalty of the Spanish colonies in
South America. Earlier, at Nootka Sound (1790), conflicting British
claims on the Pacific coast of North America were challenged by the
Spanish, and William Pitt had listened to Miranda's proposals with
interest; but he turned at that time to a friendly settlement in accordance with a policy of making peace with Spain. Subsequently, Britain
was again on the verge of supporting Miranda, even when Spain was
technically an ally, but always decided against it. Spanish American
revolutionaries had trouble understanding this ambivalent British
policy.

Relations with British North Americans

Harry Bernstein has shown that by the eighteenth century colonial
leaders in New England, New York, and Pennsylvania were keenly
interested in Latin America and its trade possibilities. Judge Samuel
Sewall of Boston proposed a missionary program to convert Spanish
America to Protestantism, and his friend, the Reverend Cotton

Mather, wrote in Spanish (which he says he learned for the purpose) *An Essay to Convey Religion into the Spanish Indies*.[7] North Americans had begun to read books about travel in Latin America and works describing the Indian civilizations and the flora and fauna of the area. Letters were exchanged by scholars and scientists north and south. The economic basis of this growing interest lay in the expanding trade the colonists developed, some of it legal but much of it contraband. The North Americans shared largely in the flourishing slave trade, both between Africa and Spanish America and between the Spanish West Indies and the British colonies, both island and mainland.[8]

After independence, the United States, although inheriting and sharing the momentum of the British expansion into Latin America, also became a rival of the British, as in various moves related to Florida and Cuba. When Napoleon withdrew from Haiti and sold Louisiana to the United States (1803), the United States at one step made a major intrusion into former Spanish territory. This was soon to be followed (during the era of Latin American independence) by the purchase of Florida (1819). To many Spanish Americans, it must have seemed that the independence of the United States had given added impetus to the older British intrusion, and to breaking up the Spanish empire.

A Note on the Slave Trade

The important role of the British and their North American colonists in the African slave trade calls for a special comment. By mid–eighteenth century the British had a virtual monopoly of the trade from the African west coast, except for the Portuguese control of the trade between Angola and Brazil (sometimes drawing on African regions north of Angola) and the French operations in the Senegal-Gambia region. British North American slavers shared this trade about equally with those of the mother country. Roland Oliver and T.

7. Cotton Mather's *An Essay to Convey Religion into the Spanish Indies* was published in Spanish in 1699 and in English in 1704, in Boston, New York, and Philadelphia.
8. Harry Bernstein, *Origins of Inter-American Interest, 1700–1812* (Philadelphia: University of Pennsylvania Press, 1945). Chapter 14 deals with the growth of cultural and scientific interest.

D. Fage estimate the number of slaves carried to America in the seventeenth century at 2,750,000 and the number in the eighteenth century at around 7,000,000.[9] Sentiment against the slave trade grew, on humanitarian grounds as well as because it tended to destroy all other trade with Africa. By 1808, as the movement for independence in Spanish and Portuguese America began (but after the independence of Haiti), both the United States and Great Britain outlawed the international slave trade, introducing an issue into the Ibero-American scene that would trouble hemisphere international relations for years to come.

9. See Roland Oliver and T D. Fage, *A Short History of Africa* (Baltimore: Johns Hopkins University Press, 1962). Philip D. Curtin, *The Atlantic Slave Trade: A Census* (Madison: University of Wisconsin Press, 1969), compares the various estimates.

3 International Aspects of Independence

HAROLD EUGENE DAVIS

The power conflicts and relationships inherited by Latin America from the colonial era were discussed in the previous chapter. We now turn our attention to those conflicts that occurred during the American and French Revolutionary-Metternich era (1775–1825) and which affected the efforts of the newly emerging nations to win their independence and to secure international recognition.

Three Phases of the Movements

From the standpoint of international relations, the independence movements must be considered in three distinguishable, though closely related respects. In the first place, they are to be seen as a continuation of the earlier colonial conflicts. In the second place, they appear as a product of new forces released in Europe and America by the American-French democratic revolutionary movement.[1] Ironically, Great Britain, against whom her North American colonies had just successfully rebelled, and who opposed the slave insurrection in Haiti, became a major source of support for Spanish American and Brazilian independence, as France did only briefly. Britain was also to become a major exponent of the suppression of the international slave trade and the abolition of slavery in the Americas. Third, the several movements in Spanish, Portuguese, and French America (and British

1. See R. R. Palmer, *The Age of the Democratic Revolution: A Political History of Europe and America, 1760–1800* (Princeton: Princeton University Press, 1964), especially Chapter 1.

America in a certain sense) must be considered in relation to each other.

These independence movements occurred in the main between 1775 and 1825—a revolutionary half-century. The first phase, as far as Latin America is concerned, is characterized by repercussions in Spanish America of the North American revolution, such as the rebellion of the *Comuneros* in New Granada, in protest against tax and other reforms, and the Indian rebellion led by Túpac Amaru in Peru, both in 1781. Although it was not a repercussion after the fact, a rebellion of Africans and Indians took place in São Thomé and São José de Maranhão, Brazil, in 1772. In passing, it may be noted that the Count of Aranda, then Spanish ambassador to France, was sufficiently impressed by the implications of the Spanish support to the independence of the British North American colonies to insist again upon his farsighted plan for the liberation of the Spanish colonies as independent kingdoms, tied dynastically to Spain—a plan that helped to shape the ideologies of the Spanish American independence movements.

The second phase, that of the French Revolutionary and early Napoleonic years, from 1789 to 1804, produced the most radical revolution, in a social sense, of the whole revolutionary period in America—the successful slave insurrection in Haiti and the failure of Napoleon's LeClerc expedition to restore French authority (and slavery) there. The Haitian rebellion was accompanied by slave insurrections in Martinique, Guadeloupe, Jamaica (British), and Venezuela. In the last named, the "zambo," José Leonardo Chirines, led a slave insurrection proposing independence in 1795.[2]

The third phase is roughly that of the later years of Napoleon, from the invasion of Portugal (1807) and Spain (1808) to the Battle of Waterloo. This phase coincides with the Spanish rebellion against Napoleon, a rebellion supported later by Great Britain in the Peninsular War, and the removal of the Portuguese court to Brazil (1807–1808) with British aid. Two of the Spanish American movements succeeded definitively during these years, those of Argentina and Paraguay.

2. Pedro M. Arcaya, *Insurrección de los Negros de la Serranía de Coro* (Caracas: Comité de Origines de la Emancipación, Instituto Panamericano de Geografía e Historia, 1949).

Others, in Chile, New Granada (including Ecuador and Venezuela), Uruguay, and Mexico, succeeded briefly but were later defeated by royalist forces, in general after the Spanish adoption of the constitution of 1812, drawn up by the Liberal party leaders, and the restoration of Ferdinand VII to the Spanish throne. Brazil remained loyal during this third phase, as did the Spanish colonies in the Caribbean and the remaining British colonies in North America and in the Caribbean. The French islands of Martinique and Guadeloupe were returned to France after a short occupation by British forces.

During the fifth phase, that of the Metternich era after 1815, Brazil and all the Spanish colonies except Cuba, Puerto Rico, and Florida achieved independence. To some extent, although often in quite different ways as we shall see, the foreign relations of the new Latin American countries, as they were coming into being and seeking international acceptance, were influenced by the conflicts and shifts in power of these several phases, as well as by the tensions and rivalries developing out of their independence movements. From time to time they elicited support or opposition from the European powers in conflict (and from the United States), but they enjoyed no formal alliances.

The objectives of the emerging nations (still undefined as nations) in rebellion during part or all of phases two through five just noted may be stated simply as follows. (1) They sought recognition of independence by their mother countries. In the case of Brazil and much of Spanish America this meant independence as monarchies related dynastically to those of the mother country. But Bolívar's Colombia sought recognition as a republic, as did Argentina after 1819. In Haiti two contradictory movements competed, one republican, the other monarchic. (2) They all sought regularization of their relationship to the Church international, (3) support for their independence from any and all possible sources in the form of credits, arms, recruits, or vessels of war, and (4) trade agreements to replace the trade with the mother countries interrupted during the French Revolutionary-Napoleonic years. This latter objective was less true in the case of Brazil, whose trade, basically with Britain and Portugal, was little interrupted by independence. The revolutionary movements had their agents in the various countries in conflict, including the United States. In some cases—for example Manuel Torres, longtime agent of revolutionary Colombia in the United States—these agents advanced revolutionary theories of open diplomacy based upon international law.[3] But since, however, these policies were at best ill defined, and foreign relations were pursued largely on an opportunistic basis, it seems best in this chapter to consider the problems involved from the standpoint of the power relationships of the era.

Power Relationships

What were these power relationships? The example set by the United States in acquiring independence in a military alliance with France was not lost on the Latin Americans, who sought European support in various ways. In Haiti, Toussaint L'Ouverture played off Spain, France, and Britain against each other. Brazil enjoyed British support as a kind of offshoot of the Anglo-Portuguese alliance. But Spanish America, while getting foreign support in several ways, was much less fortunate on the whole. Miranda, Bolívar, and San Martín each sought a British alliance without success. The reasons for their failures must be sought in the power politics of the times.

When France brought Spain into the War of the American Revolution, the latter was more concerned with recovering Florida and with reestablishing her position in the Mississippi and Río de la Plata valleys than in supporting the independence of the United States. She feared, indeed rightly, that United States independence would set an undesirable example for her own American colonies. By her reconquest of Florida she kept that colony from becoming part of the United States and thus created a troublesome problem in her later relations with the new nation. But this was a Pyrrhic victory, since Florida, as well as Louisiana, were soon to pass to the United States.

Nor had the French support of the English colonists been merely ideological or altruistic. The French policy that brought this support

3. Alberto Miramón, *Diplomáticos de la Libertad* (Bogotá: Empresa Nacional de Publicaciones, 1956), 90. "A nuestros modestos representantes cabe la no pequeña gloria de haber hecho cambiar la diplomacia secreta de las viejas cancillerías por la política exterior nacional; el que, en el campo de derecho de gentes, no solamente se sirviera al estado, sino también a los pueblos."

had been calculated to recover French losses in the Seven Years' War. Aware of this French interest, General Washington refused to approve collaboration in a French move against Canada, which an earlier expedition of the colonial rebels in 1776 had failed to bring into the independence movement. Moreover, when the United States commissioners in the peace negotiations came to suspect that France might take advantage of a Russian offer of mediation, they turned to direct conversations with the British, in disregard of their instructions. These were portents, if properly understood, of the difficulties the Spanish American nations were to encounter.

France and Latin American Independence

The French alliance had been a major, if not the determining, factor in United States independence. But France had no intention in the postwar years of extending her support of independence movements into the colonies of her ally, Spain, any more than into her own island colonies. She correctly interpreted the outcome of the War of the American Revolution as a stalemate, since she had not recovered Canada, and since the French fleet which made possible General Washington's victory at Yorktown was subsequently defeated by a British fleet in the Caribbean. For France, this British-French rivalry in America was to be a continuing determinant of policy throughout the years of the struggles for independence in Latin America. Even Waterloo did not end this competition, as we shall see.

French policy toward Spain and her empire changed, however, with the shifts in Spanish alignment during these years. Spain was an ally up to the outbreak of the French Revolution. Then, briefly, she was an enemy, joining with Britain against the Revolution. Again she was an ally after 1795 and again she was an enemy, after 1808. During the first years of the French Republic, "Citizen" Genêt, as French minister in the United States, used his post to fit out privateers and establish contacts with Spanish American elements of discontent.[4] But, during the Napoleonic period until 1808, as we shall see, France had a seemingly ambivalent objective of either protecting the Spanish

4. See Harry Ammon, *The Genêt Mission* (New York: W. W. Norton and Co., 1973).

empire or getting part of it for herself. In either case she was intent upon strengthening Franco-Spanish relations rather than upon supporting independence movements. Later, however, for a brief period only, she seemed to support the independence movements.

The relations of France with the United States, crucial in some respects to Latin American independence, also shifted during these years. As the French Revolution began, France regarded the United States, under the treaties of 1778, as an ally in the power struggle, and this relationship seemed borne out by the prompt recognition of the French Republic in 1792, by the enthusiastic reception accorded Genêt upon his arrival in Charleston, and by President Washington's authorizing advance payments on the debt to France for the aid she had given during the war for independence. The chief use of the United States in French policy at this time was as a rival of Britain. Her usefulness as a threat to the territories of Spain in America varied with the changing relations of France and Spain.

After the breach in United States–French relations consequent to the Jay Treaty (1795) of the U.S. with Britain, the United States for a time not only threatened to support revolutionary activity in Spanish America, but even gave support to Toussaint L'Ouverture in Haiti, despite the fact that under the treaty of 1778 the United States was bound to give support to France in her possessions in America. That treaty and this pledge were superseded in 1800 by a new treaty of friendship and commerce; but still the United States was eventually drawn into the War of 1812 against Britain, thus giving some support to Napoleon at this time in his life-and-death struggle with Britain. Earlier, during the Madison administration, the United States gave somewhat ambiguous support to French ambitions in Spanish America while giving at least moral support, and sometimes more, to the growing elements of discontent there.

During the first years of the French Revolution, the interests of France in American affairs remained peripheral, except for Haiti and her other colonies in the West Indies. Her main preoccupation was at this time with survival in Europe; after the Terror it was with the expansion of French power in the Continent. Genêt's activities in the

United States were contemporary with the efforts of the French commissioners in Haiti to deal with the slave insurrection there after 1791, and with threats of Spanish and British intervention. There French policy took a revolutionary turn when first the commissioners and then the Convention decreed the abolition of slavery. The policy of emancipation was later reversed under Napoleon, and slavery was restored in the French islands (except Haiti which again rebelled). But the pre-Napoleonic French policy in Haiti may be credited with beginning the process of Negro emancipation in Latin America. One of its effects at the time, which was counter productive, however, was to bring a British military expedition from Jamaica, led by General Thomas Maitland, at the invitation of the antirevolutionary and pro-slavery white planters in Haiti. The Maitland expedition occupied part of Haiti for five years, until driven out by the forces of Toussaint L'Ouverture. Its effectiveness was greatly limited, however, by the concurrent black insurrection in Jamaica, which prevented adequate reinforcement of the army in Haiti.

Moved partly by the success of the slave insurrection and partly by her changing relationship to France, Spain ceded the Spanish half of Hispaniola to France. Then, in 1801 Toussaint L'Ouverture invaded this area and freed the slaves. After the independence of Haiti (1804), the Spanish colonials rebelled and drove out the Haitians with British support. But after the Napoleonic wars this Spanish province (today the Dominican Republic) was returned to Spain. Then in 1821 this Spanish colony rebelled against Spain and gained its independence.

Spain had also been forced to cede Louisiana to France by the Treaty of San Ildefonso (1800) on the eve of Napoleon's move to restore French authority in Haiti. This he did by sending an army of 22,000 veterans under his brother-in-law, General Charles Victor LeClerc (1772–1802), accompanied by the mulatto generals André Rigaud and Alexandre Pétion, old enemies of Toussaint. Napoleon even persuaded pro-French President Jefferson to stop trade and supplies to Haiti, reversing previous United States support to Toussaint against Rigaud. Napoleon contributed in no small degree to the failure of this move to restore French empire in both the West Indies and North America by decreeing the restoration of slavery in Martinique and

Guadeloupe, leading the Haitians to believe (as was true) that the same action was intended in Haiti.[5]

France made no serious effort to reconquer Haiti after the surrender of French forces there in 1803, and Haitian independence was declared the following year. But France kept open the threat of intervention in Haiti by withholding recognition during the years of the Spanish American wars for independence (and the independence of Brazil). Only in 1825 did she make a treaty with Haiti recognizing the black nation's independence, but providing for an indemnity to France of 150 million francs, payable in five years. (The legend of Haitian *richesse* persisted.) The collapse of Haiti's economy made the payment of such a sum virtually impossible; the first payment was provided by a French loan, with a face value of 30 million francs, of which Haiti actually got 24 million, having to scrape up the balance out of scarce national funds while facing increased interest charges on the loan. But President Jean Pierre Boyer felt the payment was a means of staving off a possible French invasion, even at this late date.[6]

French policy toward Latin America during the years from the Napoleonic invasion of Portugal (1807) to the end of the Napoleonic era was determined in large measure by the French occupation of the Iberian peninsula and the consequent Peninsular War. After Admiral Nelson's defeat of the combined Spanish and French fleets off Cape Trafalgar in 1805, French activity in America, both commercial and political, was severely limited by Britain's sea power. Just as she was unable to restore control in Haiti, so she was unable to extend control over the Spanish colonies in America after assuming control of the Spanish peninsula. Despite the existence of pro-French elements, such as those surrounding Santiago de Liniers in Argentina, all the Spanish colonial governments, with British backing, rejected Napoleon's envoys who came to incorporate them in the Napoleonic satellite system.

According to W. S. Robertson, Napoleon had decided, by 1811, to

5. Rayford Logan, *Haiti and the Dominican Republic* (New York: Oxford University Press, 1968), 91–94; Paul Reussier (ed.), *Lettres de Général LeClerc* (Paris: Leroux, 1937).
6. Logan, *Haiti and the Dominican Republic*, 95–96.

encourage the independence of Spanish America, provided the new states did not form alliances with Britain. During the Madison administration, the Spanish minister, Luis Onís, reported from Washington that United States policy seemed to support the Bonapartist regime and those elements in Spanish America favoring it, while at the same time favoring Spanish American independence. Harold D. Sims has recently written connecting Napoleon's interests at this time with the Hidalgo revolt in Mexico and with the activities of Liniers and his friends who were executed at Córdoba by the first Buenos Aires Triumvirate.[7] But the only tangible support Napoleon got from the United States that had a bearing on Latin America was the War of 1812 against Britain, with its privateer attacks on British shipping and the threat of United States occupation of Spanish Florida.

A few years after the restoration of Louis XVIII in France, and of Ferdinand VII in Spain, the wars for Spanish American independence were renewed with great vigor under Bolívar in northern South America and under San Martín in Chile and Peru. These leaders generally looked to Britain for support, while France in general supported the reactionary course of Ferdinand VII, ultimately to the extent of alienating Great Britain from the Quadruple Alliance. Three years after the Liberal Revolution of 1820 in Spain and Portugal, France, with Alliance support, sent an army into Spain to suppress the constitutional regime and restore the king to his former "absolute" power. Meanwhile, the Liberal Revolution had contributed to the success of independence in Mexico and Peru, with support from anti-Liberal forces. But the French presence in Spain raised the specter of a renewal of the war in Spanish America, producing a vigorous reaction of the British government under Foreign Secretary George Canning. Canning's actions effectively stopped the French threat, through an informal agreement incorporated in the Polignac

7. W. S. Robertson, *France and Latin American Independence* (Baltimore: Johns Hopkins University Press, 1939), 74–75. Arthur P. Whitaker, *The United States and the Independence of Latin America, 1820–1830* (Baltimore: Johns Hopkins University Press, 1941), 58–60. See also Ammon, *The Genêt Mission*, and Harold D. Sims, "Napoleón y la Independencia Latinoamericana," *Americas*, XXV (August–September, 1973), 2–10; also English and Portuguese editions.

Memorandum, and also produced the epochal policy statement of the Monroe Doctrine.[8]

Relations with Great Britain

British policy toward Latin American independence displayed an ambivalence that has led some Latin Americans to charge that it was perfidy. The British reaction to the fate of the Spanish empire was complicated, even agonizing in some respects. The first successful American colonial rebellion, leading to a republic, had been directed against Britain. Britain had been a leading opponent of the French Republic when it was proclaimed in 1792. Even when Spain was an enemy during the wars of the era, Britain was reluctant to use force to break up the Spanish empire. Yet, ironically, she became a leading, if not the major, influence in the success of independence in both Brazil and Spanish America. The irony is increased by the fact that the Spanish American nations became republics.

Even during the War of the American Revolution, Britain was accused (without grounds) of supporting the Indian uprising in Peru led by Túpac Amaru and the rebellion of the *Comuneros* in New Granada.[9] When the French Revolution spread to the French sugar islands, Britain intervened, as we have noted, to defend the white plantation owners against slave insurrections, as well as to extend British trade. After Spain returned to her French alliance in the mid-1790s, Britain was mainly concerned with the struggle against the expanding French power in Europe. The situation was one that invited annexation of Spanish (as well as Dutch and French) colonies; accordingly, she occupied Trinidad and Dutch Guiana, as well as Cape Colony in Africa, and the French Caribbean islands previously mentioned as being later returned.

8. For a comprehensive account of French relations to the independence movements, see Robertson, *France and Latin American Independence.*

9. Anne Dart Yanes, "Túpac Amaru" in H. E. Davis (ed.), *Revolutionaries, Traditionalists and Dictators in Latin America* (New York: Cooper Square, 1973), 24, citing works by Lillian Estelle Fisher, Daniel Valcarcel, and Boleslao Lewin. According to María Louisa Rivara de Tuesta, in *Los Ideólogos de la Emancipación Peruana* (Lima: Comisión . . . del Sesquicentenaria de la Independencia del Perú, 1972), 19–22, Juan Pablo Viscardo y Guzmán, a former Jesuit, urged the British consul in Livorno, Italy, to support Túpac Amaru. J. M. Henao and Gerardo Arrubla, *History of Colombia* (Chapel Hill: University of North Carolina Press, 1938), in a footnote, 170–71, dismiss the claim of British support.

But annexation by force was not the only alternative in the revolutionary climate of the times. Sir Ralph Abercromby, who met virtually no resistance in the conquest of Trinidad, reported that a more successful policy would be to move into the Spanish colonies, capturing their trade by collaborating with the colonists in their rebellion against "a decadent ruling class."[10] Sir Home Riggs Popham, who led the unsuccessful invasion of Buenos Aires in 1806, knew that the British cabinet had discussed possible support of Spanish American colonial rebels, for example as in considering support for the revolutionary plans of Francisco Miranda. But he also knew there was no agreement in British councils, on either ideological or tactical grounds, to give such support. The instructions his co-commander, General William Beresford, carried from the British commander in Capetown limited him to assuming power as a governor of the province. He had no instructions from London. Popham was convinced, probably relying on the "secret communication" of a United States sea captain, J. Wain, that all he needed to gain the support of Buenos Aires was to open the port to international trade. But, as a careful British student has observed, there is no evidence that when he had the opportunity he made any move to encourage a declaration of independence. The following year (1807), however, having established themselves in Montevideo, the British published *La Estrella del Sur*, advocating Latin American independence.[11]

The British experience in the Caribbean in trying to stem the tide of slave insurrection was hardly one to encourage collaboration with American rebels. The result was an ambivalence in British policy throughout most of these years of conflict with the French Revolutionary and Napoleonic regimes: a drive to take over Spanish commerce in which a tendency to annex, or at least occupy, territory vied with the temptation to support Spanish American rebels.[12]

After 1810 Britain joined the revolutionary forces opposing French

10. The Abercrombie dispatch is quoted in H. S. Ferns, *Britain and Argentina in the Nineteenth Century* (Oxford: Clarendon Press, 1960), 11, citing the published *Correspondence . . . of Viscount Castlereagh*.

11. Jerry W. Cooney, "Paraguayan Independence and Doctor Francia," *The Americas*, XXVIII (April, 1972), 407–428.

12. Ferns, *Britain and Argentina in the Nineteenth Century*, 11–12, 22 ff.

rule in Spain and demanding the return of Ferdinand. She sent Spain an army under the Duke of Wellington to fight side by side with Spanish forces in the Peninsular War. After making this alliance with revolutionary Spain, Britain maintained a careful policy of neutrality in relation to the wars for independence, rejecting the request of the Venezuelan mission led by Simón Bolívar and Andrés Bello for British support. But this neutrality did not stand in the way of making profitable trade agreements with the revolutionary regimes; nor did it stand in the way of making it possible for professional Spanish soldiers, such as José de San Martín, Carlos de Alvear, and the wealthy Chilean Bernardo O'Higgins, to go to South America to provide leadership for the independence movements. After the restoration of Ferdinand to the Spanish throne, Britain continued this policy of neutrality, while Spain restored her control in America, except for the Río de la Plata region. This return to loyalty was based upon the Spanish Liberal constitution of 1812; but when Ferdinand suppressed this constitution he soon encountered a renewal of the wars of independence. The Quadruple Alliance, as we have noted, turned its attention to suppressing Liberal revolts in Europe and began to consider taking military action in Spanish America. At this point the policy of Britain shifted again. She continued her efforts to persuade Spain to accept independent monarchies in the New World, but now relaxed her neutrality laws sufficiently to permit Spanish American revolutionaries to purchase supplies, negotiate loans, and recruit veterans of the Napoleonic wars for service in the independence armies.

When George Canning became foreign minister in 1823 he carried forward the reorientation of British policy begun by his predecessor, Viscount Castlereagh. This policy was one of utilizing the existence of a balance of power in Europe to follow an independent British policy. In this policy he envisioned a role for the growing power of the United States, a growth he also hoped to restrict. After the Revolution of 1820 in Spain Canning hoped to influence the new Spanish regime to accept the independence of the American nations as constitutional monarchies. But the Spanish Liberals were as obdurate as Ferdinand in this respect; they rejected out of hand the monarchy proposed in Mexico by Agustín Iturbide and accepted tentatively by the Spanish Viceroy Juan O'Donojú, as well as the overtures of General San Martín in Peru.

Canning's opportunity came when France, as noted, sent an army into Spain with the blessing of the Quadruple (now Quintuple) Alliance in 1823. Although he still hoped to persuade the Spanish Liberals to accept Spanish American independence, his immediate objective was to keep France from using her position in Spain to resume active warfare against the American rebels, or even to annex part of the Spanish empire by collaborating with conservative forces there. For some time Tsar Alexander of Russia had been urging a special meeting of the alliance to agree upon a course of action toward the Spanish empire. The United States had rejected his invitation to attend, but it was now rumored that such a meeting might well be held in 1823.

At this opportune moment Canning took two bold steps. He invited the United States, only recently a wartime enemy, to take a joint stand renouncing any designs on Spanish territory and opposing intervention by any other power. More significantly, by threatening use of the British navy to stop any expedition leaving Spain for America, he elicited from France the Polignac Memorandum, a French pledge not to intervene in Spanish America. From this point on Britain's neutrality in the conflict between Spain and her colonies became increasingly friendly to the colonies, looking to recognition of Spanish American independence and the negotiation of favorable treaties of commerce, such as the treaty of 1825 with Argentina. But she avoided commitments in the nature of an alliance with the new nations. In the Panama Congress of 1826, as we shall see, the British observer was instructed merely to see that the United States did not establish close political ties.[13]

British policy in respect to Brazilian independence was both more straightforward and more successful than that relating to Spanish America. Britain's close ties with Portugal largely explain the difference. When Napoleon's forces invaded Portugal in 1807, Britain per-

---

13. *Ibid.*; William W. Kaufmann, *British Policy and the Independence of Latin America, 1804–1828* (New Haven: Yale University Press, 1951), Chap. 7; J. B. Lockey, *Pan Americanism: Its Beginnings* (New York: Macmillan, 1920).

suaded the prince regent, later King João VI, to move the court to Brazil and provided a British fleet to carry them there. British influence, exerted through the Portuguese court in Brazil, had considerable influence on the Spanish American independence movement in the Río de la Plata area, especially in moderating the designs of Queen Carlota of Portugal-Brazil, sister of the deposed King Ferdinand, who conspired to get Spanish American leaders to accept her as regent in the name of her brother. With British support, a Portuguese-Brazilian force occupied French Guiana.[14]

After expelling the French from the Iberian peninsula, British forces stayed on in Portugal, in support of the provisional government. King João and his court stayed in Brazil until, following a revolution in Portugal in 1820 similar to that of Spain, the leaders in Portugal called for the king's return to govern under a Liberal constitution. Reluctantly, for he had come to like Brazil, King João accepted British advice to return, leaving his son Pedro as regent in Brazil, which had been made a kingdom under King João.

The independence of Brazil, which soon followed, had an important source in a struggle within the constitutional Cortes in Lisbon—a struggle that pitted Brazilians against Portuguese Liberals in an unsuccessful move to make Brazil one of three autonomous kingdoms within the Portuguese empire. The feeling became so intense that the Brazilian delegates, believing their lives were in danger, found it necessary to leave secretly.[15] In Brazil, Pedro put himself at the head of the independence movement by his *Grito de Ypiranga*, assuming control of an independent nation in an almost bloodless revolution.

Thereafter, British influence in Brazil and Portugal accounted for the prompt recognition of Brazilian independence by both Britain and Portugal in treaties negotiated simultaneously by the British minister to Lisbon, Sir Charles Stuart, who went to Rio de Janeiro for this purpose. The convention with Great Britain negotiated by Stuart was rejected by Canning because Brazil did not specifically grant the

14. See John A. Hutchins, "Portugal and the Plata: The Conflict of Luso-Hispanic Interests in Southern Brazil and the North Bank of the Rio de la Plata, 1493–1807" (Ph.D. dissertation, The American University, 1953).

15. George Boehrer, "The Flight of the Brazilian Deputies from the Cortes Gerais of Lisbon," *Hispanic American Historical Review*, XL (November, 1960), 497–512.

trade privileges Britain had enjoyed with Portugal and did not undertake to suppress the slave trade. A new treaty negotiated the following year included these provisions. Brazil had little difficulty in securing recognition from other powers, including members of the Quadruple Alliance. Not only was Brazil a "legitimate" monarchy, but the new empress was an Austrian Hapsburg. Even Metternich favored recognition. Between December, 1825, and March, 1826, Brazil was recognized by Austria, France, the Holy See, Sweden, Switzerland, the Hanseatic States, Holland, Hanover, and Prussia. In January, 1825, recognition of the independence of the Spanish republics was included in King George III's speech to Parliament.[16] Recognition by the United States had come earliest (1824).

By a happy circumstance, the Brazilian relationship with the Vatican was never broken. Upon the death of King João in 1826 Pedro inherited the Portuguese crown, which he later transferred to his daughter, Maria da Gloria. But, meanwhile, the Vatican had dispatched a new nuncio to Pedro in Rio, and there he remained, despite some Papal apprehension as to tampering with the status of the Church by the Brazilian parliament. Because of the close identification of Britain with Brazilian independence, British influence in Brazilian diplomacy and trade was paramount throughout the nineteenth century.[17]

Russia and Latin American Independence

Francisco Miranda, the forerunner of Spanish American independence, spent some time in Russia, later going to England in the capacity of a representative of the Empress Catherine. He got no support from Russia for his dream of Spanish American independence, but Russia could not be immune to the significance of the breaking up of

16. Elizabeth Longford, *Wellington, Pillar of State* (New York: Harper & Row, 1972), 110.

17. Alan K. Manchester, *British Pre-eminence in Brazil: Its Rise and Decline* (Chapel Hill: University of North Carolina Press, 1933), especially Chapter 8; Kaufmann, *British Policy and the Independence of Latin America*, 182–92. See also Manoel de Oliveira Lima, *O Reconhecimento do Imperio* (Rio de Janeiro and Paris: Libraria Garnier, 1902). On recognition of Brazil by the United States, see Hildebrando Accioly, *O Reconhecimento do Brasil pelos Estados Unidos de America* (2nd. ed.; São Paulo: Editora Nacional, 1945); for Brazilian early relations with the Vatican, see his *Os Primeiros Nuncios no Brasil* (São Paulo: Instituto Progresso Editorial, 1949).

the Spanish empire. (She, too, had an American colony, Alaska.) As late as 1818, at the Congress of Aix la Chapelle, at which it was agreed that the occupation force commanded by the Duke of Wellington should be withdrawn from France (and France admitted to the Quadruple Alliance), Tsar Alexander still dreamed of bringing the Americas, both North and South, into his Holy Alliance.[18]

Relations with the United States

United States policy toward Latin American independence displayed some of the same ambiguity shown by British policy, with the additional complication, during most of the period, of the inability of the United States to pursue an independent policy, caught up as she was in the conflicts of the great powers. As early as the War of 1812 United States expansionists were urging that the nation annex Florida, despite the Pinckney Treaty, and that she claim Texas as part of the Louisiana Territory. Aaron Burr tried to interest Napoleon in his proposed move into Texas, perhaps in the liberation of Mexico. The United States was competing for Latin American trade with Great Britain, including the slave trade until 1808, and was engaged in whaling and fishing activity in the South Atlantic, leading to political relations in Chile and Argentina.[19] In the later years of the independence movements, United States activity was complicated by negotiations with Spain looking to the purchase of Florida and settlement of the Louisiana Territory boundary.

Since the Louisiana Territory brought with it a claim to Texas, it became United States policy to get Spain to recognize that claim. Sparsely settled Florida was a natural harbor for smugglers, who also traded with the Indians and encouraged Indian raids across the border into the United States. The United States also claimed West Florida as far as the Perdido River, as part of Louisiana, and the breaking up of the Spanish empire after 1808 encouraged U.S. expansionists to think of annexing it outright. By a secret act of 1811 Con-

18. Longford, *Wellington*, 50–51. Russell H. Bartley, in "The Inception of Russo-Brazilian Relations," *Hispanic American Historical Review*, LVI (May, 1976) 217–40, has called attention to the expansion of Russian interest in Latin America at this time.

19. Eugenio Pereira Salas, *Los Primeros Contactos entre Chile y los Estados Unidos, 1778–1809* (Santiago: Editorial Andrés Bello, 1971), especially Appendices 1 and 2, pp. 315–53.

gress authorized the president to use the armed forces to occupy part or all of West Florida, and it became a part of national policy to acquire the whole peninsula by purchase from Spain. The United States also became concerned lest parts of the disintegrating Spanish empire, such as Cuba, fall into French or British hands. This apprehension found expression in a resolution of Congress stating the "no transfer" policy—the United States would oppose transfer of any Spanish colony to another power. When the United States intervened in Amelia Island, off the coast of Florida, in 1817, to suppress an "insurgent" movement, this policy was an operation in opposition to possible British annexation of Florida or Cuba, since the island was occupied by Gregor McGregor, a British subject, but also a lieutenant of Bolívar. Some Latin Americans, however, have seen in this United States action a move to prevent the independence of Cuba. Given these complications of her relations with Spain, the United States was in no position to respond with an independent policy to Latin American overtures until the time of Canning's reaction to French intervention in Spain in 1823.

The independence movement in Haiti produced special problems for United States policy in the 1790s. As the French Revolution got under way, the United States was tied to France by the two treaties of 1778, calling for support in the defense of French possessions in America. The Jay Treaty (1795) with Britain started a process of alienation between the United States and France that culminated in the "XYZ Affair" and the "Undeclared War" of 1798. These hostilities with France gave the United States an excuse for furnishing supplies to Toussaint L'Ouverture in the civil war that made him the undisputed master of the island, as well as for an informal trade agreement. It also caused Alexander Hamilton, in the Adams cabinet, to listen with sympathy to Francisco Miranda's plans to liberate Spanish America. Mariano Picón Salas, Venezuelan historian, has remarked that this proposal of Miranda was "fantastic in its flimsy basis," backed by relatively unknown persons. Yet the proposal for an alliance with Britain and the United States to achieve the independence of a Spanish American constitutional kingdom, headed by an Inca, had elements of *realpolitik* in it as well. A loan of some thirty million dollars was to be made by a London bank, which would establish branches in Lima and Mexico. The United States and Britain would enjoy identical trade privileges in the new nation. The United States would receive the territories of Florida and Louisiana. Cuba would be retained by the *Incanata*, but the other Caribbean islands would be divided between Britain and the United States.[20]

The Jefferson administration was generally pro-French, especially after the fortuitous acquisition of Louisiana. Hence, it generally refrained from aid to the Haitians against the LeClerc expedition of 1802, although at the same time sought more trade with Haiti. After the withdrawal of French forces from the island, and the declaration of Haitian independence in 1804, the taint of a slave insurrection was enough to prevent United States recognition. Despite her commitment to the de facto principle, she withheld recognition until the time of the U.S. Civil War. In 1806, in accordance with this pro-French policy, Congress enacted a law forbidding trade with Haiti. According to Rayford Logan, this law, in effect until 1809, permitted Britain to monopolize Haitian trade until after the War of 1812.[21]

The United States, a small struggling republic, could not be expected to swing the balance of power in the wars for independence, even if she had entered into a treaty alliance, as France had done in that of the United States. But Spanish American independence leaders looked to the United States for sympathy, and frequently found support in the form of credits, ships, supplies, arms, and (volunteer) mercenary soldiers and sailors. Francisco Miranda attributed the motivation of his revolutionary career to his participation as a young soldier in the Spanish expedition that supported the American Revolution. Later, in 1784, he had visited the United States, meeting Henry Knox, Alexander Hamilton, and possibly President Washington. When he finally led an unsuccessful invasion of Venezuela in

20. Mariano Picón Salas, *Miranda* (Caracas: Ediciones Edime, 1953), 382–86. Picón Salas based his account on William S. Robertson, *Francisco de Miranda and the Revolutionizing of South America* (2 vols.; Washington: American Historical Association, Annual Report for 1907, published 1908).

21. Logan, *Haiti and the Dominican Republic*, 99, citing Alain Turnier, *Les Etats-Unis et le Marché Haitien* (Washington, D.C.: n.p., 1955), 103–118. See also Logan's classic *The Diplomatic Relations of the United States with Haiti, 1776–1891* (Chapel Hill: University of North Carolina Press, 1941).

1806, his party included two hundred volunteers from the United States. Upon landing he distributed a pamphlet by the former Jesuit Juan Pablo Viscardo y Guzmán describing the North American revolution. United States citizens participated actively in the revolutionary movements in various ways, and U.S. privateers, as Curtis Wilgus has pointed out, played an important role in the sea warfare.[22]

The demands of her growing commerce and her divided political sympathies pulled the United States back and forth between France and Britain during the first half century of her independence. Under the Federalists she drifted into the "Undeclared War" of 1798 against France, as we have seen; she then furnished supplies to Toussaint to defeat his rival, Rigaud. This occurred just as France was beginning to think of restoring French authority in Haiti. A decade and a half later, under President Madison, the United States drifted into the War of 1812 against Britain. As noted earlier in this chapter, the Spanish minister in Washington was reporting about this time that the United States would support the Bonapartist regime and those elements in Spanish America supporting Bonaparte. Arthur Whitaker has argued that this policy ultimately led the United States into the War of 1812 on the side of France.[23]

The treaties of 1778 with France remained in effect during the slave insurrection in Haiti and until superseded by a new, non-political treaty in 1800. But despite public and official sympathy for France after the defeat of the Federalists, the United States still feared the restoration of French empire in North America. When Thomas Jefferson learned that Spain had transferred Louisiana to France by a secret treaty, he is said to have remarked that now the United States might have to "marry the British fleet." The Louisiana Purchase ended this

22. Cf. W. S. Robertson, *Hispanic American Relations with the United States* (New York: Oxford University Press, 1923), Chap. 3. See also his *Life of Francisco Miranda* (2 vols.; Chapel Hill: University of North Carolina Press, 1928); Charles C. Griffin, *The United States and the Disruption of the Spanish Empire* (New York: Columbia University Press, 1937); Whitaker, *The United States and the Independence of Latin America*; and A. Curtis Wilgus, "Some Activities of the United States Citizens in the South American Wars of Independence, 1808–1824," *Louisiana Historical Quarterly*, IV (April, 1931), 182–203.

23. Whitaker, *United States and the Independence of Latin America*, 58–60, 73, citing Robertson, *France and Latin American Independence*, 84, 86, 93–95.

fear temporarily, both in respect to North America and to Haiti. That it might not be a permanent abdication of imperialism, however, had soon appeared in connection with Latin American independence.

The pro-French policy of the Jefferson and Madison administrations gave way after the end of the War of 1812 to a policy of studied neutrality more like that of Britain. The war had been a chastening experience for the United States. It had also turned attention away from the Latin American scene for a time, except in relation to the Floridas. Hence, when the war for independence was renewed in South America in 1816, the United States adopted a cautious policy of withholding judgment on the success of the movements while investigating conditions in the centers of revolution and watching for opportunities to favor the new states. President Madison issued a proclamation of neutrality (1816) following the general lines of President Washington's proclamation of 1793. Citizens of the United States were warned to refrain from enlisting in military expeditions against the dominions of Spain.[24] The following year an act of Congress imposed more stringent regulations, while an act of 1818 prohibited United States citizens from accepting commissions to join any movement against a government with which the United States was at peace.

The Florida question revolved around border problems, but also included problems of Indian relations, made worse by the weakness of Spanish authority in the area. Florida had been recaptured by Spanish forces during the U.S. War of Independence. A secret agreement between the United States and Britain, not incorporated in the Treaty of Paris (1783), had provided two alternative northern borders for Florida, depending upon whether the territory remained in British possession or passed into Spanish hands. In ceding the territory to Spain in 1783, Britain had specified neither of these boundaries. The Pinckney Treaty subsequently fixed the border at the thirty-first parallel, as agreed with Great Britain in the second of the two alternatives, the one more favorable to the United States.

24. Robertson, *Hispanic American Relations*. On background of U.S.-Spanish relations see Norman Fulton, *Relaciónes Diplomáticas entre España y los Estados Unidos a Fines del Siglo XVIII* (Madrid: Facultad de Filosofía y Letras, 1970).

In 1810, the inhabitants of West Florida (led by immigrants from the United States) declared their territory independent and applied for annexation to the United States. West Florida was the area on the Gulf of Mexico between the Mississippi and Perdido rivers. It was claimed by the United States as part of Louisiana, although it had not been surrendered by Spanish authorities to the French at the time of the Louisiana transfer. Madison ignored the request for annexation, but ordered General W. C. C. Claiborne to take possession on the grounds of the U.S. claim under the Louisiana treaty. The territory was incorporated into the State of Louisiana.

In 1812, despite efforts to remain neutral in the desperate warfare of Napoleonic Europe, the United States was drawn into war against Britain. Expansionist ideas in respect to Canada and Florida lay behind the war sentiment in the United States. Hence, during this second war with England, Mobile, in West Florida, was occupied by American troops and made a part of Alabama. In 1814, General Andrew Jackson also invaded East Florida to prevent the British from seizing Pensacola. (Spain and Britain were allies at this time.) Thus by the end of the Napoleonic period, the United States had occupied Florida as far east as the Perdido River. At various times she had also asserted concern for Florida as a whole.[25]

When the United States suppressed the "insurgent movement" in Amelia Island (1817) (off the Atlantic coast of Florida, as previously mentioned), it was to drive out Gregor McGregor, a British subject and former lieutenant of Miranda and Bolívar, who had occupied the island. He was presumed to be acting under the direction of a group of Latin American representatives in the United States; but Madison elected to regard the actions of McGregor as unauthorized, since none of the Latin American governments concerned (Mexico, Venezuela, Argentina, Colombia) would admit responsibility. McGregor was soon replaced by the adventurer Louis Aury, fresh from buccaneering efforts in Galveston.[26] J. B. Lockey argues that this occupa-

25. See Isaac J. Cox, *The West Florida Controversy, 1789–1791* (Baltimore: Johns Hopkins University Press, 1918).

26. Philip C. Brooks, *Diplomacy and the Borderlands* (Berkeley: University of California Press, 1939), 86–87, gives the background of Spanish policy. See also Fulton, *Relaciones Diplomáticas entre España y los Estados Unidos.*

tion of Amelia Island was probably encouraged unofficially by Britain, and that Xavier Mina, the Mexican independence leader, was involved with Spanish authorities in plans to prevent Florida from falling into United States hands at this time. After ineffectual efforts of Spanish officials to dislodge the U.S. settlers, President Madison in 1817 ordered its occupation on the grounds that it was a center of smuggling, lawlessness, slave trading in violation of the prohibition of the international slave trade, and piracy. The island was held by the United States on the basis of these claims until the purchase of Florida in 1819.[27]

In the same year as that of the occupation of Amelia Island, General Andrew Jackson was dispatched to the Florida border of Georgia with a command of Georgia and Tennessee militiamen to suppress an Indian uprising. He pursued marauding Seminole Indians across the border into East Florida, where he captured and executed two British subjects whom he accused of inciting the Indian warfare: Alexander Arbuthnot and Lieutenant Robert C. Armbrister of the Royal Colonial Marines.[28] Jackson had not been authorized to cross the Florida boundary, and his unauthorized action was hotly debated in the Monroe cabinet. This action took place while negotiations for the Florida treaty were going on, and some people feared that Jackson's raid would provoke Britain to retaliate, disrupting the Florida negotiations. But Britain denied responsibility for these acts of her subjects and the danger passed.

Under the treaty of 1819, Spain ceded Florida to the United States in exchange for a payment of five million dollars in claims of U.S. citizens against Spain. The United States gave up her claim to Texas as part of Louisiana, accepting a boundary drawn along the Sabine River to the thirty-second parallel, then north to the Red River. Following the Red River westward to a point 100 degrees west, it then turned north to the Arkansas River, following this river to its source, then north or south as the case might be (ran the treaty) to the forty-second parallel; thence the boundary proceeded west to the Pacific. In accepting this boundary Spain gave up all claim to the Oregon

27. Lockey, *Pan Americanism: Its Beginnings*. 187 ff.
28. L. Ethan Ellis, *A Short History of American Diplomacy* (New York: Harper, 1951), 120.

country. She had effectively yielded considerable territory that might have become part of a later independent Mexico, and left the United States with an unsatisfied claim to Texas that would later cause trouble.

The provision of the 1819 treaty yielding Texas to Spain was much criticized by southerners in the United States who felt that Adams had betrayed their interests. As a matter of fact, in the negotiations Adams strove hard, though unsuccessfully, to get Spain to agree that Texas was part of Louisiana. Ironically, as Philips C. Brooks has shown in his previously cited study of the Florida treaty, the Spanish minister, Luis de Onís, had instructions from his government to yield at least part of Texas if pressed hard enough.[29]

During the negotiations, Spain endeavored to get the United States to promise not to recognize the newly independent Spanish American states. Agreement might have led to further Spanish concessions— even Texas! But Adams would not yield on this question of Latin American recognition, even when the Spanish Council of State delayed ratification and recalled Onís from Washington. Adams' position was strengthened at this point by congressional adoption of Henry Clay's resolution endorsing the president's sending diplomatic representatives to the Latin American republics when he saw fit.

Scholars in the Spanish American countries have charged that the United States intentionally withheld support of Latin independence in order to acquire Florida. This is borne out in only a limited sense, if one looks carefully at the United States–Spanish negotiations. The Spanish delay in ratification of the treaty, partly because of the Revolution of 1820, came at an embarrassing time for the United States; it is important, however, to notice that the United States had already determined upon a course of early recognition.[30] The uncertainty of the military and political situation in Latin America, together with developments in Europe, and Spanish delay in ratifying the treaty of 1819 were the major factors in postponing recognition, rather than any reluctance of the United States to act. Moreover, it should be

29. Brooks, *Diplomacy and the Borderlands*, Chap. 4, especially 155.

30. Cf. Samuel Flagg Bemis, *John Quincy Adams and the Foundations of American Foreign Policy* (New York: Alfred A. Knopf, 1949), 323–44. The standard work on the Florida treaty is Brooks's *Diplomacy and the Borderlands*.

remembered that the United States was the first nation to recognize the independence of the Spanish American nations.

The Monroe Doctrine and Latin American Independence

The Monroe Doctrine and the power structure that produced it are an essential part of the international history of Latin American independence. It was a product and expression of the international situation both in Europe and America, in which Latin, and especially Spanish American independence occurred. It also stands as a significant statement of United States policy toward that independence. In the course of the negotiations for the Florida treaty, as we have seen, the United States had refused to promise Spain to withhold recognition of the new states. The Spanish delay in ratifying the Florida treaty delayed United States recognition, but after this ratification the way was clear. On January 30, 1822, Congress requested from the president the correspondence concerning recognition. The president's message transmitting this correspondence showed that he had already decided to recognize five countries that were "in full enjoyment of their independence." These were the United Provinces of Río de la Plata (Argentina), Chile, Peru, Colombia (including present-day Venezuela, Ecuador, and Panama), and Mexico, then including Central America. The congressional act approving recognition of these five countries (March 4, 1822) also appropriated funds for diplomatic missions. Colombia was recognized in 1822, Mexico in 1822, the United Provinces of Río de la Plata in 1823, and Chile in 1823. Peruvian recognition was delayed to 1826. Central America, which separated from Mexico in 1823, was recognized in 1824. Brazil declared its independence by the *Grito de Ypiranga* on September 7, 1822, and was recognized in 1824.

It was while this action for recognition was shaping up that the United States received from the British government, in August 1823, the startling proposal of the British foreign minister, George Canning, that the United States and Britain join in stating that they had no designs on the territory of the Spanish empire, that they regarded Spain's recovery of her colonies as hopeless, that recognition was "a question of time and circumstance," that they would not oppose peaceful efforts of Spain and her colonies to agree, but that while they did not aim to acquire any of the territories for themselves they could not look with indifference upon transfer of any of them to another power. U.S. Minister Benjamin Rush replied to Canning that he did not have authority to join in such a statement, but would refer the proposal to Washington. He pointed out that the United States favored immediate recognition and said that if Britain would immediately recognize Latin American independence, he would take the risk of stating that "his government would not remain inactive under an attack upon the independence of those states by the Holy Alliance." Canning replied that Britain was not prepared to take this action.

In many respects, the interests of the United States in Spanish America coincided with those of Britain. The long U.S. border with Spanish territory had just been agreed upon, and Spain could thus be assumed to be a friendly power. The United States well understood that a preponderance of sea power gave Britain a special role in America and was disposed to accept Britain's exercise of this role in the development of the new nations. But the interests of the United States and Britain also differed. The United States, for example, looked with special apprehension upon the possibility of Cuba passing into the hands of either Britain or France. Moreover, she had come to feel that her own future as a nation was in a real way identified with the cause of Latin American independence, in the sense of keeping European colonial powers out of America.

The United States had successfully objected to an extension of Russian claims down to California on the west coast and was negotiating a treaty (1824) by which Russia accepted the line of 54° 40′ as the southern boundary of Alaska. (The Oregon territory had been gained from Spain by the treaty of 1819.) In the course of these negotiations Secretary Adams had told the Russian minister "that the American continents are no longer subjects for any new European colonial establishments." Earlier, as we have seen, Adams had refused an invitation from the Russian government to join in a meeting of the Quadruple Alliance powers to consider the future of the Spanish empire in America. Subsequently, a Russian note of October 16, 1823, in refusing to consider recognition of the new republics, implied that if the United States departed from neutrality Russia might support Spain. Adams was not moved, seeing that a balance of the powers in Europe gave the United States an independence she had not previously enjoyed.

The lines of the United States reply to the Canning proposal had already been laid down in U.S. policy, and the United States, accordingly, accepted all the Canning proposals except the second, which left recognition to "time and circumstances." There were those in the United States, of course, who were eying Texas and other northern Mexican territories with envy. But the United States position, as Adams wrote to Canning, was that these countries "were of right independent of all other nations and that it was our duty so to acknowledge them." The U.S. reply to Britain was accompanied by separate notes to Russia and France in which the United States principles were stated explicitly.[31]

Meanwhile, both Britain and Spain had rejected the French proposal at the Council of Verona (1823) for a congress to oblige Ferdinand to approve autonomous monarchies in America.[32] Canning, as noted, had reached an informal agreement with France that was formulated in the Polignac Memorandum, in which France promised that she would not intervene by force in Spanish America. This Canning-Polignac agreement effectively dissipated the threat of any effective action by the Quadruple Alliance in Spanish America, making it unimportant for Britain to have United States support. Because of the slowness of communications, however, Monroe and Adams did not know of this Anglo-French agreement when Monroe's message was delivered to Congress on December 4, 1823, even though Canning had told Minister Rush of the agreement and had published the memorandum in October of that year.

Adams persuaded Monroe to adopt a less militant tone than he first intended in the foreign policy statement in his annual (1823) message to Congress. President Monroe was motivated by his own desire to

31. See Dexter Perkins, *The Monroe Doctrine, 1623–1826* (Cambridge: Harvard University Press, 1927) Chap. 4.

32. Pedro de Leturia, *Relaciones entre la Santa Sede e Hispanoamérica* (3 vols.; Rome and Caracas: Sociedad Bolivariana de Venezuela, 1959), III, 230.

state an independent policy, but much of the language he used was that of Secretary Adams. Thus, Adams was responsible for Monroe's deleting two statements in the message: a reproof to France for suppressing the revolution in Spain and a demand for recognition of the independence of Greece. Adams' view was expressed in a clear statement of the policy of nonintervention in Europe, a position, moreover, which had its roots in policies of Washington and Jefferson.

The moderate statement on the revolutionary movements of Europe was an echo of both Washington and Jefferson:

> Our policy in regard to Europe, which was adopted at an early stage of the wars which have so long agitated that quarter of the globe, nevertheless remains the same, which is not to interfere in the internal concerns of any of its powers; to consider the government de facto as the legitimate government for us, to cultivate friendly relations by a frank, firm, and manly policy meeting in all instances the just claims of every power, submitting to injuries from none.

The statement of the principles of noncolonization and nonintervention by Europe in the Americas stood out in striking contrast to the United States policy of nonintervention in Europe.

> . . . that the American continents, by the free and independent conditions which they have assumed and maintain, are henceforth not to be considered as subjects for future colonization by any European powers. . . . We owe it, therefore, to candor and to the amicable relations existing between the United States and those powers to declare that we should consider any attempt on their parts to extend their system to any portion of this hemisphere as dangerous to our peace and safety.[33]

Although the effects could not be seen at the time, and were not recognized until much later in Europe, Adams had left an indelible imprint on United States policy and upon the foreign relations of all the Americas. "The ground I wish to take," he had said, "is that of earnest remonstrance against the interference of European powers by force in South America, but to disclaim all interference on our part in Europe, to make an American cause and adhere inflexibly to that."[34]

---

33. The text is available in Ruhl J. Bartlett (ed.), *The Record of American Diplomacy* (New York: Knopf, 1964), 181–83.
34. Quoted in Bemis, *John Quincy Adams*, 389.

He had his way, and the "combined system of polity" he formulated was to be not only the most persistent element in United States policy towards Latin America, but an inescapable element in the foreign policies of the Latin American nations as well.

Policies of the Independence Movements

Some of the general objectives of the revolutionary governments of the independence movements in their relations with the United States and with the nations of Europe have been noted earlier in this chapter. It remains only to note some of the more specific objectives of the individual movements and something of their relations with each other.

The Haitian movement, in its early years under Toussaint L'Ouverture, was more concerned with the end of slavery and with foreign trade than with independence. Under Toussaint, who professed loyalty to France, the political objective became recognition of Haitian autonomy—not formal independence—with Toussaint as governor for life. After her declaration of independence, as we have seen, Haiti was not successful in gaining recognition from France until 1825, and then under onerous terms. Division of the country into a black monarchy under Henri Christophe and a mulatto republic under Alexandre Pétion complicated the problem of recognition, as did Haiti's aid to Bolívar on the condition of his proclaiming freedom of the slaves in Spanish South America.

In respect to Brazil, as we have seen, Brazilian agents in the United States and Britain succeeded quickly in gaining recognition for the new monarchy. Thus, Brazil started off her independent national life with the advantage of a profitable trade with Britain, a growing trade with the United States, and good relations with the mother country and other nations of Europe—even with the Vatican. But she also had troubles. The treaty with Britain, although ratified by the emperor of Brazil, was never submitted to the Brazilian parliament, probably because of the trade privileges granted Britain and because of the treaty's provision for suppressing the African slave trade to Brazil. Thus the Brazilian parliament continued to insist that the treaty was not binding.

Independence also confronted Brazil with complicated problems in her relations with independent Paraguay and Argentina, including the question of the expanding Portuguese territorial claims in the Plata valley. Portuguese-Brazilian influence had helped bring about the independence of Paraguay. The latter's independence was, in part at least, a counter product of a Brazilian mission that offered armed support to a governor of Paraguay who supported the Spanish regency against the Revolution of May in Buenos Aires, but who also opposed the Paraguayan criollo desire for control of the province. In effect, Paraguay got her independence both by defeating Buenos Aires pretensions and by resisting the extension of Portuguese-Brazilian power.[35] The Banda Oriental (Uruguay) had been held by Portuguese troops since they defeated the Uruguayan independence leader, José G. Artigas, in 1816. The problem of the loyalty of this army in Uruguay was scarcely settled by the withdrawal of the Portuguese soldiers when Argentina (late 1825) came to the support of the Uruguayans (the "Thirty-three Immortals") who were renewing their struggle for independence. The resulting war between Argentina and Brazil was a stalemate, although it was regarded by the Argentines as a victory. Mediation by the British minister in Brazil, Lord Strangford, resulted in a treaty (1828) in which both Brazil and Argentina recognized the independence of Uruguay.

Spanish America was fatally divided and was plagued by the differences in political objectives of the several independence movements. No one voice—leader or congress—could speak for the whole of Spanish America. Not until Bolívar's Panama Congress of 1826 did the Spanish American nations really endeavor to form a united front to negotiate recognition by Spain. But this congress, as we shall see in the next chapter, broke up in failure because of the jealousies of Mexico and Colombia.

These Spanish American wars for independence need to be understood as vicious civil wars, pitting the rebels against loyalists who wished to retain the tie with Spain and to retain the colonial institutions unchanged. It should be noted that many Indians and *castas* supported them, regarding the Spanish crown and the Church as

35. Cooney, "Paraguayan Independence and Doctor Francia."

their protectors. Many of the rebels, moreover, were not republicans; they hoped by establishing constitutional monarchies, with Bourbon or other princes, to retain the existing social structure. Yet the new Spanish nations became republics after the civil war in Argentina in 1819 and after the failure of the Iturbide monarchy in Mexico. This republican trend was welcomed by the United States, but was looked on with less favor by Britain. Republics were even more thoroughly disapproved of as too revolutionary by the other powers of the Quadruple Alliance. Although the international Church supported Spain, many priests had joined the revolutionary movements. Anticlerical measures, including the appropriation of religious foundations, were common in the course of the independence movements. These developments gave rise to serious issues in seeking recognition of the new republics by the Vatican and in reaching agreement on Church policy, both fundamentally important for these Roman Catholic countries.

During the long war years, Spanish markets for Spanish American products had disappeared, and Spanish sources of new capital had dried up. These needs had been supplied, but only partly, by the growing trade (much of it illegal) with Britain and the United States. The need of the new governments for foreign credits to revive agriculture and mining was met to some extent by loans negotiated with London bankers in 1825, on the eve of British recognition, and by the negotiation of British treaties of commerce, such as that with Argentina in 1825. But the British optimism in respect to Spanish American investments was soon dissipated, because the new governments promptly defaulted on the loans. Spanish American agreement with Britain to suppress the international slave trade was a much less serious problem than that in the case of Brazil, since all of Spanish America (except Cuba as a Spanish colony), immediately embarked on a program of emancipation, either gradual or immediate.

The great diplomatic failure of the Spanish American independence movements was the failure to achieve their major objective—prompt acceptance of their independence by Spain and by the Vatican. Some Latin Americans like to blame this failure of the diplomacy of the independence movements, and the consequent "Balkanization" of

Spanish America, on the ambivalence of British and United States policy, together with the blind opposition of the reactionary powers of Europe in the Metternich era. But, in all fairness, it should be seen that no small part of the blame is theirs, as we shall see in the next chapter, for their failure to agree among themselves in the Panama Congress of 1826. Spain, too, must bear a share of the blame, because of King Ferdinand's unreasonable and blind refusal to recognize Spanish American independence for more than a decade (in some cases longer) after this independence was a fact.

Spanish policy in dealing with the independence movements after the end of the Napoleonic wars is best characterized as one of failure. Rejecting British mediation, and fearful of Portuguese-Brazilian expansion, she missed the opportunity to check the growth of British (and subsequent United States) influence by coming to terms with her former colonies as independent states, as Britain did in the case of the United States. The course she followed opened the way to a growth of British influence, a virtual predominance of Britain, in the nineteenth century. A more intelligent course would have forged a Spanish family of nations capable of maintaining its independence of both Britain and the Metternich-dominated alliance of European powers.[36]

36. On this failure of Spanish policy see the excellent article by Enoch Resnick, "A Case in Futility: The Spanish Expedition to the Rio de la Plata (1814–1820)," *Revista Portuguesa de Historia* (Coimbra), XV (1974), 71–87.

4　Relations During the Time of Troubles, 1825–1860

HAROLD EUGENE DAVIS

Problems of Peace and Recognition

The first problem faced by the new nations in their international relations was to achieve acceptance into the community of nations. This involved making peace with their respective mother countries, securing recognition by other countries, and adjusting their relations as Catholic nations with the Holy See. For all countries except Brazil these proved to be baffling and frustrating problems for many years. Later they would need to seek independence of policy, liquidating the international ties and compromises incurred while gaining independence. But for many of the nations this goal was not achieved during the years covered in this chapter.

Meanwhile, the states had to agree upon and demarcate boundaries with their neighbors and to recognize the independence of new states breaking off from the old. They had to reach agreement upon Church-state policy both within the nations and with the Holy See. This was a special difficulty for the Spanish American states, involving frustrating relationships with the Vatican. All the nations, but Brazil especially, had to confront the questions involved in the abolition of the international slave trade, an issue inescapably raised by the independence movements and by British nineteenth-century policy.

One of the most difficult problems for the new nations was that of establishing sound and profitable commercial and financial relations with each other, with the United States, with Great Britain, and with the other nations of the Old World upon whose markets and financial resources they had depended and would continue to depend. These problems of international economic relations were linked closely, of course, to the achievement of national fiscal stability. This was an especially agonizing problem since some of the wars for independence had continued more than a decade, leaving national finances in a state of near chaos.

As has been suggested earlier, the new world nations tended in certain respects to reinforce basic trends in the international law and policies that had developed within the European family of nations— particularly those trends expressing the enlarging concept of national sovereignty and a broader scope of international relations both in war and peace. Thus, the Treaty Plan adopted by the United States in 1776, which aimed to enlarge freedom in international trade through "the most favored nation" clause and to broaden the freedom of the high seas, even in time of war, had such precedents in the past as the Franco-British treaty of 1713. When the plan found expression in the commercial treaty of 1778 with France, it was following the lines of this earlier Franco-British agreement in its trade provisions.[1] In Latin America a similar economic policy trend, which had found expression in the treaty of 1750 between Spain and Portugal, provided a model for the new nations.

In other respects, however, the New World nations helped to initiate new trends in international policy. They did in fact adopt in many respects the United States Treaty Plan of 1776, with its most-favored-nation principle and its emphasis on the rights of neutral maritime trade. The obvious ultimate objective of this plan was a society of nations whose basic economic relations would be governed by a uniform structure of legal rights and obligations. From the beginning the Latin American nations displayed a comparable dedication to the concept of a world of nations also governed in political aspects by international law, but their legal heritage, based on the tradition of Francisco Vitoria (1480–1546) and Francisco Suárez (1546–1617), Spanish fathers of international law, differed as noted from that of

1. Julius W. Pratt, *a History of United States Foreign Policy* (New York: Prentice Hall, 1955), 70, citing Department of State, *Policy of the U.S. toward Maritime Commerce in War*. For the U.S. Treaty Plan of 1776 (modified in 1784) see Pratt or Robert H. Ferrell (ed.), *Foundations of American Diplomacy, 1775–1872* (New York and Evanston: Harper & Row, 1968), 44–48.

their northern neighbor. They did not agree among themselves on Church policy, but in general they wanted from the Holy See an extension of the *patronato*, including the right of their national governments to regulate and reform certain institutional aspects of the Church.

Even more revolutionary was the assertion of the right of self-determination of peoples as a guiding principle of policy. This principle was a fundamental rejection of the system of colonialism. Latin American adoption of its corollary, the recognition of de facto governments originating in revolution, had been expressed in French recognition of the United States by the Treaty of Alliance between France and the United States (1778) and more clearly by the United States recognition of the French Republic in 1792. This principle was a revolutionary challenge of the principle of "legitimacy." Thomas Jefferson, as United States secretary of state, declared on that occasion that the United States acknowledged "any government to be rightful which is formed by the will of the nation substantially declared."

But while the Latin American nations generally followed this principle of de facto recognition, some notable exceptions occurred. Argentina and Brazil withheld recognition from Paraguay, the latter until 1840 and the former until 1852. Mexico refused for a decade to recognize the independence of Texas. Yet fundamentally the Latin American nations had welcomed President Monroe's 1823 statement (the Monroe Doctrine) that the emerging state system in the Americas was "essentially different" from that of Europe.

Long after independence, most of the nations continued to be plagued by internal problems, including factional disputes, fiscal difficulties, and unresolved constitutional issues. These factors affected adversely their capacity to conduct foreign relations and often raised serious questions in the minds of Europeans as to the viability of the new nations. They also seemed to invite foreign intervention.

In these respects Brazil enjoyed a more favorable position than the Spanish American countries or Haiti, because she came into existence with a higher degree of acceptance or approval by Portugal, Britain, Austria, and the Vatican. But her course was disputed during these early years by the "Portuguese Question" (the inheritance of the Portuguese crown by Pedro I in 1826 upon the death of his father, King João). This problem contributed to the abdication of Pedro I, and to the civil war of these years in Portugal. Haiti was belatedly recognized by France in 1825; but her inability to make the promised indemnity payments, increased by the terms of a French loan for the first payment, delayed the negotiation of a treaty regulating her relations with the mother country until 1838. Recognition of Haiti by the United States was delayed even longer—until the 1860s. Meanwhile, she was torn by civil strife and lived in fear of foreign intervention, while trying to absorb Spanish Santo Domingo and ultimately losing it.

All the nations began their national existence with large foreign and domestic debts from the wars for independence which they had to refund and amortize. These obligations usually increased in succeeding years by the addition of foreign claims growing out of the revolutionary violence of the post-independence years. During the early 1820s most of the nations negotiated loans in Europe to refund their debts or to finance deficits they expected. British investors, the principal creditors, supplied credits totaling over twenty million pounds sterling between 1818 and 1825. Interest on these loans was usually 6 percent, but in reality it was much higher, since the bonds were invariably sold at much less than their face value (58 to 89.75 percent). By the end of the decade, payments on most of these loans were in default, and the tightness of credit in London made it difficult for the countries to refund them. Some British capital flowed into Latin America during the following decades, but only in small amounts until the 1860s.[2]

Domestic financial problems were likewise difficult. Some of the old Spanish taxes had been abolished, and such new taxes as had been imposed had not produced sufficient revenue to service the debts and support the more extensive political systems which independence entailed, including the cost of the armies inherited from the wars for independence. A long depression in the mining industries, almost all

2. J. Fred Rippy, *British Investments in Latin America, 1822–1949* (Minneapolis: University of Minnesota Press, 1959), Chap. 2.

of which needed new capital and modernization, together with a decline in exports to foreign markets during the Napoleonic wars and the wars for independence, militated against an increase in tax revenues in many countries, even when the new governments were strong enough to impose the necessary tax laws. It became apparent that Spanish America no longer enjoyed the favorable balance in trade which had made American colonies a major source of Spain's wealth in the eighteenth century. Lack of economic development contributed to this lack of fiscal stability, but irresponsible management of the national debt and credit structure was also a major cause of the political instability that plagued most of the nations. Fiscal stability was impossible, of course, without political stability and vice versa. Only a few nations achieved some practical resolution of this difficult dilemma during this "time of troubles," and only these few achieved any real autonomy in their external policy.

The Panama Congress of 1826

The Panama Congress of 1826 was Bolívar's effort to get the new nations to deal jointly with their problems. Its failure highlights the tragedy of the independence of Spanish America—its fractioning into eighteen sometimes turbulent and frequently quarreling nations. The congress was a major, some would say a fatal, disappointment of the Spanish American aspiration for union. But its results were not entirely negative; it also had a positive significance in the sense of setting the stage for subsequent relations of the American nations with each other.

In their very origin, the independence movements had been linked with the idea of confederation. In the late eighteenth century, the exiled Peruvian Jesuit Juan de Vizcardo y Guzmán, in his *Carta a los Españoles Americanos*, had urged that independence with confederation would create a great American "family of brothers" (*un gran familia de hermanos*). The unsuccessful revolt of Gual y España in Venezuela (1797) was carried out in the name of *"el pueblo americano,"* as was the Mexican revolution of 1810 led by Miguel Hidalgo. In one form or another the concept of Spanish American union was expressed by leaders of the movements in every sector of Spanish America. Francisco Miranda of Venezuela, Juan Egaña and Juan Martínez de Rosas of Chile, José Cecilio del Valle of Central America, José J. Fernández de Lizardi of Mexico, Juan Puerreydón and José de San Martín of Argentina, and José Artigas of Uruguay all spoke of union. As early as 1815, Bolívar, in his "Jamaica letter" envisaged a league or union of a family of independent nations. The early leaders of independence in Argentina adopted the style, "the United Provinces of America." In 1813 Mexico declared the independence of *"la América Septentrional"* (North America), and the first proposal for a Mexican constitution (1814) referred to *"los pueblos de esta América"* as the region to be governed.

Thus the plan for a congress of the new American states to organize an American confederation was more than a hasty improvisation of Bolívar's fertile imagination. Rather, it expressed one of the fundamental underlying assumptions of the independence movement as a whole.[3]

On the surface, conditions seemed ideal for the congress to which Colombia invited the nations of America in 1826. The war for independence in South America had ended in a decisive defeat of the Spanish forces at Ayacucho in December, 1824. Bolivian independence had followed. Spanish power in America was now confined to Cuba and Puerto Rico. Even the Dominican Republic had achieved its independence, though only to be conquered immediately by Haiti. The Canning-Polignac agreement, followed by the Monroe Doctrine, gave reasonable assurance that the Quadruple Alliance would not be able to support Spain or any other European power in restoring empire in America.

Yet this very decline in external danger, as Juan B. Alberdi was to

3. Cf. Antonio Gómez Robledo, *Idea y Experienca de América* (Mexico: Fondo de Cultura Económica, 1958) 35–43; Francisco Cuevas Cancino, *Del Congreso de Panamá a la Conferencia de Caracas, 1826–1954* (2 vols.; Caracas: n.p., 1955), I, 51–163; Victor Andrés Belaunde, *Bolívar and the Political Thought of the Spanish American Revolution* (Baltimore: Johns Hopkins University Press, 1938); J. M. Yepes, *Del Congreso de Panamá a la Conferencia de Caracas, 1826–1954* (2 vols.; Caracas: n.p., 1955), I, 37–136; Augusto Mijares, *El Libertador* (Caracas: Ed. Arte, 1965), 490–93; and Daniel Guerra Iñiquez, *El Pensamiento Internacional de Bolívar* (Caracas: "Ed. Ragón," 1955).

point out a few years later,[4] made the proposed defensive alliance seem to many of the nations, preoccupied as they were with internal problems and plagued by political instability, less urgent in 1826 than in the immediately preceding years. The basis for the conference had been laid in a series of treaties negotiated by Colombia with the United Provinces of La Plata, Peru, Chile, Central America, and Mexico. But Argentina had resolved to go her own way. By 1820 she had rejected even the San Martín policy of a league of independent monarchies linked to a European dynasty. She was engaged, moreover, in a war with Brazil for control of Uruguay initiated by the "Thirty-three Immortals," out of which an independent Uruguay was to emerge in 1828. Her fear of Bolívar's ambition to unite Spanish America had led her to reject the latter's offer in 1825 to lead an army against Brazil in this war. Meanwhile, Chile was torn by internal political conflict. Moreover, she was disinclined to follow the lead of a Bolívar who had usurped for Colombia the influence previously exercised in Peru by the Chileans who, with San Martín had brought about Peruvian independence.[5]

Mexico agreed to attend the conference; but Mexican ideas ran counter to those of the leadership of Colombia and of Bolívar. Hoping to be the spokesman of the other nations in negotiating peace with Spain, Mexico was not ready to relinquish leadership to Bolívar. Haiti, the second oldest republic in America, was not invited.[6] Brazil was invited belatedly and accepted the invitation. But she did not send a representative to the congress, probably because of her involvement in war with Argentina over the Banda Oriental. The invita-

4. In a thesis presented at the College of Law, University of Chile: Juan B. Alberdi, *Memoria Sobre la Conveniencia i Objectos de un Congreso Jeneral Americano*. Santiago: Imprenta del Siglo, 1844. See Harold Eugene Davis, "Juan Bautista Alberdi, Americanist," *Journal of Inter-American Studies*, IV (January, 1962), 53–65.

5. See Benjamin Vicuña MacKenna, *San Martín, la Revolución de la Independencia del Perú* (Santiago: Universidad de Chile, 1938); Ricardo Piccirilli, *San Martín y la Política de los Pueblos* (Buenos Aires: Ediciones Gure, S.R.L., 1957; and Vicente G. Quesada, *Historia Diplomática Hispanoamericana* (3 vols.; Buenos Aires: La Cultura Argentina, 1918–1920), I, 329.

6. Félix G. Fernández-Shaw, *La Organización de los Estados Americanos* (2nd ed.; Madrid: Ediciones Cultura Hispánica, 1963), 100–101. On Mexican policy see Carlos Bosch-García, *Problemas Diplomáticos del México Independiente* (Mexico: El Colegio de México, 1947), and *Relaciones Diplomáticos Hispanomexicanos, 1839–1898* (Mexico: El Colegio de México, 1949).

tion to Brazil, like that to the United States, had been an afterthought of the Colombians, for Bolívar had originally conceived of a conference of Spanish American states only, one which might engage the political support of Great Britain as "the natural ally of Hispanic America" in negotiating peace with Spain. Delegates attended from Colombia, Peru, Central America, Mexico, and the United States (arriving late), with observers from Britain and the Netherlands.

Disappointed in her efforts to mediate a settlement between Spain and Spanish America, Britain was settling down to a policy of furthering British trade interests and preventing the intrusion of a rival power into such strategically important areas as Cuba, the Central American Isthmus, and the Río de la Plata area. Along with Holland, she was invited to send an observer to the conference, and did so, as noted. But the instructions to her representative were far short of the undertaking to underwrite Spanish American independence that Bolívar had hoped for. The British observer was instructed chiefly to ascertain whether the United States intended to enter into a league with the Hispanic American states.

British policy had been successful in dealing with Brazilian independence, as we have seen, and had laid the basis for a predominant British influence in Brazilian policy throughout the nineteenth century. Her Spanish policy was less successful. In 1823, as previously noted, Canning had tried, with only partial success, to enlist United States support for Britain's Spanish American policy. Suspicious that the Canning proposal would stand in the way of a growing interest of the United States in the area, Adams and Monroe had insisted upon immediate recognition of Spanish America and asserted the independent policy known as the Monroe Doctrine. The power balance which Canning had brought about in the Polignac agreement, with this partial United States support, achieved some but not all of the British objectives. But its success partially explains the do-nothing attitude adopted by Britain in the Panama Congress. British policy becomes even clearer when read in the light of the confusion in the relations of the Hispanic nations among themselves and of the British need to avoid provoking further French and Spanish adventures in America. In this situation British interest required nothing more from the

United States at Panama than an assurance that she would not disturb the balance of power by entering into an alliance with the new states.

In the United States the invitation to the Bolivarian congress produced mixed reactions. Having rid herself of the French alliance, the United States had committed herself to a policy of neutrality opposed to permanent alliances. After the War of 1812, the balance of power in Europe and America enabled the United States to pursue this policy with more assurance. But Henry Clay, then secretary of state, persuaded President John Quincy Adams that participation in the Bolivarian congress need not involve such an alliance and that it would be in the national interest to participate. Participation, he argued, could bring the support of the Hispanic nations for the objectives the United States was seeking concerning the rights of neutrals to trade in time of war, restriction of blockades, maximum freedom in international trade, and the right to change citizenship. These were the objectives later stressed in Clay's written instructions to the delegates.

The president decided to nominate two delegates, but the nominations met a hostile reception in Congress, setting off a prolonged debate in both houses. Among other things, Clay had to explain to Congress that the statement of Joel Poinsett, United States Minister to Mexico—to the effect that the Monroe Doctrine was a "pledge" to protect Spanish America—was in fact not a promise of alliance.[7] The nominations of Richard Anderson and John Sergeant were finally approved in March, 1826, but funds were not approved by Congress until April, too late for the delegates to arrive in time to participate in the congress. Anderson died along the way, at Cartagena, Colombia. Sergeant had not yet set out for Panama when news arrived that the congress had adjourned to Tacubaya, outside Mexico City. In Tacubaya he found only a frustrated rump meeting of the conference, which had no support from home governments.

The Panama Congress had framed a Treaty of Perpetual Union, League and Confederation, in accord with the Bolivarian plan. It had then adjourned while envoys carried copies of the treaty to their respective countries, seeking approval. Only Colombia ratified the trea-

7. Randolph Campbell, "Henry Clay and the Poinsett Pledge," *The Americas*, XXVIII (April, 1972), 429–40.

ty. The adjourned congress in Tacubaya lingered on for months, hoping for Mexican congressional approval of the treaty that never came. Mexican opposition to Colombian leadership and Argentine aloofness had doomed it to failure.[8]

But the Panama Congress was not a total loss, for it had brought out the importance of some kind of Hispanic or Spanish American union, and was to be followed during the nineteenth century by a series of hemispheric conferences that were to result finally in the Organization of American States. The subsequent conference at Lima in 1847/48, although it too failed to produce a lasting league, served to keep the objective alive. Common problems, common interests, and common backgrounds of language, culture, and religion kept alive in Spanish America the need for union symbolized by the Bolivarian project, so that, consciously or unconsciously, it formed part of the policy orientation of the new nations. The Colombian J. M. Yepes has called the treaties of Panama "one of the principal sources of American international law."[9]

In each succeeding decade some move in the direction of union was sponsored by one or more nations. In the early 1830s, under the direction of Lucas Alamán, Mexico tried to make herself a spokesman for all the nations of Spanish America in negotiating for Spanish recognition; but she had little success in enlisting other countries to follow her lead. For all practical purposes, this Bolivarian movement ended when Mexico negotiated recognition unilaterally.[10] Thereafter, under the somewhat more liberal Spanish regime that followed the death of Ferdinand, the threat of Spanish intervention, the principal motivation for union, almost disappeared. It reappeared in

8. J. B. Lockey, *Pan Americanism: Its Beginnings* (New York: Macmillan Co., 1920), is a standard work on the Panama Congress; but see also Charles G. Fenwick, *The Organization of American States: The Inter-American Regional System* (Washington, D.C.: n.p., 1936), Fernandez-Shaw, *La Organización de los Estados Americanos*, Yepes, *Del Congreso de Panamá a la Conferencia de Caracas* (I, 81–115), and Cuevas Cancino, *Del Congreso de Panamá a la Conferencia de Caracas*; also S. G. Inman, *Inter-American Conferences 1826–1954: History and Problems* (Washington: University Press of Washington, D.C., 1965), Chap. 1, and Oscar Barrenechea y Raygada, *El Congreso de Panamá, 1826* (Lima: Ministerio de Relaciones Exteriores, 1942).

9. Yepes, *Del Congreso de Panamá a la Conferencia de Caracas*, I, 111.

10. On the Mexican policy see Bosch-García, *Problemas Diplomáticos del México Independiente*.

mid-century, however, when threats of Spanish, French, British, and United States intervention prompted the previously mentioned Spanish American congress in 1847/48, during the war between Mexico and the United States, at a time when European intervention also seemed to threaten. A series of similar gestures for Spanish American union were to be made during the fifties and sixties, but with little tangible result.

Spanish Recognition

After the rebellion of the Riego expedition in 1820 and the restoration of constitutional government in 1820, Spain was unable to put together another expeditionary force. In America the defeat of the loyalists in the battles of Junín and Ayacucho in 1823 and 1824 ended the war for practical purposes, leaving the Spanish forces in control of only Cuba and Puerto Rico. But Spain was no more able to negotiate peace than to wage war. King Ferdinand seemed blind to the possibilities of a policy such as was pursued by Portugal and Britain in reestablishing profitable relations with their former colonies. No Spanish American states achieved recognition of independence until after Ferdinand's death in 1833. Under the regency of María Cristina, which followed, a more liberal attitude prevailed in Spain (and more conservative political forces prevailed in the New World). Mexico was the first to be recognized in 1835. Colombia was recognized in 1838 and Ecuador in 1840. Spanish recognition of the other nations was delayed much longer, thus closing the most natural avenue for the Spanish American states to assume a full role in their relations with the European powers, tending to throw them into the arms of Britain, or occasionally into those of France or the United States.[11]

Relations with the Holy See

During the years following 1810, in which Napoleon flirted with the Spanish American independence movements, the Vatican, under

11. Yepes, *Del Congreso de Panamá a la Conferencia de Caracas*, I, 141, gives the following dates of Spanish recognition: Mexico 1835, Bolivia 1847, Nicaragua 1850, Argentina 1858, Costa Rica 1859, Guatemala 1863, El Salvador 1865, Peru 1865, Paraguay 1880, Colombia 1881, Uruguay 1882, Honduras 1894.

French influence, also seems to have cast a favorable eye on the revolutionary movements, while avoiding specific commitments. Enrique D. Dussel writes of an encyclical of Pius VII (1813) to the Latin American clergy, entitled *"En pro de la Revolución."*[12] After the restoration of Ferdinand, papal policy tended to follow that of Spain and of the Holy Alliance, by withholding recognition. Bolívar was able to gain the ear of the Pope in 1827, however, and in 1831, even before the death of Ferdinand, an encyclical, *Solicitudo Ecclesiarum*, proposed a more independent policy to the effect that political vicissitudes should not prevent the Holy See from providing for such spiritual needs as the appointment of bishops. This statement, occasioned by the civil war then going on in Portugal between the two royal brothers, Miguel and Pedro, was protested by the Spanish Chargé d'Affaires in Rome, but the Pope's reply kept the door open for action in Spanish America.

The Pope had recognized Brazil in 1825, receiving a Brazilian minister without any question, following Portuguese recognition by treaty in 1825, and in accordance with the example of Austria. (The Brazilian queen was an Austrian Hapsburg.) The decision to recognize was intimately related to the question of the possible union of the crowns of Portugal and Brazil.[13] A nuncio appointed to the court in Rio de Janeiro was given general jurisdiction over all of South America. In 1833 the Pope recognized (de facto) the republic of New Granada by receiving her minister in Rome. This action was followed in quick succession by the recognition of Mexico (1836), Ecuador (1838), and Chile (1840).

In 1836 the Pope named an internuncio to Bogotá, and a few years later gave him general jurisdiction over all of Spanish South America. Recognition of other countries was delayed much longer, the grounds for the delay often being cited as political instability. But recognition

12. Enrique D. Dussel, *Historia de la Iglesia en América Latina* (Barcelona: Editorial Nova Terra, 1972), 109.
13. Hildebrando Accioly, *Os Primeiros Nuncios no Brasil* (São Paulo: Instituto Progresso Editorial, 1949), 205–208. Pedro de Leturia, *Relaciones entre la Santa Sede e Hispanoamérica* (3 vols.; Rome and Caracas: Sociedad Bolivariana de Venezuela, 1959), III, 60 ff. See also John L. Mecham, *Church and State in Latin America* (Chapel Hill: University of North Carolina Press, 1966), and Wilfred H. Callcott, *Church and State in Mexico, 1822–1857* (Durham, N.C.: Duke University Press, 1926).

also involved such difficult substantive issues as the exercise of the *patronato* by the new republics, the suppression of religious orders, charitable foundations, and schools, the secularization of the state, and the rising demand for religious toleration. Recognition did not necessarily mean agreement on such issues, which awaited the negotiation of a treaty (concordat) recognizing Roman Catholicism as the national religion and regulating Church-state relations. These concordats came much later, generally after mid-century, if at all,[14] so that the Church in Latin America, a major part of the world Roman Catholic Church, lived in semiisolation during much of the nineteenth century.

Agreements with the Holy See on church policy were important, if only because of the historical importance of the Church as a social institution in the area. But a number of factors stood in the way of

---

14. See Leturia, *Relaciones entre la Santa Sede e Hispanoamérica,* III, 60 and *passim.* According to Angelo Mercati, *Raccolta di Concordati: Su Materie Ecclestiastiche tra la Santa Sede e la Autorita Civili* (2 vols.; Citta del Vaticano: Tipografia Poligiotta Vaticana, 1954), concordats have been negotiated as follows:

Guatemala:	7 October, 1852 Concordat
	2 July, 1884 Concordat
Costa Rica:	7 October, 1852 Concordat
Haiti:	28 March, 1860 Concordat
	25 January, 1940 Convention
Honduras:	9 July, 1861 Concordat
Nicaragua:	2 November, 1861 Concordat
San Salvador:	22 April, 1862 Concordat
Venezuela:	26 July, 1862 Concordat
Ecuador:	26 September, 1862 Concordat
	2 March, 1881 New Version of 1862 Concordat (suspended in 1887)
	8 November, 1890 Concordat
	24 July, 1937 Modus Vivendi and Convention
Colombia:	31 December, 1887 Concordat
	20 July, 1892 "Convención Adicional" to 1887 Concordat
	"In 1898, and following at ten year intervals, supplementary conventions were negotiated establishing the amount the government should appropriate to the Church." Cf. Mecham, *Church and State in Latin America,* 132.
	1902 Convention (concerning missions)
	1942 Convention (which modified 1887 Concordat)
	1953 Concordat
	According to *Diario las Américas* (22 July, 1967), President Pastrana told Congress that negotiations would begin in a few days in Bogotá with the Vatican to reform the 1887 Concordat to be more consonant with the modern social conditions and the Vatican II.
Dominican Republic:	16 June, 1954 Concordat.

successful negotiations to establish national political relations with the Vatican, so that concordats were not negotiated until after mid-century. One factor was the reforming zeal of some of the republican leaders, who urged various anticlerical measures, including levies upon church wealth. Another factor was the reluctance of the Vatican to negotiate with republics. The desire of the Holy See to liberate the church from the *patronato*, under which the Spanish crown had controlled ecclesiastical appointments, was a major difficulty. The continuing Spanish influence on Vatican policy, as we have seen, further prolonged the delay so long as Spain was refusing recognition of the new states. In general, Brazil escaped these difficulties as we have noted.

Boundary Problems in the Relations of the New States

The new nations faced serious problems in their early relations with each other. Such rivalries had appeared as early as the Panama Congress, as we have seen. Difficulties multiplied as Central America broke up into five small nations and Colombia into the three states of Venezuela, New Granada, and Ecuador, while Argentina failed to weld the former viceroyalty of La Plata into a single state and Mexico faced the secession of Texas (and the unsuccessful secession of Yucatán), as well as the loss of Central America.

All of the nations had troublesome boundary problems to confront. These problems were of several kinds. For the Spanish American states, the basic problem was that of identifying the boundaries of the Spanish viceroyalties, captaincies general, and provinces as of the year 1810, in accordance with the generally accepted Bolivarian principle of *uti possidetis juris*. Spanish American national boundaries were defined in these terms in the negotiations for recognition by the United States, and the Spanish treaties of recognition, when made, incorporated the principle. The breaking up of the nations as originally constituted created some new problems, as in the secession of Central America from Mexico in 1823.

Central America was allowed to go in peace, but the secession of Texas resulted in two wars—one for Texan independence and one with the United States resulting from the latter's annexation of Texas. Colombia allowed Venezuela and Ecuador to withdraw without serious opposition, even agreeing to a just division of the national debt. Argentina and Brazil warred over Uruguay, and Argentina withheld recognition from Paraguay until 1852. Chile, with Argentine support, went to war in 1836 to prevent the union of Bolivia and Peru.

The separation of Venezuela and Ecuador from Colombia in 1830 made Venezuela heir to the unsettled boundary with British Guiana, while Ecuador inherited the troublesome boundary problem of Gran Colombia with Peru concerning the territories of Jaén and Maines. In the breakup of Colombia, as in the breaking up of the Central American Federation a few years later, boundary questions, such as that of Cauca, annexed to Ecuador by the revolution after 1810, had to be settled among the former national partners. Guatemala had a problem of boundaries to settle with Mexico in respect to the province of Chiapas and with Britain in respect to Belize.

Separation of the viceroyalty of La Plata into the nations of Argentina, Uruguay, Paraguay, and Bolivia gave rise to a number of difficult questions. The territorial extent of Uruguay was fairly well settled by the treaty of 1828, except for the territory of Misiones. But this latter question and that of the boundaries of Argentina with Paraguay and Bolivia were to plague international relations for half a century; that of Bolivia and Paraguay did so until the Chaco War in the twentieth century.[15]

Bolivia was a problem in itself. She had been made a part of the viceroyalty of La Plata in 1776, but she had been reannexed to the viceroyalty of Lima by Viceroy Abascal in 1810.[16] Both Argentina and Peru were forced to acquiesce in the separate national existence, de-

15. On the boundary controversies, see the two standard works by Gordon Ireland: *Boundaries, Possessions, and Conflicts in South America* (Cambridge: Harvard University Press, 1938) and *Boundaries, Possessions, and Conflicts in Central America and the Caribbean* (Cambridge: Harvard University Press, 1941). But for a Spanish American (Argentine) view, see Quesada, *Historia Diplomática Hispanoamericana*, I, 95–114, 304 ff; III, 350 ff. On the principle of *uti possidetis* see Begnigno Checa Drouet, *La Doctrina Americana del "Uti Possidetis" de 1810* (Lima: Imprenta Gil, 1936).

16. John Lynch, *The Spanish American Revolutions, 1808–1826* (New York: Norton, 1973), 116–62.

creed by Bolívar, of what had once been Charcas. An Argentine mission had agreed with Bolívar and Sucre to accept the independence of Upper Peru (Bolivia), but a boundary problem ensued when Bolivia insisted on retaining the Department of Tarija, which Argentina claimed, under the principle of *uti possidetis*, as part of the intendency of Salta, a retention to which Bolívar had agreed. Not until the 1830s, however, when Chilean armies defeated and broke up the federation of Peru and Bolivia formed under Andrés Santa Cruz, was it certain that Bolivia would remain a separate nation; she existed precariously within a balance among the rival power ambitions of Argentina, Chile, and Peru. The boundaries of Paraguay with Argentina, Uruguay, and Brazil were to be settled ultimately by the Paraguayan War (1865–1870), except for the controversy between Brazil and Argentina over the territory of Misiones, ultimately settled by arbitration.

Brazil inherited an ill-defined boundary extending some 3,000 miles through territory sparsely inhabited in many parts by uncivilized natives and touching every nation of South America except Chile. The rule of *uti possidetis* as of 1810, as followed by the Spanish American states, could not apply to boundaries between Spanish and Portuguese territories. But Brazil developed her own version of *uti possidetis* in dealing with these boundary questions. Her rule of *uti possidetis actual* emphasized de facto occupation as the basis for a claim to territory. This rule served to justify Brazilian expansion into unoccupied lands claimed by the Spanish crown, while the Spanish Americans based their claims on the Spanish-Portuguese treaties of 1777 and 1778. Even before independence, the Brazilian principle had been accepted at least partially in the frustrating Portuguese-Spanish negotiations for the treaty of 1750 and the later agreements of San Ildefonso in 1777 and 1778, confirming Portuguese territorial expansion at Spanish expense. This Portuguese expansionism, inherited by Brazil, was to be a source of increasing apprehension to her Spanish American neighbors in South America, with all of whom, except Chile, she had boundaries to settle.[17]

17. On the Spanish-Portuguese treaty of 1750 see the classical work of Jaime Cortesão, *Alexandre de Gusmão e o Tratado de Madrid (1750)* (8 vols.; Rio de Janeiro: Ministerio de

Problems of the Plata Region

The internal problems of the Plata area during the decades immediately following independence had two basic roots. The first was that of the colonial rivalries of Spain and Portugal. The second cause, arising in the struggles for independence, included the failure of the old viceroyalty of La Plata to achieve unity as a nation and the failure of the new Spanish American nations of the region, for several decades, to achieve recognition of their independence by Spain.

In this latter respect, the situation of Argentina and Paraguay was especially tragic, because they alone among the Spanish American states had maintained independence after the restoration of Ferdinand in Spain. Argentina vainly sought recognition as a monarchy with a European prince acceptable to Spain, after declaring independence formally in 1816; in the course of doing so she became embroiled in a civil war that cost her all chance of uniting the viceroyalty. She had to watch Bolivia become independent under the aegis of Bolívar, but without recognizing that independence. She had to accept the independence of Uruguay as a buffer state between her and Brazil. She saw Paraguay remain independent but, as long as Rosas governed in Buenos Aires, refused to recognize that independence. She saw Paraguay collaborating with some of the Argentine interior provinces against the never-too-secure leadership of Buenos Aires in the loosely structured union of caudillos who ruled the country under Rosas.

Rosas could do little about Bolivia because of its remoteness, although he maintained the claim to Tarija; he gave what support he could, as we shall see later, to the war waged by Chile in 1837 to prevent the union of Bolivia with Peru. Paraguay continued, both under the dictator Francia (José Gaspar Rodríguez de) and under his successor (after 1840), Carlos Antonio López, to play off Brazil against Buenos Aires, while seeking political support in Uruguay and in the interior provinces, which were jealous of Buenos Aires. To combat

Relações Exteriores, Instituto Rio Branco, 1950–1960). On the Brazilian concept of *uti possidetis* see João Pandiá Calogeras, *A Política Exterior do Imperio* (2 vols.; Rio de Janeiro: Imprensa Nacional, 1927), I, Chap. 7. See also Quesada, *Historia Diplomática Hispanoamericana*, I, 95–114.

Rosas' policy of closing the Río de la Plata to Paraguayan commerce, Francia adopted a policy of economic isolation which virtually excluded all foreigners and foreign influence. López relaxed this policy somewhat, but the issue of the free access of Paraguay to the use of this river (and of its use by Brazil) was not resolved until after the overthrow of Rosas in 1852, when the new Argentine regime, under Justo José Urquiza, recognized Paraguayan independence. Only under the second López, Francisco Solano, did Paraguay depart from her by now traditional policy of carefully balancing Brazilian power against that of Argentina. The result, in the Paraguayan War, was to be disastrous to Paraguay.

When Argentina went to war against Brazil (1825) in support of the Uruguayan movement for independence led by the "Thirty-three Immortals," as we have noted, the British minister in Brazil had mediated to effect an end to the war, thus preventing the annexation of Uruguay by Argentina. This mediation indirectly helped to precipitate the breakup of the short-lived centralist union in Argentina under Bernardino Rivadavia (1826). Two years later the independence of Uruguay was recognized by both Brazil and Argentina under a treaty sponsored by Great Britain. Under this treaty neither nation gave up its political interest in Uruguay, however, and during the next quarter century Uruguay experienced a series of interventions by her neighbors. It is worthy of note that Britain did not guarantee Uruguay's independence by treaty. France later proposed to give such a guarantee, but was turned down.[18]

Prior to the British treaty of 1827, the Argentine government had negotiated a loan of one million pounds through Baring Brothers of London. The loan required 13 percent of the anticipated revenue of the government for its service and was backed by a pledge of income from the public lands. Anticipated British investments in mining at this time failed to materialize, and the Argentine government soon defaulted on the loan payments. Thus Britain had a continuing dispute with Argentina during the Rosas years, a major element in which was this defaulted loan. Other subjects of dispute were the British

18. H. S. Ferns, *Britain and Argentina in the Nineteenth Century* (Oxford: Clarendon Press, 1960), gives the best account of these early British-Argentine relations.

occupation of the Falkland Islands and British demands for the right of British Protestants in Argentina to exercise their religion.

The government of Rosas was usually short of money and probably did not have a balance of trade sufficient to meet foreign obligations. In any case, Rosas seemed to prefer to use such funds as he had for paying soldiers rather than meeting foreign debts. The British claim to the Falkland Islands had a basis in a problematical claim dating from the eighteenth century. In 1820 Argentina asserted sovereignty over the islands and a few years later appointed a governor. Governor Luis Vernet's arrest of three United States sealing-whaling vessels brought a brief occupation of the islands by U.S. forces in 1831, giving rise to a dispute which was never really settled, merely allowed to die. The British reoccupied the islands in 1832; Argentina protested and thus the matter stood. The religious issue with Britain was exacerbated by Rosas' policy of publicly emphasizing the Catholic character of the nation, although he lacked a formal agreement with the Holy See.

France, in accordance with the Spanish and Metternich policy, withheld recognition of Argentina until after the Orleanist Louis Philippe came to the throne in 1830. In 1834 she proposed an Argentine treaty that would have given her commercial privileges like those of Britain, but the treaty was disapproved in a secret session of Rosas' legislature. Thereafter Franco-Argentine relations deteriorated, France tending generally to support the enemies of Rosas.[19]

In 1837, on the eve of Argentina's unsuccessful participation in the war against Peru-Bolivia, a dispute over the actions of a French cartographer who had been asked to make a map for the campaign resulted in the expulsion of a French vice-consul. A French fleet which appeared in the harbor of Buenos Aires to negotiate a settlement furnished supplies (and French marines) to assist Fructuosa Rivera in driving President Oribe (a friend of Rosas) from Montevideo, forcing him to seek exile in Argentina.

In 1838 Rosas intervened in the civil war in Uruguay, supporting the Blanco party and the restoration of their president, Manuel

19. Emilio Ravignani, *Rosas: Interpretación Real y Moderna* (Buenos Aires: Pleamar, 1970), 27, 36.

Oribe, in order to have a friendly ruler in the presidential office—possibly looking to the ultimate annexation of Uruguay, despite the treaty of 1828. At this time a French fleet on the Plata sided with the party of Rivera *(Colorados)* and assisted in the temporary defeat of Oribe and Rosas. Under British pressure, France then came to an agreement with Rosas and withdrew.

Subsequently, in 1843, Rosas continued the struggle in Uruguay in the "Great War," which included an eight-year siege of Montevideo (1843–1851). British and French fleets stationed off the coast tried unsuccessfully to end the siege and the accompanying Argentine blockade of Montevideo. The United States Chargé d'Affaires in Montevideo collaborated in these efforts with his good offices, and two successive United States commanders of ships stationed in the Plata estuary went even further, claiming for U.S. citizens the same rights of trade as for the nationals of Britain and France. In the second of two incidents arising from these claims the U.S. commander (Pendergast) acted against the advice of the U.S. Chargé d'Affaires, William Brent, Jr. In both cases the commanders were reprimanded for their action by the United States secretary of the navy.

The early efforts of the British and French commanders to end the Argentine blockade and siege of Montevideo failed. Thereupon, the two countries, in a further effort to force Rosas to make peace with Uruguay, declared a blockade of Buenos Aires itself. This action was protested in the name of the United States by Brent, who called it "this so called and misnamed blockade."[20] The revolutions of 1848 and subsequent events in Europe caused both Britain and France to call off the blockade and to make peace with Rosas in 1850. Rosas was overthrown two years later (1852), not, however, it should be noted, by the British and French intervention. He was overthrown rather, as we shall see, by a union of Brazilian and Uruguayan *(Colorado)* forces with those in Entre Rios and Corrientes, led by Governor Justo José Urquiza. In part, Rosas' defeat must be attributed to Brazilian expan-

20. Ferns, *Britain and Argentina in the Nineteenth Century*, gives a good account. For the intervention by the U.S. commanders see *House Documents*, 29th Cong., 1st Sess., No. 212, p. 35, quoted in Graham T. Stuart, *Latin America and the United States* (5th ed.; New York: Appleton-Century-Crofts, 1955), 358.

sionism. But it was also due to the fact that he was no longer able to unite Argentines against this intervention.

The policy of Argentina changed in several important respects after the overthrow of Rosas. The independence of Paraguay was recognized; the Río de la Plata river system was opened to international commerce, in accordance with the demands of France, Great Britain, the United States, Brazil, and Paraguay. In 1853 the United States Navy undertook a scientific survey of the rivers of the Plata system, assigning a specially constructed vessel, the U.S.S. *Water Witch*, under Lieutenant Thomas Jefferson Page, to the mission. Both Argentina and Brazil accepted the operation of this mission, but the *Water Witch* was subsequently fired on by the Paraguayans, leading to an intervention of the United States by force to secure an apology and the payment of damages.[21]

Under President Urquiza, Argentina was recognized by Spain and strengthened her friendly relations with the United States, France, and Great Britain, while maintaining a policy of acting independently of the other Spanish American states. Juan B. Alberdi, as Urquiza's principal ambassador, played a large role in working out this new policy. Its success was limited, however, by the subsequent defection of Buenos Aires from the confederation. The rivalry of Brazil and Argentina in Uruguay and Paraguay did not end at this time, continuing up to the War of the Triple Alliance.[22]

Brazil

The central characteristic of the foreign relations of Brazil during these years is what Alan K. Manchester has appropriately termed

21. The (Page) *Report of the Exploration and Survey of the River La Plata and Its Tributaries* was published in Washington, D.C., in 1856 by Cornelius Wendell. For knowledge of the importance of the expedition and of the contemporary astronomical expedition led by Lieutenant James M. Gillis, U.S.N., and sponsored by the U.S. Navy, the American Philosophical Society, and the Smithsonian Institution, the author is indebted to two unpublished research papers by Joan R. Challinor on the two subjects respectively. See also Pablo Max Ynsfran, *La Expedición Norteamericana Contra el Paraguay, 1858–1859* (2 vols.; Mexico and Buenos Aires: Editorial Guaranía, 1954, 1958).

22. On Río de la Plata relations during these years see Quesada, *Historia Diplomática Hispanoamericana*, II, Chaps. 8 and 9. On Paraguay see Cecilio Báez, *Historia Diplomática del Paraguay* (2 vols.; Asunción: Imprenta Nacional, 1931–1932).

"British pre-eminence." The theme includes the efforts of Brazil to assert independence in policy and to escape from this British influence.[23] A major aspect of this close relationship with Great Britain is that of commerce. Under the Anglo-Brazilian treaty of 1827 Britain enjoyed essentially the same privileged position in Brazilian trade she held under Portuguese rule. This included a low duty of 15 percent on British imports and continuation of an extraterritorial jurisdiction under a "Judge Conservator for the British Nation." No country, except Portugal, was to be given a lower import duty. These trade provisions caused resentment among Brazilian merchants, as did the excessive privileges the crown proposed to give to such British merchants as the Diamond Company. Their resentment continued, even though the low-duty advantage was gradually whittled away as Brazil negotiated trade treaties containing the most favored nation clause with other countries, including the United States (1828).

Closely linked to the question of trade privileges as a source of tension in relations with Britain was the British-determined action to suppress the international slave trade. Under the treaty of 1827 Brazil agreed to permit the search and seizure of vessels carrying slaves from Africa to Brazil, as under previous agreements of 1815 and 1817 with Portugal. But this treaty, ratified by the emperor on his own authority as we have seen, was never approved by the Brazilian Parliament. Nor was an effective law passed by the Parliament to implement the treaty provision for suppressing the trade. The result was a series of conflicts arising from British seizures of vessels and cargoes of slaves, sometimes in Brazilian coastal waters. Manchester argues that the efforts of Pedro I to collaborate with the British under this treaty, a collaboration which Britain had made a condition of her recognition of Brazil, was a major cause of Pedro's abdication.

The slave trade, far from diminishing, had been increasing rapidly since the arrival of the Portuguese court in Brazil. It continued to grow after Brazilian independence, despite British efforts to suppress it, because of a growing market for Brazilian sugar. The importation of

23. Alan K. Manchester, *British Pre-eminence in Brazil: Its Rise and Decline* (Chapel Hill: University of North Carolina Press, 1933), Chaps. 7–12.

slaves is said to have doubled between 1820 and 1827 and to have tripled by 1829.[24] But the British were adamant. Even after the expiration of the treaty, British actions continued to add friction. Fifteen Brazilian ships were seized by British cruisers between October 13, 1845, and May 16, 1846. Between August, 1849, and May, 1852, ninety Brazilian ships were seized.[25] Only after a drastic Brazilian law for suppression of the trade was enacted by the Parliament, under a Conservative party government, was it possible to suppress the trade effectively in 1856. By this time Britain had withdrawn her controversial orders authorizing seizures in Brazilian waters—a major source of controversy—since the Brazilians were now at last enforcing the prohibition.

A fourth aspect of Brazilian international relations during the early years of this period, as earlier noted, is the "Portuguese Question," before and immediately following the abdication of Pedro I. This question was basically that of the political relation of Portugal to Brazil. It involved the settlement of the dynastic question of the inheritance of the two thrones, a question left in suspension by the treaties of 1825. As already noted, it was also an issue in the relations of Brazil with the Vatican, resolved by concessions on both sides. This Portuguese Question was settled by Pedro's abdication of the Portuguese crown in favor of his daughter, Maria da Gloria, after the death of King João in 1826. The less tangible but more persistent conflict between the Conservative and Liberal parties was resolved, as far as it was in any sense settled, through the political process in both countries.

A fifth major aspect of Brazilian foreign relations concerned the Banda Oriental or Uruguay, including its relationship to the Brazilian province of Rio Grande do Sul and to Brazilian claims to Misiones. During the time of the independence movement in Argentina the British minister in Rio de Janeiro, Lord Strangford, had restrained the efforts of Princess Carlota to assume the regency of the Viceroyalty of La Plata; he had also held off Portuguese moves to occupy the

24. Lawrence F. Hill, "Abolition of the African Slave Trade to Brazil," *Hispanic American Historical Review*, XI (May, 1931), 169–97.

25. These Brazilian figures are cited in Manchester, *British Pre-eminence*, 254–255.

Banda Oriental. After Strangford left, and after the capture of Montevideo by the Uruguayan independence leader José Artigas, the Portuguese began to move into the region. Ultimately they defeated Artigas, forcing him to seek exile in Paraguay, where he lived until his death in 1850.

After Brazilian independence the Portuguese troops were withdrawn from the Banda Oriental, but Brazilian troops remained until forced out by the rebellion under the "Thirty-three Immortals" supported by the Argentines. British mediation brought this war to an end with the treaty of 1828, under which, as we have seen, both Brazil and Argentina recognized the independence of Uruguay. This withdrawal of Brazil, leading to the establishment of Uruguay as a buffer state between Argentina and Brazil, was a triumph of British policy for the area. But it was a major setback for the new Brazilian monarchy and another cause of the abdication of Pedro in 1831. As a side effect of the war in the Banda Oriental, a French fleet had appeared off Rio in 1827, bombarding the port to force the payment of French claims, some of them arising out of the conflict in Uruguay. But the French presence was also an indication of that country's continuing interest in the whole area.

Brazilian relations with the United States during these years were friendly, on the whole, and involved no really serious issues. The United States had been first in recognizing Brazilian independence, and Brazil hoped that the Monroe Doctrine meant a willingness of the United States to enter a treaty of alliance, which would have strengthened Brazil's position in relation to both Portugal and Britain. Although this hope had been disappointed, Brazil had ratified a commercial treaty with the United States. She was reluctant, however, to agree on an arrangement for the extradition of criminals, possibly fearing that it would be used to restrict the right of political asylum. A few questions arose concerning the rights of United States citizens to practice their Protestant religion or to carry on missionary work.[26] In 1851 the appearance on the Amazon River of two United States navy lieutenants, William Lewis Herndon and Lardner Gibbon, aroused

26. See David Vieira, "The Protestant Element of the Religious Question in Brazil, 1872–1875" (Ph.D. dissertation, The American University, 1972).

what was to be a recurrent Brazilian fear of losing the Amazon valley to a foreign power. The purpose of the expedition, however, was merely to explore the river from the standpoint of its commercial use and to call attention to the demand for opening it up to international traffic.[27] In this respect it was comparable to the Thomas Page exploration of the Plata. This U.S. purpose, in fact, complemented in a way the Brazilian desire to open up the Plata system for trade with her territories on the Paraguay and Paraná rivers.

By 1850 Brazil felt free enough, after British and French withdrawal, to join a campaign to overthrow Rosas in Argentina, signing a treaty to this effect with Uruguay and the Argentine provinces of Entre Rios and Corrientes, and furnishing troops to the tri-national army that defeated Rosas in the Battle of Caseros (1852). The year before she had signed a treaty of alliance with Paraguay, in which Brazil agreed to come to the aid of Paraguay if she was attacked by Argentina, and both nations agreed in demanding that the Río de la Plata be internationalized. This treaty, as we shall see, displayed a newly aggressive policy of Brazil in the area.

After the overthrow of Rosas, the new Argentine government of President Urquiza recognized Paraguay and opened the Río de la Plata to navigation by vessels of all nations. The Argentine-Paraguayan treaty following this recognition accepted the Paraguayan title to the Chaco, but did not define its boundaries. Other boundary lines were set, however, and the controversial Misiones territory was ceded to Argentina. (It had also been ceded by Uruguay to Brazil and its fate was to be settled later by arbitration.) One interesting consequence of this internationalization of the Río de la Plata came a few years later, when President Urquiza of Argentina mediated the dispute between the United States and Paraguay over the *Water Witch* incident.[28]

Paulino Soares de Souza, the principal author of the newly aggressive Brazilian policy in the Río de la Plata region, had been convinced that, because Rosas was free from French and British intervention

27. William Lewis Herndon and Lardner Gibbon, *Exploration of the Valley of the Amazon* (2 vols.; Washington: Robert Armstrong, Public Printer, 1853).

28. See Page, *Report of the Exploration . . . of the River La Plata*, and Harris Gaylord Warren, *Paraguay* (Norman: University of Oklahoma Press, 1949).

after 1850, he would control Uruguay and, unless stopped, would probably seek to reincorporate Paraguay into the confederation. The independence of Uruguay would disappear for all practical purposes, he believed, and Rosas would "come over us with greater forces." To prevent the consolidation of this solid transcontinental block of power, and thus to settle Brazilian claims in the Plata region became the Brazilian objective. Ably seconded by young José Silva Paranhos, soon to be the Count of Rio Branco, he proceeded to divert Paraguay from an understanding with Rosas by the treaty of 1850. He then negotiated a treaty of alliance with the *Colorado* government in Uruguay (opponents of Oribe and Rosas) and with the provinces of Entre Rios and Corrientes in Argentina pledged to overthrow Rosas. In return for arms and credits and an armed force promised to Uruguay for this purpose, Brazil received the Uruguayan surrender of its claims to Misiones. In effect, Brazil was moving in to take up the interventionist role, recently abandoned by France, as a major opponent of the power ambitions of Rosas.[29]

In later years Rosas complained bitterly of what he termed a Brazilian betrayal, since he had withheld support of rebels in Rio Grande do Sul; he also, rightly, blamed Brazil for opening up the Río de la Plata to international traffic, in accordance with the Brazilian-Paraguayan treaty of 1850.[30] A second Brazil-Paraguayan treaty (1856), negotiated by Silva Paranhos in Asunción, settled the dispute over navigation on the Paraguay and Paraná rivers, giving reciprocal rights to the vessels of both nations in each other's territories.

The international position of Paraguay was enhanced by these developments, so that in 1859 the president of Paraguay mediated in a civil war in Argentina, bringing the province of Buenos Aires back into the Argentine confederation. This internal union of Argentina thus achieved was an obvious key to peace in the area; but the appearance of peace was illusory. Juan Bautista Alberdi later expressed the illusory character of this settlement in his *History of the Paraguayan War*, when he wrote that the overthrow of Rosas and the

29. Quesada, *Historia Diplomática Hispanoamericana*, II, 191–215.

30. Rosas to Josefa Gómez, Southampton, April 5, 1865 in José Raed, *Rosas: Cartas Confidenciales a su Embajadora, Josefa Gómez, 1853–1875* (Buenos Aires: Humus Editorial, 1972), 59–62.

immediately subsequent events also presaged the disastrous Paraguayan War of the following decade.[31]

The Question of Bolivia (1836–1839)

Like Uruguay and Paraguay, Bolivia is a buffer state. The province of Charcas (Upper Peru) was held by the forces of the viceroy of Peru throughout the wars of independence, turning back invading revolutionary armies from Argentina, who claimed the province as part of the Viceroyalty of La Plata. Bolívar, after the final defeat of the Spanish forces, created Bolivia as a buffer between Peru and Argentina and got the agreement of Argentina to Bolivian independence in return for a promise to give back Tarija to Argentina. Bolivia was also a buffer between expanding Brazil and Spanish America. In a limited sense she was also a buffer between Peru and Chile, long-time rivals and potential enemies, holding a section of the Pacific coast line between the two. Her boundaries remained largely unsettled during the period here considered, despite the general acceptance of the principle of *uti possidetis juris* of 1810. Later these unsettled boundaries were to give rise to two of Spanish America's most bloody wars.

When President Andrés de Santa Cruz of Bolivia arranged a federal union with Peru in 1836, both Chile and Argentina were alarmed at the prospect of this expansion of their old rival, Peru. Chile's ire was increased by Peruvian default on a Chilean loan advanced during the time of San Martín and by Peruvian support of the Chilean exiles, including former president Ramón Freire, in their efforts to regain the government of Chile. Andrés de Santa Cruz, the ambitious independence leader and lieutenant of Bolívar, was believed to have the ambition of bringing all of the old Viceroyalty of Peru (including Ecuador and possibly Chile) under his control.

Chile attempted to come to terms, sending Mariano Egaña to negotiate unsuccessfully with Santa Cruz. She demanded that Peru

31. Juan B. Alberdi, *Historia de la Guerra del Paraguay* (Buenos Aires: Ediciones de la Patria Grande, 1962). Earlier editions under various titles. On Brazilian relations during these years see José Honório Rodrígues, *Brazil and Africa*, trans. Richard A. Mazzara and Sam Hileman (Berkeley: University of California Press, 1965); Manchester, *British Pre-eminence in Brazil*, and Ricardo Levene, *History of Argentina*, trans. W. S. Robertson (Chapel Hill: University of North Carolina Press, 1937, 1963).

guarantee independence of Bolivia and Ecuador, undertake the payment of the old debt and of Chilean claims arising from Peruvian military support of Freire's plans, accept a limitation of Peruvian naval forces, and enter into a reciprocal trade treaty, including the most-favored-nation clause.

When this effort failed, Chile enlisted the support of Argentina, who had an unsettled claim to the territory of Tarija, to break up the confederation. The Bolivians turned back an invading Argentine force, but the Chileans pursued the war aggressively, sending two amphibious expeditions against Peru and Bolivia. She did this successfully, despite a plot within the army, possibly instigated by Peruvians, that brought the assassination of the minister of war and strong man of the Chilean government, Diego Portales. The first expedition landed at Arica and proceeded to Arequipa, where an agreement was made which the Chilean government rejected, because it did not provide for the separation of Bolivia and Peru. A second expedition, accompanied by Peruvians, including the former president Augustín Gamarra, landed at Callao, occupied Lima, and finally defeated the army led by Santa Cruz in the bloody and decisive battle of Yungay, north of Lima. Gamarra was reinstated as president of Peru, and Santa Cruz was forced to take refuge in Ecuador, later going into exile in Europe.[32]

The Dismemberment of Mexico

The unhappy course of Mexico's international relations during her first four decades of independence is all the more tragic when considered in light of her ambition, as we have seen in connection with the Panama Congress in 1826, to play the role of the senior spokesman for Spanish America in making peace with Spain. The record illustrates

---

32. The Chilean side may be read in Francisco A. Encina, *Resumen de la Historia de Chile*, Redacción . . . de Leopoldo Castedo, (2nd. ed., 3 vols.; Santiago: Zig Zag, 1956) II, 895–946; or in Luis Galdames, *History of Chile* (Chapel Hill: University of North Carolina Press, 1941, 1963). For Peru see Jorge Basadre, *Historia de la República del Peru, 1822–1899* (Lima: n.p. 1939). *La Misión La Torre en Bolivia, 1831–1835* and *Confederación Peru-Boliviana, 1835–1839*, both with a prologue by Carlos Ortiz de Zevallos Paz-Soldán (Lima: Ministerio de Relaciones Exterior del Perú, 1911 and 1912), Vols. VIII and IX of *Archivo Diplomático Peruano*.

the disastrous effects of the Spanish Liberal government's rejection of the Iturbide-O'Donojú proposal of Mexican independence as a monarchy. Internal factionalism was another cause of this poor record. The feuding within the ruling class, a small minority of criollos who controlled the wealth of the nation and ruled over inert Indian masses, made stable government next to impossible. In some respects this factionalism, and the *caudillismo* it bred, were a product of the manner in which Mexico gained independence—the defeat of the popular uprising of Hidalgo and Morelos by royalist forces (1810–1814), the continuation of the independence movement as guerilla warfare under such leaders as Vicente Guerrero and Guadalupe Victoria (Manuel Félix Fernández), and finally the achievement of independence through a kind of *golpe* executed by a Spanish army officer (and Mason), Agustín Iturbide. Had Mexico gained independence through such military victories as those achieved by the forces of San Martín and Bolívar in South America, Mexico would have had a more solid nationalism on which to build a state. In the final analysis, however, an even more important reason than the foregoing for the disastrous course of Mexico's foreign relations during these early years was the expansionism of the United States, which British policy opposed. The question of Texas thus became a focal point in United States-British rivalry.

Independent Mexico in 1821 extended from Oregon to the Isthmus of Panama, including half the population and half the wealth of Spanish America. Two years later, when the empire of Iturbide was overthrown, the Central American Federation declared its independence, supported by General Vicente Filísola, who commanded a Mexican army in the region. A decade later, when another revolution in Mexico replaced the federal republic with a centralized state, a successful independence movement occurred in Texas (1835). At the same time, Mexico almost lost Yucatán to a separatist movement in that independence-prone province.[33] A decade later, a war with the United States, following U.S. annexation of Texas, resulted in the loss

33. See Mary Wilhelmina Williams, "Secessionist Diplomacy of Yucatán," *Hispanic American Historical Review*, IX (May, 1929), 132–43.

of New Mexico and upper California. This last catastrophe came at a time when a series of rapid changes in government had reduced the Mexican state to a condition of nearly helpless anarchy.

Mexican monarchism did not die when Iturbide, returning from exile in 1824, was captured and executed. Conservative elements in the upper class were Spanish in their sympathies. Alienated by the political unrest under the republic and by the republican church policy, they gravitated toward monarchism, even after recognition of the Mexican republic by Spain, and wished to protect and strengthen the Church as a basis for social and political stability. They found a spokesman in Lucas Alamán and a military-political leader in Antonio López de Santa Anna. Reformers like Valentín Gomez Farías and José Joaquín Herrera, on the other hand, stood for republicanism, usually in a federal pattern. They were anticlerical, favoring a lay society and more liberal economic policies. Anti-Spanish, they aften tended also to be pro–North American.

The colorful and erratic Joel R. Poinsett went to Mexico as the first United States minister in 1825 under instructions to purchase Texas, which the United States had relinquished to Spain by the treaty of 1819. But the treaty he negotiated (1828) confirmed the 1819 boundary line instead. By nature an adventurer, he made the mistake of identifying himself too closely with the liberal and federalist *Yorkinos* (York rite Masons), of whom Vicente Guerrero was the head. After the overthrow of Guerrero, these political activities of Poinsett caused Mexico to demand his recall, leaving a note of bitterness in United States–Mexican relations. His successor, the "vain, ignorant, ill-tempered, and corrupt" Anthony Butler, further alienated Mexicans by brazenly seeking the acquisition of Texas until his recall on the eve of the Texas revolt in 1835. The question of Texas was further complicated at this time by what the Mexicans have called "the Pastry War," a French armed intervention for the collection of claims in 1838.

The Texans defeated the Mexican army sent to suppress their uprising in 1839, capturing President Santa Anna, the leader of the army. They released him, however, on his promise to secure Mexican recognition of Texas independence, a promise he later repudiated. Texan independence was recognized by the United States in 1837 and subsequently by France, Great Britain, and the Netherlands. But Mexico continued to refuse recognition and renewed the war to suppress the rebellion in 1842. Again Santa Anna was the army leader and again he failed. The following year (1843), realizing that annexation sentiment was strong in Texas and the United States, the Mexican government served notice upon the United States that annexation would be considered a hostile act. Meanwhile, in the United States President Van Buren had withheld from the Senate a treaty for annexation and the Senate had subsequently rejected ratification when the treaty was presented by Van Buren's successor. This congressional action was inspired partly by fear that annexation might lead to war with Mexico, partly by Great Britain's involvement in the controversy, and partly by the opposition of antislavery forces in Congress. John Quincy Adams, earlier advocate of the acquisition of Texas, as we have seen, now denounced the annexation freely in the House of Representatives, calling it a plot of the southern "slavocracy."

Responding to Texas advances, Great Britain tried to persuade Mexico to grant recognition in exchange for a Texan promise not to join the United States; Mexico remained unwilling, however, until the United States Congress, by joint resolution in 1844, approved annexation, circumventing the need for a two-thirds majority to ratify a treaty. Texas had balked at the British proposal to abolish slavery, but now reluctantly agreed to include in a treaty an agreement for the suppression of the international slave trade. At the height of the crisis in 1845 Britain was able to present to the Texans the choice between a Mexican treaty including the Texan promise not to seek annexation to the United States and the United States offer of annexation. A constitutional assembly in Texas chose annexation. The Mexican minister in Washington immediately demanded his passport and left the country in accordance with the Mexican ultimatum of the preceding year.

The Republic of Texas claimed the territory of New Mexico, and Britain's interest in Texas was not unrelated to this territory and to California as well. Moreover, the United States was still disputing possession of the Oregon country with Britain when President Polk assumed office in 1845, having promised in his campaign to secure both Oregon and Texas for the United States. Both Britain and the

United States seemed to assume that Mexico could not maintain effective control over California. The United States suspected a British design to create a buffer to U.S. expansion in the Southwest by creating a British-dominated zone extending from Texas to California. This suspicion and the Oregon problem lay behind Polk's bold reassertion of the Monroe Doctrine in his inaugural address in 1845, in which he warned that the Texas question was exclusively an American one and spoke of the peaceful expansion of the United States to the Pacific Coast. While the latter reference related most clearly to Oregon, it was not without implications for California as well.

Mexico had defaulted on the payments due on some two million dollars awarded to United States citizens in 1843 by a U.S.–Mexican mixed claims commission. Polk's policy, taking advantage of Mexico's difficulties, was to settle the dispute over Texas, including Texan claims to New Mexico and a Rio Grande boundary, and to acquire California, in exchange for these unpaid claims, paying an additional sum if necessary. Meanwhile, a war party had gained control in Mexico in 1846, and Mexico was determined to use force against the union of Texas with the United States. This regime was shortly succeeded, however, by that of the Liberal statesman José Joaquín Herrera, a regime more inclined to seek a peaceful solution of the Texas controversy. Herrera's regime was too weak, however, to be able to accept the surrender of territory beyond what Mexico considered to be the bounds of the province of Texas.[34]

While the basic causes of the war which followed are quite clear, the question of how war was precipitated is more debatable. The Mexican view is that it was precipitated by the United States sending an armed force under General Zachary Taylor into the disputed territory between the Nueces and Rio Bravo (Rio Grande) rivers. The U.S. view is that Mexico provoked the war by sending her forces into the area to challenge those of the United States. Fundamentally, however, as the

34. On political changes in Mexico during these years, see Herbert I. Priestly, *The Mexican Nation, a History* (New York: Macmillan, 1923); Henry B. Parkes, *A History of Mexico* (New York: Houghton Mifflin, 1969), 211–221; Thomas E. Cotner, *The Military and Political Career of José Joaquín de Herrera* (Austin: University of Texas Press, 1949), 110–71; and Alfonso Teja Zabre, *Historia de México: Una Moderna Interpretación* (Mexico: Secretaría de Relaciones Exteriores, 1935), 316–26.

British historian R. A. Humphreys has pointed out, the cause was Mexico's inability to establish a stable political regime. The outbreak of war was symbolized, as J. F. Rippy has remarked, by the corrupt and irresponsible Antonio López de Santa Anna.[35] Mexicans insist that the avowed expansionism of President Polk, of his southern supporters, and of the aggressive settlers in Texas provided the basis for the final clash. It seems likely that Mexico would have lost Texas in any case. But corruption, incompetence, and factional strife in Mexico, as Mexican historians today point out, provided the opportunity for U.S. expansionists to gain control, not only of Texas, but of Mexico's other tenuously held northern territories as well.

Mexico had a larger standing army than the United States and had inherited the proud Spanish military tradition. Some Mexican leaders, ignorant of the newly acquired professional competence of the United States armed forces, boasted that they would dictate a peace in Washington. These vainglorious attitudes made the subsequent defeat all the more humiliating. The United States carried the war into Mexico with two invasions. General Zachary Taylor led the invasion from the north. General Winfield Scott led a seaborne expedition which landed in Vera Cruz and moved up through the precipitous mountains to the Mexican plateau. The inconclusive Battle of Buena Vista in northern Mexico, claimed as a victory by both sides, was the immediate background of this Scott expedition. The United States invaders under General Scott showed their superiority in training, equipment, organization, and supply, while the Mexican army showed little or none of the power to resist which they demonstrated against French invaders a decade and a half later. Mexico lost the war mainly because of her failure to offer an effectively organized and directed defense, except briefly at the Battle of Cerro Gordo.

The Treaty of Guadalupe-Hidalgo (1848) was negotiated by the United States envoy Nicholas Trist, after his authority to negotiate had been withdrawn! It incorporated virtually the terms President Polk had offered prior to the war. By the treaty, Mexico recognized

35. R. A. Humphrey, in *Cambridge Modern History* (14 vols.; Cambridge: Cambridge University Press, 1957–75), Vol. X, Chap. 23; J. F. Rippy, *Latin America* (Ann Arbor: University of Michigan Press, 1958), 206.

the Rio Bravo boundary of Texas, accepted the incorporation of Texas into the United States, and ceded New Mexico and upper California. In return, the United States agreed to pay claims of $3,250,000 by the U.S. citizens against Mexico and to pay Mexico the sum of $15 million for the ceded territories. President Polk and his advisors had considered making more extensive demands on Mexico, but wisely decided to accept the unauthorized treaty negotiated by Trist.[36]

Santa Anna returned to power by a *golpe de estado* in 1853 at the invitation of a newly invigorated Conservative party that was monarchist and pro-Church in ideology. This was the administration, seriously pressed for funds, that agreed in 1853 to sell to the United States the Mesilla Valley (Gadsden Purchase), desired by the United States as a southern route for a transcontinental railway. A Liberal uprising led by General Juan Alvarez drove Santa Anna into exile the following year and launched a movement of profound reforms in the army, the Church, the government, education, and land ownership. The new movement also gave rise to new issues in Mexico's foreign relations.

Under Benito Juárez, during the ensuing War of Reform (1858–1861), a civil war that merged into the struggle against French intervention and the empire of Maximilian, the Mexican government found sympathy and support in the United States. Fortunately for both sides, the McLane-Ocampo Treaty, authorized by Juárez during the War of Reform in 1859 when his cause was at low ebb, was rejected by the United States Senate. This treaty would have given the United States a right-of-way across the Isthmus of Tehuantepec in return for a payment of two million dollars. Even though defeated, this proposed treaty gave the critics of Juárez grounds for branding

36. See G. L. Rives, *The United States and Mexico, 1821–1842* (2 vols.; New York: Charles Scribner, 1913); J. H. Smith, *The War with Mexico* (2 vols.; New York: Macmillan, 1919), I, 62, who argues that Polk was trying to avoid war; James M. Callahan, *American Foreign Policy in Mexican Relations* (New York: Macmillan, 1932). For a Mexican view of the war see Zabre, *Historia de México*, 319–26, and Alberto María Carreno, *México y los Estados Unidos* (2nd. ed.; México: Edición Jus, 1962), especially p. 18. Glen W. Price, *Origins of the War with Mexico* (Austin: University of Texas Press, 1967), sees California as the main objective of Polk. José Fernando Ramírez, *Mexico during the War with the United States*, trans. Elliott B. Scherr (Columbia: University of Missouri Press, 1950), gives a revealing account of the political chaos in Mexico during the War.

him "one who despoiled the Church with one hand and sold his country with the other." Even the substantial aid he later received from the United States in opposing Maximilian was not sufficient to erase the stigma.

Power Conflicts in Central America and the Caribbean

The rivalry of the United States and Great Britain in the Caribbean and in Central America, following Latin American independence, presented serious problems to the new nations of the area. This rivalry included competition for the carrying trade, competition for markets and for the trade in sugar and rum, complicated by difficulties over suppression of the contraband slave trade. The rivalry also extended to the establishment of river steamboat lines in Central America, the construction of railroad lines, and the prospective building of a canal across Central America at some yet-to-be-determined point. The rivalry found expression in competitive negotiations with the Central American countries for the control of the Isthmian routes and their strategic approaches, as well as in competition for desirable sites for naval bases. It was also a rivalry for control of the strategic Caribbean approaches to America, to which Cuba and Hispaniola were important keys.

Britain had retained important possessions in Central America and the Caribbean after the independence of the United States, including such important Caribbean colonies as the Bahamas, Trinidad, Jamaica, the lesser Antilles, British Guiana, and the present territory of British Honduras, or Belize. Before the inflow of British investment capital began going largely to Brazil and southern South America, Cuba and the former Spanish colonies in Central America and the Caribbean had a larger relative importance in British policy than they came to have later.

English freebooters had seized logging settlements in Belize in the eighteenth century, and Britain secured a right of occupation, though not a clear title to the area, in treaties of 1783 and 1786 with Spain. In 1840 Britain enlarged her territorial claims for Belize and gave it the status of a crown colony. Both Mexico and Guatemala also claimed the territory, as heirs of Spain, but Mexico relinquished her claim in favor of Guatemala. Britain later reached a treaty agreement with Guatemala in 1859, establishing her right of possession. As part of the agreement Britain promised to join with Guatemala in developing a cart road and/or river transportation between the Atlantic and Guatemala City. An additional convention signed in 1863 limited the British contribution for this purpose to £50,000; but Guatemala did not ratify this additional convention within the prescribed time, and Britain refused to extend the ratification period, declaring the matter closed.[37] Unfulfilled provisions of this treaty are the basis, as we shall see later, of Guatemala's twentieth century claim to the territory.

Meanwhile, Britain had extended her claim to include the Bay Islands off the Honduran coast and in 1835 had proclaimed a protectorate over the "kingdom" of the Mosquito Indians living along the Caribbean coast of Nicaragua. In 1847, British forces occupied the port of Greytown on the Caribbean coast at the mouth of the San Juan River, one of the best routes for an interoceanic canal. Two years later a British naval officer laid claim to Tigre Island in Fonseca Bay, regarded as a possible Pacific terminus of a canal. The Central American states, feuding internally with each other, seemed powerless to prevent these intrusions.

In 1846 Colombia had entered into the Bidlack Treaty with the United States, when it was feared that former President Flores of Ecuador might engage British and/or Spanish support for an imperialist venture in the Panama Isthmus. The treaty guaranteed freedom of transit across the Isthmus of Panama. United States agents were soon negotiating transit treaties with several Central American countries, including Nicaragua. Britain disavowed the occupation of Tigre Island at U.S. insistence, but United States-British competition in the area increased in intensity. A Nicaraguan appeal to the United States for protection against British encroachment on the Mosquito "Kingdom" area finally led to the 1850 Clayton-Bulwer Treaty between the United States and Britain. In this treaty the two countries agreed to cooperate in encouraging the construction of a canal over which neither would exercise exclusive control. The treaty also con-

37. Kenneth J. Grieb, "Jorge Ubico and the Belize Boundary Dispute," *The Americas*, XXX (April, 1974), 452.

tained a clause by which both parties promised not to "occupy," "colonize," or exercise "dominion" over "any part of Central America."[38]

Viewed objectively, and within the climate of the times favoring European expansion, this treaty was a significant triumph for the Monroe principle of noncolonization. But expansionists in the United States regarded it as an ignoble surrender and for the next half century sought its renegotiation. The treaty pledge of noncolonization was vague, but the United States was able to insist successfully upon British withdrawal from the Nicaraguan coast, though not until an incident of mob violence against a United States diplomatic officer resulted in U.S. bombardment of Greytown. Supported by the Liberal party in Nicaragua, the filibuster William Walker led a group of American adventurers into that country, making himself its ruler between 1855 and 1857. But Walker failed to secure the support of the United States government and was defeated by a general uprising of the Central American nations in a "national war of Central America," as well as by the opposition of Cornelius Vanderbilt's transit company and of British and French agents.[39]

The Cuban Question

The independence of Cuba and Puerto Rico had been an objective of the leaders of the Mexican, Venezuelan, and Colombian independence movements. But their half-hearted moves to achieve this end had failed for various reaons, including the lack of vigorous support of the islands, the presence of strong Spanish forces there, and the coldness with which the revolutionary moves were viewed by the United States, Britain, and France. After the defeat of Napoleon and the restoration of Ferdinand in Spain, independence moves encountered

38. Key provisions of the Bidlack Treaty are conveniently available in Ruhl J. Bartlett (ed.), *The Record of American Diplomacy* (New York: Knopf, 1948), 244–45. Essential provisions of the Clayton-Bulwer Treaty are likewise in Bartlett, 251–53, and in Henry S. Comager (ed.), *Documents of American History* (2 vols.; New York: Crofts, 1938) I, 326–27.

39. See Mary Wilhelmina Williams, *Anglo-American Isthmian Diplomacy, 1815–1915* (Washington, D.C.: American Historical Association, 1916), and J. Fred Rippy, *Rivalry of the United States and Great Britain over Latin America, 1803–1830* (Baltimore: Johns Hopkins University Press, 1929). On Walker see William O. Scroggs, *Filibusters and Financiers: The Story of William Walker and his Associates* (New York: Russell and Russell, 1969), originally published 1916, and Marco A. Soto V., *Guerra Nacional de Centroamérica* (Guatemala: Ministerio de Educación Pública, 1957).

sporadic sympathy in neighboring Spanish American states and in the United States. But British policy and factional divisions within the islands, exacerbated by the conflict of Cuban abolitionist and proslavery forces, prevented both the success of the insurrectionary movements and the possible transfer of the islands to any other power. The preoccupation of the Spanish American nations with their internal problems and problematic relations with their immediate neighbors made the Cuban question during these years much less a Latin or Spanish American matter than a question of power politics involving European powers and the United States.

The island's prosperous agricultural economy was increasingly devoted to the cultivation of sugar (with the use of Negro slave labor) after the independence of Haiti brought the collapse of the Haitian sugar economy. Despite this prosperity, Cuba was torn by political discontent and by protest against Spanish rule. She was unstable politically, much like Spain and the nations of Spanish America. A large Spanish garrison was stationed in the island, so that, as in Spain, the military had come to play a dominant role in government. The island's strategic importance athwart the sea routes to and from the Gulf of Mexico and the Caribbean made Spain refuse stubbornly to consider any proposal, either for Cuban self-government or for transfer of the island to some other power.

An illicit African slave trade continued, in spite of Spain's long-standing agreement with Britain to suppress it. But although Spanish policy on slavery and the slave trade vacillated, permitting slavery and the slave trade to continue, the ever-present possibility that Spain would abolish slavery, together with the activity of abolitionists in Cuba, was great enough to arouse apprehension from time to time among the slaveowners, inspiring movements for independence that sought support among southern slave holders and proslavery expansionists in the United States. Not all of the support for independence in Cuba came from these slaveholders, of course, but they were a link with the "Manifest Destiny" expansionism in the United States.

Meanwhile, Cuban policy of the United States was dictated basically by the "no transfer" policy resolution adopted by Congress in 1810, expressing concern lest this prosperous and strategically important island pass into the hands of Britain or France. No nation or combination of nations in Spanish America was strong enough or determined enough to support Cuban independence effectively, although Spanish Americans generally sympathized with independence leaders and offered them political asylum. After the United States acquisition of Florida, Louisiana, Texas, and California, however, the Spanish American attitude was more ambiguous, some Spanish Americans fearing that United States support of Cuban independence might mean United States annexation of Cuba to protect the slave-holding interest.

Revolutionary expeditions for the liberation of Cuba were organized in the United States in 1849, 1850, and 1851 by Narcisco López (1798–1851), a Venezuelan soldier of fortune. In the last of these invasions López was captured and executed. When the Cuban leaders planning another uprising began to seek United States support among such southern proslavery leaders as Senator R. B. Rhett of South Carolina, the neutrality policy of the United States hardened and steps were taken to insure that no expedition should depart from the United States. To divert attention, Pierre Soulé was sent to Madrid to attempt to purchase the island.[40]

Britain had a long-standing interest in Cuba, having occupied the island temporarily during the Seven Years' War. When a French fleet touched at Havana in 1825, the British foreign minister, George Canning, remonstrated to the French government, adding that Britain wished Cuba to stay with the mother country and that "the Americans (Yankees I mean) think of this matter just as I do."[41] Later, Britain feared that Napoleon III might seek to purchase the island from Spain as the basis for restoring French empire in America. Neither Britain nor France wished to see Cuba fall into United States hands, either by purchase or by independence and annexation. Accordingly, in 1852 they jointly invited the United States to join in a treaty to insure Spanish possession of the island. The United States rejected the offer,

40. See Amos A. Ettinger, *The Mission to Spain of Pierre Soule, 1853–1855: A Study in the Cuban Diplomacy of the United States* (New Haven: Yale University Press, 1932) and C. Stanley Urban, "The Africanization of Cuba Scare, 1853–55," *Hispanic American Historical Review* (February, 1947), 29–45.

41. Quoted in Stuart, *Latin America and the United States*, 176.

saying candidly that she could not make such an agreement because it was her long-settled policy to acquire Cuba under certain conditions.

In 1853, the year following the French-British proposal, Louis Cass of Michigan introduced into the United States Senate a resolution disclaiming designs on Cuba, but stating that acquisition of Cuba by a third party would endanger the southern coast of the United States, who would resist it by all the means in her power. Senator Stephen A. Douglas of Illinois, trying to reconcile conflicting sectional interests in the Democratic party, opposed the Cass resolution in a speech that is one of the classic "Manifest Destiny" statements.

Meanwhile, Pierre Soulé was trying unsuccessfully to persuade Spain to sell Cuba to the United States. But United States-Spanish relations had been aggravated by a series of incidents involving United States vessels engaged in illicit trading in Cuban waters, notably the *Black Warrior.* Spain, therefore, bluntly refused to entertain Soulé's proposals. Secretary Marcy then instructed Soulé to consult with the United States ministers in London and Paris, James Buchanan and John Y. Mason. Their consultation produced the Ostend Manifesto. Supposedly, the manifesto was intended to be a confidential statement to the secretary of state, but it was allowed to reach the press, intentionally or unintentionally, appearing in papers in Europe and America as the outcome of the conference of these three ministers. The U.S. government disavowed it, but the language of the Ostend Manifesto was generally taken to be a statement of United States designs on Cuba. It helped, incidentally, to make Buchanan an acceptable presidential candidate in 1856. Two sentences are the gist of the position stated:

> After we shall have offered Spain a price for Cuba far beyond its present value, and this shall have been refused, it will then be time to consider the question, does Cuba, in the possession of Spain seriously endanger our internal peace and the existence of our cherished union? If the answer is yes, then we act on the same basis that would justify a neighbor in tearing down the burning house of another neighbor, if there were no other means of preventing the spreading of the flames.[42]

42. The essential text is in Bartlett, *Record of American Diplomacy*, 240–42; see *House Executive Documents*, 33rd Cong., 2nd Sess., No. 98.

Both British and United States policy worked to prevent United States acquisition of Cuba at this time. British policy supported Spain in opposing the sale of Cuba, and the judicious course followed by the United States presidents and secretaries of state in their negotiations to purchase Cuba curbed the expansionists. Stanley Urban has concluded that President Pierce had no illusions about the possibility of purchasing Cuba at this time, but made the bid for the island largely as a political move to divert into more proper channels the actions of southern radicals who supported Cuban independence.[43]

International Relations at the End of the 1850s

By the end of the 1850s an era was closing in the international relations of Latin America. The period of internal political chaos was passing, or had passed, giving way to some kind of consolidated national structure in most of the new nations. Argentina had achieved federal union under the constitution of 1853. Chile had enjoyed three decades of political stability under the rule of the Conservative party. Mexico was passing through another period of turbulence which would ultimately invite French intervention, but the Mexican Liberal party had laid the foundation in the constitution of 1857 for the national consolidation of a republican Mexico. Brazil had passed through the trials of the regency period that followed the abdication of Pedro I and was entering a period of vigorous expansion and growth under her young emperor, Pedro II.

Unsettled and unmarked boundaries still plagued the relations of the Latin American nations with each other and were to produce two international wars in South America in the decades just ahead. Events of the 1860s were to witness another unsuccessful effort to create a Hispanic alliance or league—a conference in Lima in 1864/65, prompted by a renewal of Spanish imperialism. In the main, however, it appears that the nations of Latin America had by 1860 reached the stage of pursuing their independent national interests with fair success under the protection of the balance of power maintained by the British fleet and supported in general by the United States, ex-

43. See footnote 40, also Pratt, *A History of United States Foreign Policy*, 295–98.

cept when domestic expansionist forces got out of hand. The delicacy of this balance would be demonstrated dramatically, however, when the United States involvement in a prolonged and bloody civil war opened the way to a renewal of French and Spanish imperialism during the 1860s.

5 Conflict and Challenge: The Transition to Power Politics, 1860–1870

F. TAYLOR PECK

The decade of the 1860s was a period of transition in the international relations of the Latin American states to a stage in which power politics was to find greater expression. It brought change both in the relations between the states of the New World and in their relations with outside powers. Thus events of this decade of challenge and conflict differed in several respects from those of the earlier years of independence, both in the seriousness of the threats to independence and in the violence of the conflicts between the states themselves. During this decade several serious conflicts occurred. France tried to impose Maximilian as emperor of Mexico. Spain attempted to reincorporate Santo Domingo into the Spanish empire. Cuba struggled for ten years in an effort for independence from Spain. Peru opened war against Spain when the Chincha Islands were seized as payment for Spanish nationals. The Paraguayan War (War of the Triple Alliance) entangled Brazil, Argentina, Uruguay, and Paraguay in one of the bloodiest wars in the hemisphere. Finally, the tensions between Chile and Bolivia began to develop, tensions that were to lead in the following decade to the disastrous War of the Pacific.

A Decade of Intervention and Conflict

The decade marks the last attempts by France and Spain to reestablish their political power, both imperial and monarchical, in the New World. During the reign of Isabel II in Spain and of Napoleon III in France, the dynamics of European politics brought about a dangerous resurgence of imperialism in the Americas. This new imperialism was generally unopposed by Great Britain, preoccupied as she was with her own imperial interests in Africa and Asia. Some writers consider this new imperialism to have been a serious challenge to the Latin American policy of the United States as expressed in the Monroe Doctrine, coming, as it did, while the United States was engaged in the Civil War. The Civil War and Reconstruction inhibited effective action by the United States against the original schemes of European monarchs, and one cannot help suspecting that U.S. weakness invited these interventions. But the United States protested in each instance and in each major case the European intervention was ultimately repulsed. To the Latin American nations the threat was more immediately important, in some cases threatening their very independence.

In the conflicts between the states of the hemisphere during this decade, the offers of United States good offices were either rejected or, when accepted, were singularly unsuccessful. The main significance of these conflicts lies in the fact that they constitute a transition to an era of increased nationalism and international power politics in the area.

Mexico: Intervention and Empire

As previously indicated, Mexico entered the decade of the 1860s in the throes of the civil wars of *La Reforma*. The widespread destruction of life and property that occurred included damages to foreign nationals. European powers vigorously pressed claims for the loss of their nationals against the government of Benito Juárez, as well as seeking assurances for the protection of life and property. European demands were intensified in some quarters by resentment toward measures enacted against the Roman Catholic Church under *La Reforma*. Tensions between Mexico and the Holy See were particularly high as a result of measures suppressing the religious orders and requiring the Church to divest itself of real property. The Mexican government, in severe financial difficulties, attempted to negotiate the issue of claims, offering to settle them for what appeared to the European powers an insultingly low figure. When this figure was rejected,

Mexico suspended entirely any further payment of claims, an action that invited intervention. This intervention was not long in coming. Paris, London, and Madrid agreed to a three-power occupation of the customhouse at Vera Cruz, the major source of Mexican governmental revenue. This occupation was accomplished in December, 1861.

Spain and Great Britain, after negotiating agreements for the settlement of their claims, withdrew their armed forces. The French, on the other hand, sent reinforcements and moved inland. Napoleon III, with the support of Mexican opponents of Juárez, was about to attempt the creation of a French sphere of influence in the New World. He hoped, also, to strengthen his relations with Austria by placing a Hapsburg on a Mexican throne. In April, 1862, the French forces began a march toward Mexico City, finally occupying the capital in June, 1863. A Mexican Conservative-army coalition then extended the invitation to the Archduke Maximilian, the intended French puppet, and the new emperor reached Vera Cruz in June, 1864.

For three years, until his death before a firing squad in May, 1867, Maximilian attempted, unsuccessfully, to rule Mexico. His failure resulted from several causes. One of these was his personality and politics; others arose from conditions in the country. The details of Maximilian's reign cannot be discussed here. The reader may consult an extensive bibliography, much of it relating to Mexico's international relations at the time. In summary, the emperor alienated his own political supporters by courting the opposition Liberals and adopting many of their Church reforms. His policies were idealistic and well-meaning, too much so for his Conservative Mexican backers, and he functioned ineffectively as an executive. His policies were unacceptable to his French supporters as well. They continued to press their claims for compensation, ultimately taking matters into their own hands, seizing Mexican assets as payment for their claims, and thereby further angering the Mexicans.

Maximilian's policies were also resented by the Church and the Holy See, because he resisted the restoration of properties of the Church and its former special privileges, or *fueros*. Further, the emperor, as a foreigner and an intruder, aroused the deep and traditional Mexican xenophobia. Nor was the institution of monarchy acceptable to Mexicans as a political and social institution. Despite chaos and misgovernment, the forty years of the Republic had left their imprint, and Mexican public opinion favored the Juárez cause.

But the final cause for Maximilian's downfall came from outside Mexico. The United States did not demobilize at the end of the Civil War, and the United States representative in Paris stressed concern for the Mexican situation. Indeed, the United States had supported Benito Juárez when it could throughout the entire period. The postwar concentration of Union troops in the southern United States now gave added force to U.S. demands for the withdrawal of French troops. Moreover, the Prussian victory in the war against Austria in 1866 changed the European power structure; a frightened Napoleon III found that he had to look to the defense of France in Europe. This defense required that he withdraw the French troops from Mexico much ahead of schedule. Without French troops, Maximilian's power disintegrated rapidly. His military defeat and execution returned Mexico to the route of *La Reforma*, under President Juárez.

The withdrawal of the French army ended French efforts to restore empire in America. Mexico and the other nations of Latin America now seemed relatively secure from further threats of European colonization. The foreign policies of the independent American states, moreover, began to display a generally increasing harmony that encouraged immigration, foreign capital investment, and national development. Latin American relations with the United States were also increasingly tranquil, though relations between Latin American states were not always so peaceful.

Some outstanding examples of arbitration and conciliation during the 1860s began to form the pattern for a variety of international agreements that were to come into being with the creation of the Inter-American System in 1889. For example, in 1868 President Benito Juárez agreed to a mixed commission, similar to that of 1843, to settle claims arising from damages to United States nationals and property during the wars of *La Reforma* and the Maximilian era. The mixed commission technique for the adjudication of claims and the settlement of disputes developed characteristics that were distinct from other diplomatic practice. This technique became one of the continuities in, and contributions to, the history of the international relations of the New World.[1]

The War of the Triple Alliance, 1864–1870

While Mexico was struggling against European imperialism, other states in the hemisphere had become embroiled in international conflicts. Among these was the Paraguayan War. This conflict, also referred to as the War of the Triple Alliance, had its origins in the international power politics of the Río de la Plata region. It had aspects of power politics previously deemed more characteristic of Europe than of America,[2] although the thoughtful student will see sources of the balance-of-power theory and practice in the balance of British and French interests before independence, as well as in the effects of the balkanization of Spanish America into numerous small and weak states.

Each participant, in its historical literature, has viewed the events from the standpoint of its national interest. Paraguayans see the war as the result of expansionist Brazilian policy and what they consider an unusual Brazilian-Argentine agreement to partition Paraguay. They see it as unusual because in the past Argentine and Brazilian policy objectives in the region had been traditionally opposed to each other. The view of the Triple Alliance (Argentina, Brazil, and Uruguay) is that they joined to oppose Paraguayan aggression against Uruguay and the threat of Paraguayan military power under the dictator-president, Francisco Solano López. Uruguay had come into being as a buffer state between Argentina and Brazil through the

1. On these Mexican developments see: Arturo Arnáiz y Freg and Claude Bataillon (eds.), *La Intervención Francesa y el Imperio de México, Cien Años Después, 1862–1962* (Mexico: Associación Mexicana de Historiadores, Instituto Francés de América Latina, 1965); Lilia Díaz (ed.), *Versión Francesa de México, 1864–1867* (4 vols.; Mexico: El Colegio de México, 1967); Arnold Blumberg, *The Diplomacy of the Mexican Empire, 1863–1867* (Philadelphia: The American Philosophical Society, 1971); Jaime Delgado, *España y México en el Siglo XIX* (Madrid: Instituto Gonzalo Fernández de Oviedo, 1950); Joachim Kühn, *Das Ende des Maximilianischen Kaiserreichs in Mexico* (Gottingen: Musterschmidt Verlag, 1965); and Luis Weckmann (ed.), *Las Relaciones Franco–Mexicanas, 1839–1867* (Mexico: Secretaría de Relaciones Exteriores, 1962).

2. On the power conflict aspect of this war see Robert N. Burr, *By Reason or Force: Chile and the Balancing of Power in South America, 1830–1905* (Berkeley: University of California Press, 1965), 99 ff.

mediation and influence of Great Britain. While maintaining economic dominance in this buffer state, Great Britain neither guaranteed Uruguayan independence nor sought to control the internal political processes of the new nation. Consequently, the partisan politics of Uruguay came to reflect the conflicting interests and interventions of her powerful neighbors, Brazil and Argentina.

Within Uruguay an Argentine faction contended with a Brazilian faction for control of the government. It had been necessary during the Rosas period for Great Britain, with French support, to interpose a blockade of Buenos Aires by naval forces to protect Montevideo, not only to pressure the Argentine president, Juan Manuel Rosas, to respect the lives and property of British and French citizens, but also to make him respect the independence of Uruguay. Meanwhile, Paraguay watched these power moves enviously; when the international situation appeared to favor the personal and imperial ambitions of her president, Francisco Solano López, she initiated a war that was to have tragic results for her.

Paraguayan ambition was no doubt stimulated by a major policy shift in the international politics of the region that had taken place before the alliance against Paraguay was formed. In 1864 Argentina had supported an armed invasion of Uruguay by an expedition composed of exiled members of the Uruguayan *Colorado* party, the political party that favored Argentine interests in Uruguay. The purpose of the expedition was to overturn the existing government of the *Blanco* party, the party that was usually supported by Brazil. Thus the two powerful neighbors seemed to be at odds on Uruguayan policy. Events were to prove this an incorrect assumption. On this occasion, Paraguay, supported by Great Britain, France, Portugal, and Italy, demanded explanation of the Argentine action. Brazil, for her own purposes, did not join the *démarche*. Argentina simply did not reply. However, Brazil took the occasion to make strong representations to the Uruguayan government concerning the protection of, and the properties of, Brazilian nationals residing in the frontier regions, which were areas of indistinct boundary demarcation and of cattle rustling and contraband trade. Argentina offered to mediate the dispute, but her offer was rejected by Uruguay. The Brazilian foreign minister was opposed to joint action with Argentina, but Argentina and Brazil now found themselves on the same side of a Uruguayan problem. With the cooperation of the Uruguayan *Colorado* party, Brazil reacted to the Uruguayan refusal to take cognizance of her representations by sending a military force into the country. The consequence of that action was the overthrow of the *Blanco* party government and the establishment of a *Colorado* government. The *Colorado* government settled the issues with both Argentina and Brazil, ultimately entering into an alliance with the two powers against Paraguay. It now became apparent that Brazil, following a newly aggressive policy, was seeking the support of the Argentine government, under Bartolomé Mitre, in an effort to achieve a definitive settlement of boundaries in the Río de la Plata area.

The Brazilian entry into Uruguay provided the president of Paraguay with the occasion for realizing a personal dream, *i.e.*, the creation of a new nation that would embrace southern Brazil, northern Argentina, and possibly Bolivia, with Paraguay as its center and Asunción as its capital. To this end he had the cooperation of the *Blanco* government in Uruguay. Paraguay, therefore, protested the military action of Brazil and informed the emperor that Paraguay considered this action equivalent to an attack upon Paraguay.

When no satisfactory reply to this protest was received, Paraguay seized an armed Brazilian vessel. In response, Brazil declared war on Paraguay. The relative power of the nations did not then differ as much as geographic size and population today might at first indicate. At that time, Paraguay probably had the largest and best-organized standing army in South America. She also had a record of virtually unbroken political (authoritarian) stability since independence. The southern provinces of Brazil had traditionally resisted the extension of imperial power and had flirted with separatist movements. Consequently, their political leaders might find the call for a new and larger Platine state, such as Solano López envisioned, quite attractive. This alienation of the southern provinces, with its attendant dangers, especially in Rio Grande do Sul, was one of the reasons for Brazil's aggressive action against Uruguay. The Paraguayan president appeared confident that Brazil would not be able to field an army in time to prevent his capture of Montevideo. He further relied on the support of separatist movements in the provinces against Buenos Aires, centering in Entre Rios, Corrientes, and Córdoba. Political leaders in these provinces had found Paraguayan political stability attractive and had shared Paraguay's resentment of the trade monopoly that Buenos Aires exercised in the Río de la Plata region. Hence, she did not expect Argentine opposition.

To reach Montevideo, however, Paraguayan forces had to cross the Argentine province of Corrientes. But the expected political cooperation there did not materialize and the Argentine government denied permission to make the crossing, despite the fact that the decision drastically shifted Argentine foreign policy from one of opposing Brazilian designs in the area to one of apparent cooperation to settle the problem of Paraguayan boundaries. Despite the Argentine refusal, Paraguay invaded Corrientes and seized two Argentine vessels on the Paraguay River.

So began the War of the Triple Alliance. The United States offered to mediate to effect a peaceful solution. Paraguay accepted the offer, but Brazil, Argentina, and Uruguay rejected it. Britain, France, Chile, Bolivia, Peru, and Ecuador also proposed mediation with similar lack of success. The war was destined to be one of the most destructive in Latin American history, continuing until the complete defeat and unconditional surrender of Paraguay.[3]

Despite the failure to rally support from dissident Argentine and Brazilian elements, the Paraguayans almost succeeded in winning the war. But their failure to capture Montevideo signaled the beginning of five years of retreat in a fight-to-the-death defense of their homeland. For a brief period Argentina exercised military leadership in the field under the guidance of president Bartolomé Mitre. But because of her internal political problems, Argentina was soon content to leave the prosecution of the war almost entirely in Brazilian hands. Brazil, as foreseen, had been slow to mobilize. The Brazilian army was small, for neither the emperor nor the party leaders had supported a large military establishment. Indeed, they had shunned both military ex-

3. Harold F. Peterson, "Efforts of the United States to Mediate in the Paraguayan War," *Hispanic American Historical Review*, XII (February, 1932), 2–17.

penditures and military display. The war forced a change in these policies, marking the beginning of a large Brazilian army and navy. As casualties mounted, largely from disease, and as expenditures climbed, Brazil found that she was waging an increasingly unpopular war. Some politicians accused the emperor of fighting for dynastic, rather than national, interests.

Paraguay was finally defeated, President López dying in the final battle, in 1870. The six-year Brazilian occupation of Asunción that followed proved unpopular with Paraguayans and Brazilians alike. For Argentina it raised even more serious questions regarding Brazil's future political ambitions in the area, questions not settled until Argentina's treaty with Paraguay setting national boundaries, but leaving the question of the Argentine-Brazilian boundary in Misiones to be settled later by arbitration. This Brazilian power threat caused Argentina to hesitate during the 1870s to exercise a moderating influence on Chile's attitude toward Bolivia and Peru in the developments that later produced the War of the Pacific. The War of the Triple Alliance is notable because for the first time Argentina and Brazil had been united against Paraguay, which had traditionally maintained her independence by playing the two powers against each other. Juan B. Alberdi, for example, denounced the actions of the Mitre government as a betrayal of both Argentine and Paraguayan interests. The consequences of this policy change were disastrous for Paraguay, i.e., defeat, humiliation, occupation, loss of territory, a startling decline in population and, finally, a policy of withdrawal into an isolation that has been one of the extremes of Paraguay's relations with her neighbors and with the world.[4]

Brazil: Postwar Foreign Policy

The War of the Triple Alliance had some internal political effects that

4. Pelham H. Box, *Origins of the Paraguayan War* (2 vols.; Urbana: University of Illinois Press, 1930), gives the best account of the diplomacy. Brazilian, Argentine, and Paraguayan works reflect more nationalistic viewpoints. For Alberdi's criticisms see his *Historia de la Guerra del Paraguay* (Buenos Aires: Ediciones de la Patria Grande, 1962). The essays were originally published separately in 1865 and following years. See also Ricardo Levene, *History of Argentina*, trans. W. S. Robertson (Chapel Hill: University of North Carolina Press, 1937), and subsequent reprint.

helped to bring about the change in the Brazilian political system from empire to republic. Some aspects of the transition took place slowly as a consequence of characteristics that differentiate Brazil from her Spanish-speaking neighbors. Among the most important of these characteristics was that of internal political tranquility. The last insurrection in the empire of Brazil had been a brief uprising in the northeast of the country in 1847–1848. Its suppression marked the beginning of forty years of civil peace. Secessionist movements stopped, and by 1848 Pedro II was in control of a unified state, although a decentralizing trend, sanctioned by the *Ato Adicional* of 1834, forecast the later federalist state.

Modest, democratic, and with an inquiring mind, Pedro was one of the eminent rulers of his age. The structure of his state was supposedly modeled after the British constitutional monarchy, but the Iberian tradition persisted. After 1847 Pedro personally appointed the prime minister and kept a firm hand on international relations. Financial order and a sound currency were the consequences of new agricultural developments in the production of cotton and coffee for export, combined with British financing of public services and industrial development. The international slave trade was finally abolished in the 1850s. Brazil then gave official encouragement to European immigration, largely from Portugal, Spain, and Italy.

The basic Brazilian international policies continued, vigorously implemented during the decade of the 1860s, as we have seen, in the War of the Triple Alliance and bearing the imprint of the foreign minister, the first Baron Rio Branco. Even after the change from empire to republic in 1887–1889 this consistency held true. The first of these policies was expansion of the national territory, now through negotiation rather than force, and based on the principle of *uti possidetis* (the Brazilian version) and on the work of excellent Brazilian geographers. The second policy was that of friendship with Great Britain for economic and commercial reasons, putting aside the remembrance of that nation's forceful suppression of the slave trade and her objections to slavery in Brazil. A third and largely new policy was that of friendship with the United States as a possible counterbalance to Britain and to Brazil's Spanish American neighbors. A fourth policy was defense of the independence of Uruguay, including the policy of maintaining influence in that country through support of a major political party there.

In this light, Brazilian apprehensions over other expansionist ambitions displayed by Paraguay after Francisco Solano López became its president (1862) are not hard to understand; nor can they be separated from Brazilian territorial claims against the state. A Brazilian declaration of war against Paraguay was logical under the circumstances, as we have just seen. This war against Paraguay, however, required the rapid expansion of the Brazilian military establishment and it left Brazil, after the war, with a military establishment that increasingly resented the emperor's efforts to reduce and control it. The extensive public criticism evoked by the war also reflected adversely on the imperial popular image. Moreover, the creation of the Third French Republic in 1870 gave Brazil a vigorous republican movement. These factors heightened the tensions and divisions within Brazil, soon to be created by a Church-state conflict and by the uncompensated abolition of slavery.[5]

Chile: Nationalism and Power Politics

Differences between Brazil and her Hispanic neighbors are evident, but none is so striking as the contrast between Brazil and one of the two countries with which she has no common border, Chile. The European revolutions of 1848 caused both ideas and immigrants to flow to the New World, and to Chile both came in numbers. A colonizing company had somewhat earlier initiated a German immigration into southern Chile, and this stream grew after 1848. European social revolutionary ideas were also transmitted to Chile through such intellectuals as Francisco Bilbao, who, returning from France in 1848, directed his energies through the Society of Equality toward the creation of a new, romantic, democratic Chile. The movement was not successful at the moment, but it left its mark. Other liberals came to

5. See C. H. Haring, *Empire in Brazil: A New World Experiment in Monarchy* (Cambridge: Harvard University Press, 1958). See also Carlos M. Delgado de Carvalho, *Historia Diplomática do Brasil* (São Paulo: Companhia Editôra Nacional, 1959), and João Pandiá Calogeras, *A Política Exterior do Imperio* (2 vols.; Rio de Janeiro: Imprensa Nacional, 1927).

Chile as exiles from the harsh rule of Argentina under Rosas, thus beginning a tradition of Chile as the haven for the politically persecuted in the southern continent. The earlier war of Chile against the confederation of Peru and Bolivia (1836–1839) had reinforced the Chilean military tradition, but the conservative and competent governmental system developed under the Chilean constitution of 1833 allowed for the peaceful transfer of power from one regime to another. Not all was tranquil, however, because Chile suffered an occasional *pronunciamento*, riot, or barracks revolt; but the constitutional regime always triumphed, and the consequences of such disturbances upon the national life were minor.

Even the Indian problem of Chile was largely solved in 1861, when the Araucanians were crushed and confined to reservations in the southern reaches of the land. International politics impinged upon internal development, however, creating an expansive nationalism that led Chile into two wars—a naval war with Spain (1865–1870) and the War of the Pacific (1879–1883). The war with Spain resulted from the Spanish seizure of the Chincha Islands off Peru in 1864 and the consequent demand of a Spanish admiral for "honors" to the Spanish flag by Chile.[6]

But before that conflict erupted another dimension of new Spanish imperialism had been extended into Santo Domingo.

Santo Domingo: The Return of Spanish Imperialism, 1861–1865

As we have seen, the relations of Spain with the New World took a newly aggressive direction in the decade of the 1860s, largely as the consequence of a political reorientation within the Spanish government under Isabel II. One new venture came from an unexpected opportunity to reincorporate Santo Domingo into the Spanish empire. That nation had regained independence in 1844 after twenty years of Haitian occupation, affirming as the keystone of its foreign policy protection against the black, French, and Creole-speaking

---

6. Albert Cruchaga Ossa, *Estudios de Historia Diplomática Chilena* (Santiago: Editorial Andrés Bello, 1962). See also William Columbus Davis, *The Last Conquistadores: The Spanish Intervention in Peru and Chile, 1863–1866* (Athens, Ga.: University of Georgia Press, 1950).

state with which Santo Domingo shared the island of Hispaniola. Political leaders in Santo Domingo sought this protection by a variety of means, one of which was annexation by a great and friendly power. But the threat from Haiti did not produce internal unity, and the island republic swung unstably between the political ambitions of personalist leaders grouped roughly under the party labels of Liberal and Conservative. One such leader was Pedro Santana, who sought both protection and stability through reincorporation of Santo Domingo into the Spanish empire in 1861.

Santana was named captain-general of the island by Spain and was granted a title of nobility; as might have been expected, the restructuring of the imperial bureaucracy brought Spanish troops, clergy, judges, *corregidores*, and new taxes. It soon became apparent that this attempt to restore Spanish rule was a disaster. Rebellion broke out, and dissidents fought a new and successful war for independence from Spain (1864–1865). Santana resigned, totally depressed, and committed suicide. Yellow fever took its toll of Spanish troops. The end of the Civil War permitted the United States to express with greater force her protests at Madrid against the Spanish occupation of the island republic, an occupation contrary to the Monroe Doctrine. In May, 1865, the Spanish government abandoned the undertaking, and Santo Domingo returned to the ranks of American republics.[7]

Cuba: The Ten Years' War, 1868–1878)

Spain's problems in the Caribbean did not end with her withdrawal from Santo Domingo. Her relations with Cuba, for example, entered a new and critical stage. The period of peace that had begun with the political accommodation of 1855 came to an end with the *Grito de Yara*, October 10, 1868. On that date a long-projected war for independence was initiated, plunging the island into ten years of deadly conflict. The *Grito*, in addition to being a call for independence, demanded universal suffrage and the gradual emancipation of slaves.

The Cuban decision for independence from Spain had not been

7. Sumner Welles, *Naboth's Vineyard: The Dominican Republic, 1844–1924* (2 vols.; New York: Payson & Clarke, 1928). Rayford Logan, *Haiti and the Dominican Republic* (New York and London: Oxford University Press, 1968), 40–43. Joaquín M. Inchaustegui Cabral, *Historia Dominicana, 1844–1941* (Ciudad Trujillo, Santo Domingo: Librería Dominicana, 1953).

reached easily or quickly. After 1810 Cuba enjoyed representation in the Spanish Cortes, despite the repressions of Ferdinand VII, until 1837, when she was denied such representation after the Spanish government suppressed its popular Liberal constitution of 1834. Cuba was supposed to have been governed by a set of special laws, but these laws were never promulgated. One apparent reason was the fear of slave revolts, a fear that deepened the lack of a consensus favoring independence. Annexation to the United States had also seemed to be wished by Cuban slave owners, but autonomy within the Spanish empire also remained a realistic possibility. Yet when a Cuban delegation went to Madrid in 1866–1867 to seek redress of grievances, it failed to resolve with the Spanish government such issues as tax reform, increased self-government, and the emancipation of the slaves. Indeed, the threat of further repressive laws strengthened in their minds adherence to the movement for independence. That European "imperialist" interest in Cuba had not ended was apparent when President Grant proposed to mediate in the war, but was strongly advised by Great Britain not to do so.

The devastating ten years of civil war ended in 1878 with a Spanish agreement for certain political reforms, amnesty for political prisoners, liberty for rebel slaves, and the gradual abolition of the institution of slavery. Except for this last reform, which became definitive by 1886, the provisions of this agreement were not carried out, however, and Spanish despotism apparently deepened. By 1895 the Cuban sentiment for independence had become essentially one of no compromise. On the basis of this principle of no compromise, the second struggle against Spain began in that year, with unexpected consequences for the international relations of the Caribbean.[8]

The Question of Belize

Under a treaty of 1859 Great Britain had agreed with Guatemala to join in opening communication between the Atlantic coast and

8. R. Guerra Sánchez, *et. al.*, *Historia de la Nación Cubana* (10 vols.; Havana: Editorial Historia de la Nación Cubana, 1952). See also Duvon C. Corbitt, "Cuban and Revisionist Interpretations of Cuba's Struggle for Independence," *Hispanic American Historical Review*, XL (August, 1963), 395–404; and Robert G. Caldwell, *The López Expeditions to Cuba, 1848–1851* (Princeton: Princeton University Press, 1915).

Guatemala City by constructing a cart road and/or opening river communication. By an additional treaty, signed in 1863 but never ratified, the British financial contribution for the purpose of constructing this road or river outlet was limited to 50,000 pounds sterling. Because of internal dissensions, the Guatemala congress had not taken up the question of ratification within the stipulated period. When Guatemala requested an extension of the period for ratification, the British Foreign Office replied that Britain considered the matter closed. The cart road/river route was never constructed, and the resulting diplomatic impasse became the basis of a new phase in the Belize controversy seventy years later when President Jorge Ubico of Guatemala reopened the controversy.[9]

Spanish Intervention in Peru, 1863–1869

The newly imperialistic and aggressive foreign policies of Spain in the decade under study embroiled her in a conflict with Peru and Chile, sometimes referred to as the First War of the Pacific, although it has no commonly accepted name. If the first conflict of Chile against Peru and Bolivia (1837–1839) is referred to as the War of the Confederation, this conflict might logically be called the First War of the Pacific (1863–1869), making the generally acknowledged War of the Pacific (1879–1883) the Second War of the Pacific. Nomenclature is not important, except for the possible confusion that arises between this conflict, which involved an extra-hemispheric power, and the later war between hemispheric nations. But it serves in this case to remind us of the continuance of Chilean concern for the power struggle of this region, as Robert Burr has reminded us in his previously cited work.[10]

Again, the conflict developed from claims of foreign nationals against a New World state. In this instance, the claims were those of Spanish nationals against Peru, claims dating from the time of Peruvian independence. Such claims were intensified by claims for the redress of grievances of Spanish immigrants who had come to Peru

9. Kenneth J. Grieb, "Jorge Ubico and the Belize Boundary Dispute," *The Americas*, XXX (April, 1974), 448–74.
10. Burr, *By Reason or Force*, 90–99.

under a national policy encouraging such immigration. Financial claims and the claims for the redress of foreign grievances present, of course, a subject of continuity discernible throughout the history of Latin American international relations, indeed, a major theme in the relations between the American states and the European powers until post–World War I. This conflict between Peru and Chile (ultimately also involving Ecuador and Bolivia) and Spain was an example of the European use of force, common at the time, to collect claims and to redress grievances of European nationals. But it had special significance as a possible effort to restore the Spanish empire in America, since Spain had not formally recognized the independence of Peru and Chile. When negotiations of the claims question with Peruvian officials broke down, the Spanish naval forces of eight warships carrying 207 cannons, then present in Peruvian waters under the guise of a "scientific expedition," seized the guano-rich Chincha Islands off the Peruvian coast. The Spaniards proceeded to mine and market the natural fertilizer, using the money from sales to pay the Spanish claims.[11]

The Second American Congress of Lima, 1864–1865

Several months before the seizure of the islands, Peru had invited the neighboring states of Chile, Bolivia, Ecuador, Colombia, Venezuela, and Brazil to meet in a congress to consider the need for a defensive arrangement against the new threats of European intervention and other measures of common interest. Peru, more than any other Spanish American country, had been sensitive to the power implications of the United States Civil War, opening the Americas to renewed threats of European intervention, as in the case of Mexico and the Dominican Republic. Only the six Spanish American states mentioned (with an unauthorized observer from Argentina, Domingo F.

11. Davis, *Last Conquistadores*, and Frederick B. Pike, *The Modern History of Peru* (New York: Praeger, 1967), Chap. 4. The active role of Chile in these developments relating to the Spanish occupation of the Chincha Islands has been carefully studied by Alberto Wagner de Reyna in two articles: "La Misíon Santa María en el Perú, Octubre 1865–Enero 1866," in *Apartado del Boletín de la Academia Chilena de la Historia* (Santiago: Imprenta Universitaria. Valenzuela Basterrica y Cía., 1952) and "La Ocupación de las Islas de Chincha y Las Relaciones Chileno-peruanos," in *Apartado del Boletín de las Academia Chilena de la Historia* (Santiago: Imprenta Universitaria, Valenzuela Basterrica y Cía., 1954).

Sarmiento) attended the congress. Its first months of meetings, contrary to expectation, were taken up with efforts to use their good offices to effect a settlement between Peru and Spain. These good offices were rejected by Spain; and Peru, as we have seen, ultimately surrendered to Spanish demands in the Vivanco-Pareja treaty. But the Peruvian government which signed this treaty was soon overturned by a *golpe* led by Ramón Castilla; the new government repudiated the treaty. Chile joined with Peru against Spain in the ensuing hostilities (with nominal support from Ecuador and Bolivia); a joint Chilean-Peruvian fleet forced the withdrawal of the Spanish fleet from Callao. The Chilean naval vessel *Esmeralda* captured the Spanish *Covadonga*. But both Callao and the unfortified port of Valparaiso were subjected to a heartless bombardment by the Spanish fleet before it finally withdrew in disgrace from American waters. The war brought victory to neither side. The Spanish fleet withdrew largely because of political changes at home that ended Spain's ill-fated revival of imperialism. But it also withdrew in part because the claims against Peru had been paid by the sale of Peruvian guano.

From the Latin American standpoint, this inconclusive war was more significant as the last serious Spanish American effort to form an alliance for their mutual defense and the maintenance of peace. After the failure of the Lima Congress' mediation in the dispute, the delegates turned their attention to the purposes for which they had assembled. They drew up four treaties: (1) Union and Alliance, (2) Preservation of Peace, (3) Postal Services, and (4) Commerce and Navigation. Like their predecessors, these treaties remained unratified, although, in accordance with the treaty of Union and Alliance, Chile, Bolivia, and Ecuador supported Peru in the war with Spain in 1865. The power conflicts summarized earlier in this chapter explain in large measure the failure of this last Spanish American effort to achieve an alliance. Mexico at this time offered no help; she was fighting for her life against French intervention. Brazil (not really wanted, as the Peruvians explained to the Chileans, but invited as a courtesy) was involved in the preliminaries of the Paraguayan War, as were Uruguay, Paraguay, and Argentina. Argentina, whose support was essential to any successful Spanish-American alliance, specifically rejected any such international collaboration; Domingo F. Sarmiento, on his way to the United States as the Argentine minister in Washington, attended on his personal initiative, and was formally reproved for his action by President Mitre of Argentina.[12]

The Bolivian model for a defensive alliance seems to have died, after some four decades of frustration, with the failure of these treaties to receive ratification. The movement for international cooperation among the states of America was to follow a different pattern in the following decades. Yet the Spanish-Peruvian conflict and the Second Lima Congress had shown that the Spanish American states still had possibilities of cooperation when faced with a real danger. The Lima Congress had also revealed their potential for agreement on means for the peaceful settlement of boundary disputes, postal cooperation, and measures for improving trade and transportation—all topics that would be on the agenda of future hemispheric conferences.

12. On the American Congress in Lima (1864–1865), see Samuel Guy Inman, *Inter-American Conferences, 1826–1954: History and Problems* (Washington: University Press of Washington, D.C., 1965), 26–29; J. M. Yepes, *Del Congreso de Panamá a la Conferencia de Caracas, 1826–1954* (2 vols.; Caracas: Tenth Inter-American Conference, 1955). I, 257 ff; and Oscar Barrenechea y Raygado, *Congresos y Conferencias Internacionales Celebradas en Lima, 1847–1894* (Buenos Aires: Peuser, 1947). Francisco Cuevas Cancino, *Del Congreso de Panamá a la Conferencia de Caracas, 1826–1954* (2 vols.; Caracas: 1955), I, 257–72.

6 Power Politics and the Consolidation of National Policies, 1870–1900

F. TAYLOR PECK

The international relations of Latin American states during the final decades of the nineteenth century reflect increasingly national and individual characteristics, but three distinct regional groupings are distinguishable: (1) South America below the Caribbean littoral, (2) Mexico, and (3) Central America and the Caribbean. For the states of South America, foreign policies sought increased relations with Europe through the encouragement of immigration, of investment, and of cultural affinities. Basically secure from threats of European intervention, these nations concentrated on internal problems and national development. Except for what we are calling the Second War of the Pacific, even interstate relations were relatively peaceful. For Mexico, her special relations with the United States were amplified and complemented by an enlarged role in hemispheric and world politics. For Central America and the Caribbean, on the other hand, these decades brought increased conflict and intervention, both from Europe and from within.

The War of the Pacific, 1879–1883

This conflict had its roots in a disputed boundary between Bolivia and Chile that was part of their imperial heritage. For administrative reasons, the territory that became the Bolivian Department of Atacama on the Pacific Ocean had been designated as part of the Viceroyalty of La Plata (Buenos Aires) when that viceregal unit came into being. When Marshall Sucre detached as a separate nation that portion of the former viceroyalty that was to be named Bolivia in honor of his illustrious patron, Simón Bolívar, he included that coastal area (with ill-defined boundaries).

The increased commercial use of guano and natural nitrates transformed this vast desert into a region with valuable natural resources. In the 1840s Peru began licensing companies to exploit the deposits in its territory (Tacna, Arica, and Tarapacá). Chile claimed the right to work the deposits on her northern frontier as far as Majillones on the twenty-third parallel, but Bolivia insisted that this Chilean claim was an encroachment upon her territory. Intermittent diplomatic exchanges and conflicts over jurisdiction in this nitrate-rich region continued until 1863, when the controversy became so intense that the Bolivian congress authorized the president to declare war on Chile at his discretion. Spain's subsequent seizure of the Chincha Islands off the coast of Peru in 1864 averted the crisis. Bolivia then joined Chile, Peru, and Ecuador in resisting Spain. Meanwhile in 1866, Chile and Bolivia signed a treaty designed to settle the boundary question. This treaty established the international boundary at the twenty-third parallel and provided that Chile and Bolivia would share in the exploitation of resources in the territory between the twenty-third and the twenty-fifth parallels south, dividing the revenues from export taxes on the products, chiefly nitrate, between the governments, and making available to each other facilities for trade. The treaty provided, moreover, that minerals, specifically nitrates, might be mined and exported without special discriminatory taxes on the Chilean producers or without hindrance from Bolivia. Still under the influences of the war with Spain, Bolivia granted a concession to the Anglo-Chilean Nitrate Company to exploit the nitrate deposits discovered by Chilean explorers a few years earlier near Antofagasta, located north of the twenty-fourth parallel. British capital was invested in this company, but, according to J. Fred Rippy, the amount was not large until after the War of the Pacific. By 1890 it had reached the sum of £5.3 million and climbed to £20 million by 1928. Moreover, in 1870 Chilean prospectors discovered a rich silver lode at Caracoles, near the twenty-third parallel. Bolivia claimed that the mines were north of the agreed dividing line and hence not within the joint benefit zone.

Chile, on the other hand, insisted that the line dividing the Bolivian-Chilean territories ran north of Caracoles.

Negotiations for clarification of a treaty, the terms of which had never been sufficiently precise to satisfy the Chilean entrepreneurs, were interrupted by political turmoil in Bolivia, so that it was not until December 5, 1872, that the Lindsey-Corral Protocol was signed. This agreement, while eliminating some of the more troublesome features of the treaty of 1866, left the condominium arrangement intact. The two countries agreed to continue negotiations, however, thereby indicating that all problems had not been solved to Chilean satisfaction. Yet even before this preliminary agreement, Chile had grown suspicious of Bolivian intentions; the rumor persisted of a secret treaty of alliance between Peru and Bolivia against Chile. Such a treaty was indeed under discussion in 1872 and was formally signed on February 6, 1873; but Chilean reaction at that time was stopped by other complicating factors in her international relations. Chief of these factors was the continuing border dispute over the Patagonian boundary with Argentina, a dispute that presented a constant threat of hostilities. Until this border problem was settled, no Chilean government dared move against Bolivia, much less against a Bolivia allied with Peru.

Meanwhile, Peru sought to bring Argentina into the alliance with Bolivia. President Domingo F. Sarmiento was reported to have favored this alliance in September, 1873, but the Argentine government, in accordance with its usual policy of avoiding entangling alliances, hesitated over adherence. Then engaged in the negotiations for a peace settlement of the War of the Triple Alliance against Paraguay, Argentina was much concerned about the possible hostile reaction of her ally, Brazil, to a Peruvian alliance. Adherence to the treaty required approval of the Argentine congress, and this approval could be neither certain nor secret. Peru was sufficiently concerned over the Argentine relations with Brazil to propose a clause to the effect that the alliance would not apply to disputes arising between Argentina and Brazil. But this was insufficient in Argentine eyes. Moreover, boundary disputes between Argentina and Bolivia further worked against Argentine adherence to the proposed secret treaty.

While Argentina hesitated, Chile learned of the secret alliance in January, 1874, through a leak from the Argentine congress. This information made the apparent Bolivian delay in the ratification of the Lindsey-Corral Protocol even more suspicious in Chilean eyes. The Chilean government reacted by ordering the two ironclads then being built for her in British shipyards to sail at once for Valparaiso, without sea trials and without the completion of their outfitting. This was done, and these two vessels subsequently tipped the scales of sea power in Chile's favor.

Despite these adverse conditions, a change in government in Bolivia brought to power President Tomás Frías, a rare phenomenon of a civilian executive. President Frías negotiated a new treaty with Chile in 1874. By the terms of this Treaty of Sucre, the twenty-fourth parallel was reconfirmed as the international boundary. It was agreed that Chile would receive one-half the revenue from the export taxes on nitrates taken from the zone of mutual exploitation. It was further agreed that no additional Bolivian taxes on exports would be imposed for twenty-five years, and that all disputes arising under the treaty would be settled by arbitration. Lamentably, Bolivia delayed ratifying the new treaty, further heightening Chilean suspicions.

The situation was further worsened by Peru when, in 1875, she nationalized all private mines in her nitrate area and created a national monopoly for the exploitation of nitrates. Chilean owners and operators in the Tarapacá province of Peru acted at once to try to exempt that area from the Peruvian national monopoly. Societies were also formed in Chile at this time, advocating the annexation of the whole nitrate region; the harassment of Peruvian and Bolivian officials in the area became common.

Nonetheless, the Chilean government was once again prevented from taking forceful action against either Peru or Bolivia because its dispute with Argentina over the Patagonian boundary flared up anew. This boundary dispute, also a result of the indeterminate demarcations under the Spanish empire, involved both land and water boundaries. Realizing the potentiality of this conflict in which she did not wish to become involved and aware of Argentina's opposition to involvement in the international politics of the West Coast (except for her frontier problems with Chile), Peru instructed her representative in Buenos Aires to cease all efforts to get Argentina to join her secret alliance.

In 1876 a new president of Bolivia, General Hilarión Daza, seeking new sources of revenue to support his regime, demanded as the price of Bolivia's ratification of the Treaty of Sucre (1874), a new tax of ten *centavos* per *quintal* (25 pounds) on all nitrates exported from the Atacama zone. He further threatened, should the tax not be paid, to seize all nitrates in the hands of exporters to compensate Bolivia for the nonpayment of the tax. This demand, in contravention of existing agreements, was unacceptable to the Chilean government; but the controversy remained unresolved for some time because of both internal and external political considerations in Chile.

In February, 1878, the Bolivian congress finally approved the concession of the Anglo-Chilean Nitrate and Railway Company which had been pending since 1873. The concession was approved, however, on condition that the company pay the new tax of ten *centavos* per *quintal* on all nitrates exported from the Atacama zone. (The 1874 treaty was ratified with Bolivian congressional approval.) The Chilean government again protested that the tax was contrary to the agreement of 1873 and the treaty of 1874.

Bolivia finally agreed, verbally, to defer the imposition of the tax until a solution of the problem could be found. But no further steps were taken to resolve the problem, and on July 2, 1878, Chile presented a note to the Bolivian government asking for compliance with the agreement of 1873 and the treaty of 1874. When no reply was forthcoming, Chile, under increasing pressure from her (nitrate) commercial interests, threatened on November 8, 1878, to abrogate the treaty and reclaim the disputed territory as far as the twenty-third parallel.

At this juncture a new incident in Patagonia occurred to complicate Argentine-Chilean relations. Chile seized a United States vessel in Argentine (Patagonian) territorial waters. The president of Argentina reacted by ordering a naval force to the Santa Cruz River in the south. Chile felt compelled to order her fleet, including the two new British-built ironclads, made ready to sail south also. But the importance of the Chilean dispute with Bolivia outweighed the importance of this conflict with Argentina, in which honor and territory were involved but no important economic interest. Consequently, negotiations in Santiago produced the Fierro-Sarrate Treaty of December 6, 1878, providing for the settlement of the Patagonian boundary dispute by arbitration, a process that led to a penultimate settlement in 1902. Upon the heels of Chile's agreement with Argentina, the Bolivian government informed Chile that the nitrate tax was to be collected. Free now to deal more strongly with Bolivia, Chile replied that this was a violation of the treaty of 1874, and that Chile would take appropriate action to prevent enforcement of the tax. Unimpressed, President Daza of Bolivia ordered collection of the tax. Still seeking a peaceful settlement, the Chilean government offered, on January 20, 1879, to arbitrate the dispute as provided in the treaty of 1874. Bolivia, for reasons that have yet to be satisfactorily explained, had already initiated action against the company. She refused the arbitration offer and ordered the concession of the Anglo-Chilean Nitrate and Railroad Company of Antofagasta to be canceled and the company property to be presented for public sale. Following the Chilean government's lead, the company had changed its position, refusing to pay the ten *centavo* per *quintal* tax, historically known as the "penny tax." The situation had now reached an impasse.

When the news of Bolivia's decision to cancel the concessions reached Santiago, the Chilean government reacted with an ultimatum giving Bolivia forty-eight hours to withdraw the cancellation of the concessions and to agree to an arbitration of the dispute. If Bolivia did not agree, Chile would reclaim all territory to the twenty-third parallel. To support the ultimatum, the Chilean fleet was mobilized at the port of Caldera. When no reply was received within the time prescribed, the Bolivian diplomatic representative in Santiago was given his passport. The Treaty of Sucre (1874) was abrogated, and the Chilean fleet was ordered to Antofagasta. The (Second) War of the Pacific had begun.

On February 14, 1879, the day set by the Bolivian government for the sale of the assets of the Anglo-Chilean Nitrate and Railroad Company, Chilean military forces occupied Antofagasta and began taking control of all the territory northward to the twenty-third parallel. A war manifesto from President Daza of Bolivia on February 27, 1879, made the conflict absolute.

The outbreak of war between Chile and Bolivia alarmed Peru. It was a conflict she had not sought or even felt directly concerned with. The alliance with Bolivia, which she was soon called upon to recognize, had been negotiated by a former government and in a very different set of international circumstances. Therefore, Peru offered to mediate the dispute, proposing that Chile withdraw from the occupied territory and submit the whole question to arbitration. Chile rejected the Peruvian proposal and, aware of the secret treaty of alliance, asked for assurances of Peru's neutrality. The war party in Peru, meanwhile, pushed the government into a hasty posture of rearming. Chile feared that Peru's mediation effort was a ruse to gain time and demanded that Peru immediately suspend its arming, abrogate the secret alliance, and declare its neutrality. Such a declaration might well have been in Peru's interest, but the pressures of internal politics made that neutrality impossible. Peru, therefore, declined Chile's request. When the Chilean minister in Lima asked for his passport, Peru assumed the character of a belligerent. Chile declared war on both Peru and Bolivia on April 5, 1879.

Chile was able to usurp Peru's control of the sea in October, 1879, thanks to her two British-built ironclads. A land defeat at Tacna, Peru, put Bolivia totally out of the conflict in May, 1880. On the diplomatic front each side tried to enlist the support of its neutral neighbors, and a number of neutrals attempted to mediate. Believing it possible that European nations would intervene in violation of the principles of the Monroe Doctrine, the United States sought to mediate the conflict in September, 1880. This attempt failed, largely because of the intransigence of the negotiators, when they met on board the U.S.S. *Lackawanna* in the harbor of Arica. The Peruvians were later to blame their intransigence on the U.S. minister in Lima, who, they claimed, misled them to believe that the United States supported their position, by stating that the United States wished to see the integrity of Peruvian territory maintained. The United States minister in Santiago also misled the Chileans by his enthusiasm for their position, repudiating that of his colleague in Lima. Ultimately, the failure of mediation led to the necessity of the attack upon and the capture of Lima by Chilean forces before that portion of the conflict could begin to come to a settlement.

After great losses by both sides in men and material, following the earlier campaigns in the Peruvian-Bolivian-Chilean desert, the decisive battle of Chorillos occurred on January 13, 1881. Neither force had really sought this engagement, because peace negotiations were already underway. But a Chilean victory was the result, leading to the fall of Lima on January 17, 1881. Two years of guerrilla warfare in the highlands followed before a Peruvian government strong enough to come to terms with the Chileans could be established. Eventually, after a long Chilean occupation of the Peruvian capital, during which the Chilean occupation troops earned for themselves and their nation the enduring hatred of the Limeños, the Treaty of Ancón was signed on October 20, 1883.

The Treaty of Ancón provided that the province of Tarapaca with all its mineral wealth should be permanently transferred to Chile, and that the Peruvian territories north of Tarapacá—Tacna and Arica—should be occupied by Chilean forces for ten years, after which a plebiscite was to be held to determine the ultimate sovereignty. This last provision led to the so-called Tacna-Arica dispute, often referred to as the Alsace-Lorraine of South America. Since Chile and Peru could not agree upon the provisions for holding the plebiscite, the controversy over the ownership of this region continued for the next forty-five years. It not only embittered Chilean-Peruvian relations but it seriously impaired the maturing of the Inter-American System, as we shall see. Chile's fear that compulsory arbitration projects discussed at the early meetings of the American states might be injurious to her claim to Tacna-Arica almost proved the undoing of the entire Pan-American movement. The Tacna-Arica question also complicated Latin American relations with the League of Nations; furthermore, it has occasionally found echoes in the United Nations long after the settlement of the dispute in 1929, because of its implications in relation to Bolivia's assertion of a right under international law for an outlet to the sea.

Although the Chilean armistice with Bolivia was concluded before the Treaty of Ancón between Peru and Chile, the final peace settlement with Bolivia was not concluded until 1904. In this treaty of 1904, contrary to the tradition of American international law, Bolivia recognized the sovereignty of Chile over a territory acquired by conquest. In compensation, Chile agreed to provide a railroad outlet and a free port on the Pacific. Bolivia thereafter tended to look eastward, turning her attention to seeking an outlet to the sea through the vast river systems of Brazil, Paraguay, and Argentina, a policy which contributed to another of the major Latin American wars in the twentieth century, the Chaco War. An interesting aftermath of the War of the Pacific was the establishment of international mixed commissions to arbitrate claims of German, French, British, and Italian nationals against Chile for losses occasioned during the war.[1]

Brazil: The Imperial Transformation

In Brazil the monarchy emerged victorious from the War of the Triple Alliance. The Brazilian political objectives of the conflict had been achieved. But, as mentioned, that war was destined to have an impact on Brazilian institutions and international relations not immediately apparent. One institution affected immediately was slavery. Slavery and the slave trade had been a point of diplomatic contention between Brazil and Great Britain ever since the latter nation undertook

1. The author is deeply grateful to Dr. John Soder, of George Mason University, for numerous useful suggestions on the War of the Pacific, based on his doctoral dissertation. The literature on the War of the Pacific is extensive. See especially Manuel Jordán López, *Historia Diplomática de la Guerra del Pacífico* (Santiago: Editorial Universitaria, 1957) and C. R. Markham, *The War Between Chile and Peru* (London: S. Low, Marston, Searle and Rivington, 1882), a contemporary account. Robert N. Burr gives a good analysis of the power aspects in his *By Reason or Force: Chile and the Balancing of Power in South America, 1830–1903* (Berkeley: University of California Press, 1965). Graham Stuart, in his *Latin America and the United States* (5th ed.; New York: Appleton-Century-Crofts, 1955), 389–99, gives an impartial account of the diplomacy. Also useful are, for an objective Peruvian view, Frederick B. Pike, *The Modern History of Peru* (New York: Praeger, 1967), 139–50, and Jorge Basadre, *Historia de la República del Perú* (5th ed., 6 vols.; Lima: Editorial "Historia," 1961–1962), V, 1876–2496 and VI, 2507–2659, and for an objective Chilean view, Francisco A. Encina, *Resúmen de la Historia de Chile*, Redacción de Leopoldo Castedo (2nd ed., 3 vols.; Santiago: Zig-Zag, 1956), II, 1387–1494, and III, 1495–1590. On the postwar claims tribunals, see Alejandro Soto Cárdenas, *Guerra del Pacífico: Los Tribunales Arbitrales* (Santiago: Universidad de Chile, 1950). On British capital investments in Latin America, see J. Fred Rippy, *British Investment in Latin America, 1822–1949* (Minneapolis: University of Minnesota Press, 1959), Chap. 11, esp. p. 134.

the suppression of the slave trade early in the nineteenth century. British warships did not hesitate, in accordance with treaty agreements with Brazil, to stop and search Brazilian vessels or to pursue slavers into Brazilian territorial waters. The difficulty did not in any sense arise because the government or the emperor approved of the institution of slavery. The international slave trade had been abolished by action of the Brazilian government. Rather, it was the Paraguayan War that raised the issue, bringing vividly to the attention of the Brazilian government the unfortunate international reputation that the continuation of slavery in Brazil gave the empire among allies and enemies alike, especially after slavery was finally ended in Paraguay under Brazil-Argentina occupation. Consequently, a Brazilian emancipation movement gathered support from the public, as well as from the official family.

Although Brazil was never as deeply affected by ultramontanism as were some of her Spanish neighbors, the empire also became involved in a controversy with the Roman Catholic Church in Brazil and with the Holy See as a result of the application of policies of the latter concerning, among other matters, Masonry. The particular incident involved what appeared to the emperor to be an infringement upon royal prerogatives and led to his disciplining two Brazilian bishops, who had made public papal encyclicals without royal approval, by brief imprisonments. The resulting crisis, and it was an important one, was complicated by the fact that prominent Brazilian Masons joined with the small Protestant minority in an endeavor to open the door to European Protestant immigrants. An ambiguous apology from the Holy See settled the matter internationally, but an important internal political consequence of this international dispute was a serious weakening of Catholic support of monarchy. Such support was further weakened by the fact that the heir to the throne was a daughter, unpopular in part because she was married to an even more unpopular prince of the French House of Orleans. When that daughter, during her father's absence in Europe for medical treatment in 1888, approved the abolition of slavery without compensation to the owners, the rural sugar aristocracy of Brazil's northeast found further reason to disagree with, and soon to abolish, the imperial system.

Despite applause from British and other international sources for the Brazilian abolition of slavery, those elements of Brazilian society that had traditionally supported the empire were generally unmoved when a military coup created the Republic in 1889. The social shock and political dislocations in Brazil as a result of this coup were, as a matter of fact, minor, if compared to the duration and destruction of the wars for independence and the civil wars revolving around republicanism of the Spanish American states.

The change from empire to republic in Brazil changed the nation's international relations into a more republican model; but the fundamentals that guided the policies of the republic were essentially a continuation of the policies of the empire, at least until World War I. An important exception was the reorientation of Brazilian policy away from Britain and toward the United States. This reorientation recognized the increasing importance of the U.S. market for Brazilian coffee, as well as the growth of United States power in the hemisphere. Such fundamentals included friendship with the United States, continual dependence upon British sources for new capital, admiration of and imitation of French culture, encouragement of European immigration and, whenever possible, friendship with the Portuguese mother country. Brazilian higher education continued to be provided in large part by universities in Portugal, France, Great Britain, Germany, and the United States. One effect of this reliance on foreign universities was that both Brazilian culture and the conduct of international relations were guided by international ideas and influences. A nationalistic xenophobia was not yet a phenomenon in this "Land of the Southern Cross."[2]

International Relations of Mexico and Central America

Border disputes and the thievery and smuggling consequent to border violations continued to trouble relations between Mexico and both her northern and southern neighbors, as did such instructions as

2. For Brazilian policy during these years, see, in addition to sources noted in footnote 1 above, João Pandiá Calogeras, *A Política Exterior do Imperio* (2 vols.; Rio de Janeiro: Imprensa Nacional, 1927–1928), Carlos Miguel Delgado de Carvalho, *Historia Diplomática do Brasil* (São Paulo: Companhia Editora Nacional, 1959), and João Frank da Costa, *Joaquim Nabuco e a Política Exterior do Brasil* (Rio de Janeiro: Gráfico Record, 1968).

the order of June, 1877, based on an agreement between Mexico and the United States authorizing the crossing of the Mexican border by United States or Mexican forces pursuing thieves or smugglers. Sensible actions by the military commanders on both sides avoided a serious clash between Mexican and U.S. troops, and the ghost of Yankee invasion that had been raised earlier was laid to rest in February, 1880, by a new agreement on reciprocal boundary enforcement. The relations of Mexico with the United States have evidenced this friendly diplomacy since the days of Benito Juárez and the early mixed commissions dealing with claims and other matters, and setting an international precedent in such matters. The most famous and enduring of these commissions was the International Boundary Commission, which began its work in 1884. The work of this commission did not begin, however, before an attempt by a president of the United States, Benjamin Harrison, to use the withholding of recognition of a Mexican government as a diplomatic device. This was the refusal to recognize the government of Porfirio Díaz. The withholding of recognition of a revolutionary government to accomplish a diplomatic objective in international politics has seldom, if ever, succeeded. This occasion was no exception; but the event was soon forgotten during the long presidency of Porfirio Díaz, to Mexicans the *Porfiriato* (1884–1911). Using the slogans of order, bread, stability, and fiscal sovereignty, the Mexican government was reorganized financially. Her foreign debt and claims payments were made promptly and fully, including those on the politically sensitive British debt. President Díaz encouraged the investment of foreign capital within the country, provided for the protection of the foreigners, and basically set about modernizing the nation.

Mexico observed an interested, yet largely uncritical, neutrality during the Spanish-American War, although public opinion and the press were sharply divided on the issue of United States intervention in the war for Cuban independence. Further, as will be seen, the growing power and prestige of Mexico were called upon to assist the United States in several attempts to mediate Latin American controversies and especially to bring peace to strife-torn Central America in the first decades of the present century. Mexico was the first Latin American state to enter the international scene, attending the First Hague Conference in 1899.[3]

Barrios and Central America

An early admirer of Mexican Liberal policies was Justo Rufino Barrios, Liberal party president of Guatemala from 1873 to 1885. Patterning the political organization of his country and his Liberal, anticlerical policy on that of Mexico, he sought to attract the kinds of foreign investment and immigration that President Porfirio Díaz had introduced to Mexico. Barrios encouraged the expanded production and export of coffee, thereby involving Guatemala in the economic and political relations internationally concerned with that product. Barrios also agreed with Mexico to abandon Guatemala's claim to Chiapas, a territory that Mexico had absorbed from the former captaincy-general when Mexican troops left Guatemala after the fall of the Mexican emperor, Augustín I, in 1822.

In the international realm in general, Barrios' efforts were less than successful. One of these efforts was to reconstitute the Confederation of Central America. He believed that in a visit to Washington in 1882 he had secured United States support for his project to unify the Isthmus politically, and for a joint policy on the Nicaraguan canal. His first target in the reunification was the neighboring and fiercely independent republic of El Salvador. Barrios invaded El Salvador in 1885, despite Mexico's open disapproval and despite the mobilization of Mexican troops on the Guatemalan frontier. Perhaps fortunately for his historical reputation, the unifier died in the first battle. El Salvador was thus saved from conquest, and a Mexican invasion of Guatemala was avoided; but the unification of the Isthmus was delayed for a century.[4]

3. For this period in Mexican foreign relations consult Daniel Cosío Villegas, *Historia Moderna de México* (6 vols.; Mexico: Editorial Hermes, 1955), Vols. V and VI, and his extensive bibliography, *Cuestiones Internacionales de México* (Mexico: Relaciones Exteriores, 1966); also James M. Callahan, *American Foreign Policy in Mexican Relations* (New York: Macmillan, 1932).

4. J. Fred Rippy, "Justo Rufino Barrios and the Nicaraguan Canal," *Hispanic American Historical Review*, XX (May, 1940), 190–97.

Chile: The U.S.S. *Baltimore* Incident

The War of the Pacific (1879–1883) provided Chile with a military hero whose political attributes led to the presidency; but this fact in itself proved no guarantee of subsequent political stability. In 1891 Chile was torn by a brief but destructive civil war that found the navy and the congress pitted against the army and the popular (civilian) president, José Balmaceda, who had antagonized the congress by his program of political and economic reform and his large programs of public works. The loss of lives and the property damage were great before the triumph of the rebel forces. Both Santiago and Valparaiso had been looted by the insurgents. The rebellion was rumored to have been backed by British nitrate interests seeking to avoid nationalization and by Chilean interests allied with them. The victors established a parliamentary system in which conservative economic forces dominated. The popular ex-president, who had taken asylum in the Argentinian embassy, committed suicide on the day his presidential term expired, leaving a political testament that provided a platform for reforming forces during the next three decades.

The victory produced an unexpected incident in international relations, reverberations of which still can be heard in Chile's relations with the United States. The insurgents believed the United States had been partial to the government forces by sheltering some members of the defeated party and by stopping a shipload of munitions to the revolutionary forces. This Chilean resentment erupted in violence in October, 1891, when a mob in Valparaiso attacked sailors from the U.S.S. *Baltimore*, then in the harbor, killing two sailors and injuring five others.

A United States naval inquiry blamed the Chilean police for having stood aside while the attack took place, and the U.S. government made a demand for reparations. Chile rejected this demand, making public the cabled demand from the United States that it considered to be highly offensive. Moreover, Chile insisted that the U.S. sailors had been at fault. She yielded to pressure, however, when President Benjamin Harrison asked Congress for authority to use force, if necessary, to secure an indemnity. Chile paid the United States $75,000, but the incident further soured Chilean-U.S. relations, partly explaining the Chilean attitude of neutrality during World War I and her later obstruction of U.S. efforts to conduct the plebiscite in Tacna and Arica after she had sought and agreed to U.S. arbitration of the dispute, an arbitration which brought the decision to hold the plebiscite.[5]

Argentina: The Other Side of the Boundary

Argentine foreign policy has been characterized by two often conflicting motivations. One is an attachment to European culture and economy relations; the second is a desire for American (Spanish American) regionalism to support her ambitions for hemispheric leadership. The former force has led her statesmen to encourage European immigration from Italy, Germany, and Spain, as well as to seek European investment, especially from Great Britain and France. European immigration, basically Italian and Spanish, produced expressions of national interests that occasionally conflicted with policy trends within the Inter-American System, both intra-hemispherically and in extra-hemispheric relations. An examination of the various meetings of the Inter-American System demonstrates those dissonances of Argentine policy, as does her nationalisitic neutral stance during World War I and her later nationalistic stance during World War II. Foreign investment provided the bases for Argentina's charges of foreign exploitation and intervention in her internal political affairs. Much of this animosity was directed toward the United States, but her major and most enduring international dispute outside the hemisphere has been with Great Britain, as previously discussed, over the sovereignty of *Las Malvinas* (Falkland Islands).

In the settlement of boundary disputes, of which she has had many in the history of her international relations, Argentina has favored arbitration over force as a means of settlement. As early as 1878 she called upon President Rutherford B. Hayes of the United States to arbitrate her boundary dispute with Paraguay in the Department of

5. See Encina, *Resumen de la Historia de Chile*; and Fanor Velasco, *La Revolución de 1891: Memorias* (Santiago: Sociedad "Imprenta y Litografía Universo," 1914), a diary of a subsecretary of foreign relations, giving interesting contemporary insights.

Misiones. Another U.S. president, Grover Cleveland, acted as arbiter in 1895 in a boundary dispute between Argentina and Brazil. A United States diplomat also served on the boundary commission that determined the Argentine-Chilean boundary in the Puna de Atacama in 1899.

The Chilean boundary question, which had been an issue since independence, was apparently settled in 1881 by a treaty that divided Tierra del Fuego between Argentina and Chile and fixed the boundary north of the fifty-second parallel south to where the highest peaks of the Andes divided the watershed. But, to Argentina's displeasure, and to Chile's delight, geographers discovered that the watershed lay some miles east of a line joining the highest peaks. Consequently, relations between the states continued to verge on open conflict, until the boundary was finally settled by the arbitration of the king of England in 1902. To symbolize lasting peace between the neighbors, a statue, the "Christ of the Andes," was then erected on the boundary line. This peace has been troubled now and again, however, by disagreement over the boundary in the Beagle Channel of the Straits of Magellan, an area named after Charles Darwin's vessel.[6]

Foreign Intervention in Central America and the Caribbean

The states of Central America and the Caribbean had troubled relations, both extra-hemispheric and hemispheric, during the last decades of the nineteenth century. Political and financial instability characterized the governments, provoking various European powers into the employment of force, or the threat of force, to collect claims of their citizens. The record during the last three decades of the century shows the dimension of European intervention in the New World and the potential threat to national independence that was present.

6. Sources useful on these Argentine boundary questions include Vicente G. Quesada, *Historia Diplomática Latinoamericana* (3 vols.; Buenos Aires: 1918–1920), I, 95–114, 304 ff; and III, 350 ff; Gordon Ireland, *Boundaries, Possessions, and Conflicts in South America* (Cambridge: Harvard University Press, 1938); H. S. Ferns, *Britain and Argentina in the Nineteenth Century* (Oxford: Clarendon Press, 1960); and Sergio Villalobos R., *La Disputa del Beagle* (Santiago: Editorial Tradición, 1968).

Venezuela: 1871–Germany, Great Britain, Italy, Spain, Denmark
                    1875–The Netherlands
Nicaragua: 1874–Great Britain
                    1878–Germany
                    1882–France
                    1895–Great Britain
Colombia: 1886–Italy
Santo Domingo: 1893–France
Haiti: 1869–France
                    1871–Spain
                    1872–Germany
                    1877–Great Britain
                    1883–France, Great Britain, Spain
                    1885–Russia
                    1887–Great Britain
                    1897–Germany

The consequences of these threats in producing U.S. interventionism and the Latin American reaction will be further discussed in the succeeding chapters.[7]

The Problem of Belize

A boundary between Guatemala and Belize was agreed to by treaty in 1859. It was never surveyed, however, although a beginning was made by a mixed commission in 1861. Two years later a convention was drawn up, substituting a money payment for the British promise in the earlier treaty to build a road from Guatemala to the Caribbean coast, but this treaty failed ratification. The road was never built, and this default was the basis of the Guatemalan claim in the twentieth century that she was no longer bound by the treaty of 1859. In 1882, Guatemala and Mexico signed a treaty confirming Mexico's title to Chiapas. Then in 1893 an Anglo-Mexican treaty fixed a boundary between Mexico and Belize, a boundary that three quarters of a century

7. Laudelino Moreno, *Historia de las Relaciones Interestatales de Centro América* (Madrid: Companía Ibero-americana de Publicaciones, 1928); Dana G. Munro, *The Five Republics of Central America* (New York: Oxford University Press, 1918); and Thomas L. Karnes, *The Failure of Union: Central America, 1824–1960* (Gainesville: University of Florida Press, 1961).

later was still the subject of some disagreement in respect to the status of Belize.[8]

The Venezuelan Boundary Dispute with Great Britain

In 1895 a dispute over the boundary between Venezuela and British Guiana (now Guyana) came to a head. It had smoldered for well over a half-century. The subject of intermittent and unsatisfactory negotiation, the dispute was thrust upon world attention after Venezuela had appealed to the United States to persuade Great Britain to arbitrate the controversy. President Grover Cleveland, thoroughly irritated by the failure of the British government to reply to various diplomatic representations and to agree to arbitration of the matter, cast the mantle of the Monroe Doctrine over the dispute and presented the British government with what appeared to be a virtual ultimatum to arbitrate.

The president's vehicle of communication was his message to Congress on December 18, 1895. In it he reported that the Venezuelan government had requested earlier that the United States use its influence with Great Britain to secure settlement of the dispute, but that what began as a simple transmission to Great Britain of the Venezuelan position had evolved into a crisis because the British government failed to respond. The British reluctance was due in part to the language used by the United States secretary of state, Richard Olney, in speaking of the nature of the Monroe Doctrine: "Today the United States is practically sovereign in this continent, and its fiat is law upon the subjects to which it confines its interposition."

So broad an assertion of influence, emphasized by the bellicose tone of the subsequent presidential message, produced a strong reaction in Latin America. Argentina, Brazil, Chile, and Mexico all expressed vigorous opposition to this "protective" diplomacy. Peru, Colombia, and Central America reacted more cordially and Ven-

8. For the Guatemalan view consult José Luis Mendoza, *Britain and her Treaties on Belize,* trans. Lilly de Jongh Osborne (2nd ed.; Guatemala: Ministry for Foreign Affairs, 1959). See also Gordon Ireland, *Boundaries, Possessions, and Conflicts in Central and North America and the Caribbean* (Cambridge: Harvard University, 1941), and Carlos Urrutia Aparicio, *Juridical Aspects of the Anglo-Guatemalan Controversy in re Belize* (Washington, D.C.: n.p., 1951).

ezuela, of course, was ecstatic. The Cleveland arbitration proposition was accepted finally by Great Britain, which agreed to arbitration in January, 1896. The bases for the arbitration were settled by the United States and Great Britain, and accepted by Venezuela. An arbitral commission was established consisting of five members—two Englishmen, two members of the United States Supreme Court, and a noted Russian scholar in the field of international law. The neutral Russian sided in general with the claims of the British, so that Venezuela lost virtually all of her claim. She ratified the arbitral award, however, in 1897. Years later, the Spanish lawyer who represented Venezuela before the commission, Severo Mallet-Prevost, dictated a memorandum in which he charged that the Russian's decision resulted from a secret agreement with the British arbitrators. This memorandum was published in the *American Journal of International Law* in 1949, reopening, in the eyes of the Venezuelan government, the validity of the 1897 award.[9]

The agreement was the first of its kind, in that a European power, although not specifically recognizing the applicability of the Monroe Doctrine, accepted its validity in practice in an extra-hemispheric dispute and yielded precedence to the United States in Western Hemisphere affairs. Even more significantly, it was the first step in the development of the Anglo-American entente against the growing power of the German empire; it also paved the way for the Hay-Pauncefote Treaty (1901) which, in turn, opened the way for United States action on and control of the Panama Canal. Thus, the Venezuelan boundary controversy, indirectly, had major policy implications for Central America and the Caribbean, setting the tone, if not the substance, of much of hemispheric relations in the twentieth century. Finally, it paved the way for British manipulation of the European diplomatic scene during the Spanish-American War to favor the United States.

9. Samuel Flagg Bemis, *The Latin American Policy of the United States* (New York: Harcourt Brace & Co., 1943); Ireland, *Boundaries, Possessions, and Conflicts in South America*; Armando Rojas, *Venezuela: Límite al Este con el Esequibo* (Caracas: Carta de Venezuela, 1965); Otto Schoenrich, "The Venezuela–British Guiana Boundary Dispute," *The American Journal of International Law*, XLIII (July, 1949), 523–30.

The Cuban War for Independence, 1895–1898, and United States Invervention

In 1895, the unhappy island of Cuba had embarked once again on a quest for independence. The quest produced a Spanish reign of terror, with garrison towns, and concentration camps under the Spanish policy of *reconcentración*. Despite the killing of several U.S. citizens and the destruction of U.S. property, the United States government observed strict neutrality for three years, while putting pressure on the Spanish government to grant concessions to the Cuban rebels. Some concessions were made by Spain, but the revolutionary groups had passed the point of compromise. For them, it was now independence or death. Public and congressional opinion in the United States became increasingly inflamed by newspaper stories of Spanish atrocities. It was the blowing up of the U.S.S. *Maine* in Havana harbor in February, 1898, that brought the break.

The United States immediately demanded reparations from Spain, the abandonment of the *reconcentración* policy, and an armistice to permit the rebels to negotiate peace through U.S. mediation. Spain ultimately acceded to these demands, but the hour for mediation had passed as far as the United States was concerned. President William McKinley, leaving the decision to Congress, received authority to intervene with force in the conflict between Spain and her colony. A joint resolution of Congress, April 20, 1898, declared that the people of Cuba were and of right ought to be free and independent. Spain was called upon to withdraw from the island, and the president was authorized to use force, if need be, to accomplish that objective. Finally, Congress disclaimed for the United States any intention to exercise sovereignty over the island, except for pacification.

Latin Americans wavered in their sympathies. Some supported the United States in its aid to Cuban independence; others were moved to sympathize with Spain as the mother country, despite their desire to see Cuba independent. In general they maintained an uneasy neutrality in the war. The surprisingly quick victory of the United States forces over those of Spain stunned most Latin American governments, however. Neither the weakness of the Spanish empire forces nor the strength of the United States had been realized. As in the case of Venezuela in 1895, the reaction among the Latin American states was mixed. Some eagerly welcomed a new sister republic. For others, a sentimental attachment to the motherland produced a heightened fear of Yankee imperialism. Despite the Spooner Amendment promising Cuban independence, few believed that the United States had really denied herself the exercise of sovereignty over Cuba. Some noted, rather, how eagerly the United States had annexed Puerto Rico and the Philippines.

If the United States–Spanish War of 1898 demonstrated nothing else to the Latin American states, it showed that the combined representations of the monarchs of Europe were ineffectual in preventing the United States from pursuing what it considered to be its vital interests and its mission in the hemisphere. Great Britain, France, Germany, Austria, Russia, and Italy had addressed a collective note to President McKinley on April 7, 1898, offering their friendly interposition in the dispute with Spain. Such interposition was respectfully declined.

Another consequence of Cuban independence was less positive. Committed to intervention in the internal affairs of Cuba by the Platt Amendment, the United States, by its subsequent military and diplomatic interventions in Cuba strengthened her image as the aggressive imperialist in the Caribbean, if not in the entire Western Hemisphere. The fact that no other New World state had the energy and organization to interpose itself between Europe and Latin America was conveniently overlooked. Even the second Venezuelan crisis (1903–1904), as we shall see, did not alter this image; rather it produced the Roosevelt Corollary, giving the Monroe Doctrine an interventionist meaning to Latin Americans.[10]

10. Herminio Portell Vilá, *Historia de Cuba en sus Relaciones con los Estados Unidos y España* (Havana: Jesús Montero, 1938–1941); David F. Realy, *The United States in Cuba, 1890–1902: Generals, Politicians, and the Search for Policy* (Madison: University of Wisconsin Press, 1963). For Mexican reactions to the War of 1898 see Charmion Shelby, "Mexico and the Spanish-American War," in Thomas Cotner and Carlos Castañeda (eds.), *Essays in Mexican History* (Austin: University of Texas Press, 1958), 13. See also Perkins, *The Monroe Doctrine, 1867–1907* and Walter Millis, *The Martial Spirit: A Study of Our War with Spain* (Cambridge: Harvard University Press, 1931).

7 Latin America Enters the World Scene, 1900–1930

F. TAYLOR PECK

Latin America entered the twentieth century faced with profound changes in international relations and world power politics. Yet in general the nations seem to have had little awareness of these changes and less appreciation of their impact upon hemispheric and extra-hemispheric affairs. Great Britain continued to be the most influential commercial, financial, and military power with which the states had relations. France had been culturally dominant for decades, exercising a fascination in taste, manners, and the radical politics among the intellectuals and the other elites. Germany had ties with her ethnic populations in Brazil and southern South America, as well as with various national military establishments; she was also much admired by the new technicians and scientists. Italy was venerated for her art and music. The cultural influences of Spain and Portugal, although less obvious, were persistent.

This chapter analyzes some of the far-reaching alterations in international relationships involved in the social, economic, and political changes taking place in Latin America during the first three decades of the twentieth century. The topics treated include changes in power relationships, both among the states of the area and with outside powers. The crises in Venezuela, especially in 1902–1903, are studied from this standpoint of power changes, as well as from the standpoint of the development of the Roosevelt Corollary of the Monroe Doctrine. Brazil, emerging during these years from under the shadow of Great Britain, is seen to be seeking a more autonomous policy in a kind of "unwritten alliance" with the United States. Both Mexico and the United States endeavor to use their good offices again to bring stability and peace in Central America, but the Mexican Revolution, causing Mexico to withdraw within herself, leaves the field open to increasing interventionism by the United States, supported by regional treaties incorporating the Tobar principle. The independence of Panama and the construction of the canal introduce not only a new phase in the commerce of the Pacific coast countries, but a new issue of "imperialism," specifically related to the United States presence on the Isthmus.

Beginning with the Second Hague Conference, and continuing in the politics of World War I, in the League of Nations, and in the conflicting issues arising within the evolving regional (Inter-American) system, the nations began during these decades to play an increasing role in international affairs, one much greater than they had played in the preceding century. All in all, the most significant diplomatic conflict of the period is that between Mexico and the United States (and Great Britain) over issues arising from the Mexican Revolution. These issues include the consequent "Punitive Expedition," led by General John J. Pershing. Even more significantly, they include the efforts of the Mexican government to regulate and control the booming petroleum industry and to break up and distribute the lands of large haciendas.

In their relationships with each other, the nations of Latin America continue many of the same power conflicts as in the nineteenth century, especially in South America. Boundary disputes still flare, some of them destined to lead to violent warfare, as in the case of the dispute between Bolivia and Paraguay over the Chaco region. Chile's expansionism seemed to have ceased with her treaties with Argentina and Bolivia, but her dispute with Peru over the plebiscite to determine the final possession of Tacna and Arica remained one of the sorest spots in inter-American relations during these three decades.[1]

---

1. See Samuel Guy Inman, *Problems of Panamericanism* (2nd ed.; New York: George R. Doran, Co., 1925), Chap. 9. One of the strongest Latin American criticisms of the United States was the book of Manuel Ugarte, *Destiny of a Continent*, trans. Catherine A. Phillips, edited with introduction and bibliography by J. Fred Rippy (New York: Alfred A. Knopf, 1925).

Changing Power Relationships

A sign of the changing power relationships appeared in the Venezuelan Crisis of 1902/03, the last major display of European force against a New World republic. The diplomacy of this crisis concluded with tacit recognition of the United States power and interests in the hemisphere, though without specific recognition of the long-contemplated Monroe Doctrine. A second sign was the implementation of the project for an Isthmian canal, bringing the creation of yet another American republic and signaling the initiation of an expanded Caribbean policy by the United States. A third sign of change emerged from within the form of the Mexican Revolution and its social and national contexts. The fourth sign was World War I and its impact on Latin America. Perforce, these relationships involved changes of various Latin American states in their relationships with the United States, both bilaterally, and, by 1930, within the newly energized Inter-American System, largely dormant since its inception in 1889. Consequently, an understanding of the conflicts and concerns that came to dominate Latin American international relations during these first decades of the twentieth century requires that major attention be given to the changing policies of the United States as they affected Latin American policies and to the Latin American reactions to these changes.

Latin American critics of United States policies and actions during this period have tended to perceive such policies and actions as if the U.S.–Caribbean pattern were being applied throughout the countries of the hemisphere. To a degree this attitude is justified by the fact that the United States public tended to conceptualize all of Latin America in terms of U.S. experience with Mexico and the Caribbean. Consequently, what was considered by one party as protective diplomacy came to be considered by the other as aggressive imperialism, intervention, and "dollar diplomacy." What was looked upon by some as the proper behavior of civilized states in international society was also seen by some as the infringement of the national sovereignty of weak states by the strong. On several occasions these conflicting conceptions almost led to the dissolution of the Inter-American System, as will be seen in the discussions of the various Pan-American conferences during the period under consideration.

The importance of the United States in the international relations of Latin America has sometimes been viewed as being in direct proportion to the proximity of a given state to the United States border. The closeness of Mexico and the Caribbean gave them both commercial and strategic importance. The policies and actions resulting from United States construction of the Isthmian canal had also made Central America a special concern. Considerations of U.S. security after the turn of the century seemed to make it essential that no republic of this region should fall under the control of any foreign power, especially any foreign power that the United States might consider a threat to its own interests. The war of 1898 had eliminated the last vestiges of Spanish power in America, but Great Britain, France, the Netherlands, and Denmark still exercised sovereignty in the islands; Great Britain still exercised naval supremacy on the seas, but was challenged by the rising German naval power. Hemispheric relations were generally far from tranquil at the turn of the century and thus, in light of the power and arms rivalries in the world politics during the final decades of the nineteenth century, the United States concern about the continued security of the hemisphere seemed to have a real basis, however unfounded such concern may seem today.

Both Africa and the Far East had undergone, or were undergoing, the partition into zones of interest that marked the climax of nineteenth century imperialism. Would Latin America be spared this fate? Many states of the New World feared that the pretext of intervention might be used to justify a permanent occupation similar to that going on in Africa and Asia. The right of a nation to intervene to protect the lives and property of its nationals in another state was firmly established in international law and practice. But the Latin American states tended to reject this principle of international law. Thus, when internal conditions of Latin American states became such as to attract or justify European intervention, many Latin American states sought to prevent the intervention by appealing for a change in international law. The Drago principle, while recognizing the general principles of international law, was this kind of proposal. United

States policy, while agreeing in general with the Drago concept, sought to eliminate the objective conditions that might provoke and justify foreign intervention. Thus, in the 1898 Treaty of Paris between Spain and the United States that ended the Spanish-American War and secured Cuban independence, the United States agreed that she was responsible for the protection of life, liberty, and property, not only of U.S. nationals in the territories relinquished by Spain, but also those of other resident foreigners.

The Roosevelt Corollary to the Monroe Doctrine expressed this policy of protective diplomacy. In order for the United States to prevent European intervention in the New World, Roosevelt argued, the United States had to assist the nations under threat of intervention, so as to eliminate the conditions for intervention and to promote governments of political stability and financial responsibility.[2]

For the Latin American states the proposed Roosevelt nostrum seemed worse than the ill; that is to say, for them the substitution of Yankee protection for a possible European intervention solved nothing. Indeed, because of geographic proximity, if nothing else, the threat of United States occupation seemed greater and the loss of national sovereignty to the United States more probable than that to Europe. Many Latin American leaders were willing to support this U.S. protective diplomacy, but this did not insure its wide acceptance, at least outside the Central American and Caribbean subregion. Instead, the U.S. policy provoked a violent reaction in the form of increasing anti-Yankeeism and of such specific propositions for international behavior as the Calvo and Drago doctrines, emanating from Argentina. For the United States, the development of this policy of protective diplomacy was not the decision of one administration or one president. It began, as we have seen, with the Venezuelan Crisis

2. For Roosevelt's reasoning see pertinent sections of his 1904 and 1905 messages in Henry Steele Commager (ed.), *Documents of American History* (2 vols.; New York: F. S. Crofts, 1938), II, 213–15. On U.S.–Latin American relations during these years see, among others, Julius Pratt, *America's Colonial Experiment* (New York: Prentice-Hall, 1950); Samuel Guy Inman, *Latin America, Its Place in World Life* (New York: Harcourt Brace and Co., 1947); Samuel Flagg Bemis, *The Latin American Policy of the United States* (New York: Harcourt Brace and Co., 1943); Antonio Gómez Robledo, *Idea y Experiencia de América* (Mexico: Fondo de Cultura Económica, 1938); and S. A. Livermore, "Theodore Roosevelt, The American Navy, and the Venezuelan Crisis of 1902–1903," *American Historical Review*, LI (1946), 452–71.

of 1895 under the Cleveland administration, and extended through World War I. After the decision to construct a canal across the Isthmus of Panama during the Roosevelt administration, the security of the canal added a further rationale for the exercise of protective diplomacy. United States policy was thereafter projected into Latin America in new and special ways.

The Venezuelan Crisis of 1902–1903

The crisis arising out of European interventions in Venezuela in 1902–1903 demonstrates the new caution exercised by European states in their Latin American relations in matters in which the United States might have an interest. As early as 1901 the German government had outlined to the U.S. State Department certain proposals for making the Venezuelan government respect the financial claims of German nationals. Disavowing all territorial ambitions, the proposal called for a naval blockade, the temporary occupation of some ports, and the diverting of customs duties for the payment of German claims. These coercive actions apparently did not alarm the administration of Theodore Roosevelt.

Germany then invited Great Britain, which had equal cause for action against Venezuela, to join the blockade. However, the project for control of Venezuelan customs was abandoned as impractical. By December 9, 1902, when the blockade was instituted, and when Italy had joined the other European powers, all parties to the action had shown great sensitivity for possible U.S. concern. On December 11, 1902, the Venezuelan government asked the United States to arbitrate the dispute. This request was transmitted to Great Britain and Germany without comment and, consequently, without the exertion of pressure.

The people of the United States became increasingly alarmed by the European action to institute a blockade, especially the action of Germany, and the attitude of the U.S. government soon changed. Although the evidence is not clear, some scholars believe Roosevelt threatened to employ force if Germany did not agree to arbitrate. Thus, by December 14, the German government had decided to accept U.S. arbitration in order that Great Britain, by accepting arbitration, might not appear more conciliatory toward the United States than Germany. Henceforth, arbitration of the dispute was accepted in principle by the European powers.

The European blockade continued, however. Action by German naval units in sinking some vessels of the Venezuelan navy and in bombarding the fortifications of Puerto Cabello touched off an anti-German campaign in the U.S. press. The heat of the aroused public opinion surprised President Roosevelt so that he urged the European powers to settle the dispute promptly, lest public opinion force the U.S. administration to take some more direct action in the matter. The blockade was lifted in February, 1903, but not before an alarmed British ambassador in Washington had informed the government of the state of U.S. public opinion and advised that good relations with the United States would be hampered by further cooperation with Germany against Venezuela. British public reaction also seems to have been largely opposed to further action against Venezuela. A United States naval concentration in the Caribbean, under the command of Admiral George Dewey, served to demonstrate the seriousness of United States purpose. As a result, the European blockade was lifted and the arbitration by the Hague Court went forward, but with some unexpected consequences for the international relations of Latin America.

During the controversy (1902), in response to a request addressed by the U.S. secretary of state to all Latin American nations, the Argentine foreign minister, Luis M. Drago, submitted to the United States secretary his proposal that all American states should adopt the principle that the public debt of a nation should not be the occasion for armed intervention or the occupation of the territory of an American state. What he sought was to abolish the traditional right of intervention under international law and to establish the complete immunity from the use of force in this sector of international relations. The Drago proposal was not originally a principle readily admissible as international law. Indeed, the right of intervention under international law received a special legal extension as a consequence of the Venezuelan arbitration.[3]

3. Drago's statement is conveniently available in Commager (ed.), *Documents of American*

This extension was a consequence of the decision of the Hague Court of Permanent Arbitration in the Venezuelan case (1904). One issue in this case was the preferential rights of payment to the claims of the intervening powers, in this case Great Britain, Italy, and Germany. The court decided that the intervening powers had a right of first access to any funds designated for settlement of the claims of their nationals. Therefore, the rights of powers that did not use force were placed after the rights of powers that did use force. This decision, putting a premium on intervention, was a rejection of the Drago principle of nonintervention. The Hague decision brought into focus the possible consequences of the political instability and financial irresponsibility of the American nations. The decision, by coincidence, came the day before the U.S. Senate consented to the treaty with the new republic of Panama containing special provisions in this respect. The Panama treaty established a virtual protectorate, giving the United States, in addition to other privileges, the right to erect fortifications if necessary for the protection of the canal; it also provided for U.S. naval bases at its approaches, in order that defense might begin as far from the actual canal as possible. The United States strategy for protecting the canal looked even farther. In the east it contemplated Cuba, Haiti, Santo Domingo, Puerto Rico, and the British, French, and Danish West Indies. In the Pacific it might include not only the coast of El Salvador, Honduras, and Nicaragua, but even the Galapagos Islands of Ecuador.

Although the American republics bowed to the international juridically sanctioned right of armed intervention, their national sovereignty and their independence were thought to be endangered by European interventions that would menace the canal and contravene the Monroe Doctrine. Certainly the individual states themselves were responsible to see that conditions of intervention did not exist. But when the state was unable to meet that responsibility, who, then, became responsible? The answer seemed to Theodore Roosevelt to be implied in the Monroe Doctrine. If the United States and the other American republics desired to keep European powers

History, II, 203–206. It was published in *Foreign Relations of the United States* (Washington: Government Printing Office, 1903), 1 ff.

from intervening in the New World, it was the responsibility of the United States, as the only American state with the power to do so, to see that the states of the hemisphere lived up to their international obligations. In the instances where they did not, then it was the responsibility of the United States to see that they did, even though this might mean intervention in the affairs of an otherwise sovereign nation. In his annual messages to Congress in both 1904 and 1905 President Roosevelt stated what became known as the Roosevelt Corollary to the Monroe Doctrine:

> Chronic wrong doing, or an impotence which results in a general loosening of the ties of civilized society, may in America, as elsewhere, ultimately require intervention by some civilized nation, and in the Western Hemisphere the adherence of the United States to the Monroe Doctrine may force the United States, however reluctantly . . . to the exercise of an international police power.[4]

In the eyes of most Latin Americans, this policy was simply the substitution of one imperialistic interventionist for another, and all under the mantle of the Monroe Doctrine. Such intervention conflicted with the general notion of Pan-Americanism and the juridical equality of states, as well as with the Argentine position expressed in the Drago Doctrine. This latter doctrine the United States came increasingly to support as a concept of international behavior, if not international law. Thus President Roosevelt instructed the U.S. delegation to the Second Hague Conference (1907) to seek an agreement to give up the right of intervention and accept the Drago principle. But the conference whittled down the proposal, adopting only a mild resolution that was meaningless in light of the Hague Court decision.

Intervention by the United States, it soon appeared, would lead to misunderstanding and animosity, strengthening the growth of anti-Yankeeism, regardless of the sensitivity with which any protective diplomacy might be exercised. What really forced the decision of the United States on its interventionist policy was the tacit recognition by the European powers of United States hegemony in the Caribbean subregion during the Venezuelan Crisis, combined with the Hague Tribunal decision (1903) requiring preferential payment of the claims

4. Quoted in Commager (ed.), *Documents of American History*, II, 213–15.

of interventionist nations in Venezuela. The ultimate consequence of these developments was the establishment of the Roosevelt Corollary (1904), that the United States would intervene when necessary to prevent political conditions that would warrant European intervention.

The implications of the Hague Court decision were soon highlighted to the Roosevelt administration when it was informed, correctly or incorrectly, that Italy was about to intervene in Santo Domingo with naval forces as it had done in Venezuela, to secure the rights and claims of Italian nationals, especially the payment of loans in default. After repeated assurances to Congress and to the public that the United States had no interest in the annexation of either Santo Domingo or Haiti, President Roosevelt arranged, by an executive agreement, for the collection of Dominican customs and the payment of the foreign debt through a United States receivership.[5] This action was another step in the development of the protective diplomacy of the United States in the first three decades of the twentieth century. Although at the time no Latin American reaction was observable, its negative impact on the Yankee image was to develop shortly thereafter. It fell to the presidency of another Roosevelt to counteract this negative impact of the Roosevelt Corollary.

Brazil: The "Unwritten Alliance"

The Baron of Rio Branco, as foreign minister after 1902, initiated a major reorientation of Brazilian policy. Seeking independence from British predominance, in accordance with what he rightly conceived to be the national interest, he cultivated what has been called by E. Bradford Burns an "unwritten alliance" with the United States. This new relationship was symbolized by an agreement to raise the status of the respective legations to embassies, and by the appointment in 1905 of the distinguished scholar-diplomat, Joaquim Nabuco, to be the first Brazilian ambassador to the United States. The new relation-

---

5. The Venezuelan crisis has been treated in many ways. See especially John Bassett Moore, *Digest of International Law* (8 vols.; Washington: Government Printing Office, 1906), Vol. VI, and Howard C. Hill, *Roosevelt and the Caribbean* (Chicago: University of Chicago Press, 1927).

ship also strengthened Brazilian relationships with her Spanish American neighbors. The cordial collaboration of Nabuco with the U.S secretary of state, Elihu Root, in the preliminaries for the Third Inter-American Conference at Rio de Janeiro in 1906, signaled what was to be a permanent feature of the power relationships within the evolving inter-American political system. Rio Branco stated the meaning of the change very succinctly: "For me, the Monroe Doctrine . . . signifies that politically we have broken away from Europe as completely as the moon has from the earth."[6]

In 1902 Brazil had initiated a policy of determining and fixing her boundaries by agreement with her neighbors. Boundary disputes, largely due to the vagueness of colonial frontiers and the constant Brazilian expansion into areas claimed by Spain under Spanish-Portuguese treaties, had been sources of potential trouble between Brazil and her (chiefly Spanish American) contiguous states. The resolution of these boundary problems, achieved in the early twentieth century, owes much to the character and ability of the Brazilian foreign minister, Baron Rio Branco. It also owes a debt to the competence of Brazilian geographers and cartographers, whose maps became the bases of many negotiations and, most important, to the Brazilian national character. The national will of Brazil to seek ways to resolve problems through discussion and compromise proved fundamental in the success of her international negotiations. Nowhere else in America, or elsewhere, had the principle of settling disputes through negotiation been more persistently, rigorously, intelligently, and successfully followed.

But Brazilian expansionism was not completely dead. Brazil had been accused of fostering revolts in the rubber-producing areas bordering on Bolivia (Acre territory), thereby posing threats to an Anglo-American concession. This territorial dispute was settled in 1903 by a Bolivian cession of the territory to Brazil, in return for which Brazil paid two million pounds sterling to Bolivia for the construction of a railway to allow access to the sea by way of the Amazon.

6. The statement of Rio Branco is quoted in Carolina Nabuco, *The Life of Joaquim Nabuco* (Stanford: Stanford University Press, 1950), 307. See also E. Bradford Burns, *The Unwritten Alliance* (New York: Columbia University Press, 1965).

Violence and the threat of violence were carefully avoided in these negotiations, although the conditions leading up to them contained some of both. As had been indicated, the settlement of the Venezuelan boundary dispute with Great Britain produced an unanticipated benefit for Brazil in the willingness of France to come to an amicable settlement of the disputed boundary of French Guiana. Major boundary settlements were also reached by Brazil during these years with Peru and Colombia and with Great Britain and the Netherlands for British and Dutch Guiana.[7]

Central America and the Caribbean: Interactions

Liberal-Conservative party struggles figured large in the international conflicts within Central America, conflicts which, in turn, increased the subregion's vulnerability to foreign intervention. This vulnerability was further accentuated by the construction of the Isthmian canal. In the early years of the present century the growing power of Mexico under Porfirio Díaz also changed the traditional patterns of relations between the Central American states.

What President Justo Rufino Barrios had done for Guatemalan coffee in the late nineteenth century, another Liberal president did for her banana production in the twentieth century. Under the regime of Manuel Estrada Cabrera (1898–1920) the development of the banana industry in the otherwise underdeveloped coastal lands was encouraged, tying the nation's future to the United States in a new and in some respects an unfortunate way. In the 1920s U.S. capital poured into Guatemala, as it did into other parts of Latin America. But Guatemala's sound currency and relative political stability prevented intervention of the kind that other Central American states experienced during these years.

As indicated by her earlier reaction to President Barrios, a basic foreign policy objective of El Salvador has always been to remain in-

7. For intervention in the Dominican Republic see Sumner Welles's classic work, *Naboth's Vineyard* (2 vols.; New York: Payson & Clarke, 1928), especially Vol. II; Rayford Logan, *Haiti and the Dominican Republic* (New York and London: Oxford University Press, 1968); Melvin M. Knight, *The Americans in Santo Domingo* (New York: Vanguard Press, 1928); Dana G. Munro, *The United States and the Caribbean Areas* (Boston: World Peace Foundation, 1934), 101–142; and his later *Intervention and Dollar Diplomacy in the Caribbean* (Princeton: Princeton University Press, 1964); and Pratt, *America's Colonial Experiment.*

dependent of Guatemalan influence. To this end, El Salvador has supported Central American unification and cooperation, usually under Liberal party leadership, even while rejecting Guatemala's dominance, as in the case of Barrios' efforts for union. Further, the importance of her relations with Honduras in El Salvador's national life and development led her occasionally to meddle in the internal affairs of her neighbor. But she was not alone in such meddling. Guatemalans and Nicaraguans also intrigued and intervened politically in Honduras.

In her international relations, Honduras has sought to maintain national sovereignty, achieve national identity, and defend the integrity of the national territory. These problems have been serious, since the threat of intervention from other Central American states has never been remote. As in the case of Guatemala, the input of foreign capital into the banana industry tied Honduras to the international commodity relations in the trade in this fruit, whether through the United or the Standard Fruit Company. In 1907 and again in 1922/23 political conditions in Honduras led to conferences, arranged with the good offices of the United States and (in the first case) Mexico, whose object was the fostering of international order and respect among the states of Central America, as we shall see a little later. In both cases it was agreed to protect the neutrality of Honduras in the Isthmian conflicts. Law and order did not find fertile soil in Honduras, and the best designs of the diplomats could not prevent a situation in 1924 that led to United States armed intervention.[8]

Nicaragua, like Guatemala, had been deeply torn by the feuds between Liberal and Conservative political parties. This factional fighting had led in the mid–nineteenth century to the filibustering of William Walker and to interventions by European powers. In the present century it brought a military occupation by the United States Marines. But Nicaragua also intervened in the affairs of her neighbors and brought Central America twice into open hostilities, if not de-

8. Howard I. Blutstein, *et al.*, *Area Handbook for Honduras* (Washington: The American University and Government Printing Office, 1971); also *Foro Hondureño*, Vol. XXII, Nos. 4–12 (September–May, 1953), in which several articles are devoted to the Honduras-Nicaragua boundary question.

clared war. The prize in this case, as it frequently had been, was to place a friendly government in control of Honduras. For example, in 1894 the president of Nicaragua, José Santos Zelaya, had helped Honduran Liberals to come to power. That regime had been overthrown in 1903. Then, in 1906, war broke out between Guatemala and her two southern neighbors, El Salvador and Honduras. The United States sought the mediation of Mexico for the restoration of peace.

Mexican mediation led to the calling of a general Central American peace conference at San José, Costa Rica; but nothing could be accomplished because President Zelaya, regarded by both Mexico and the United States as the evil genius of Central America, refused to take part. Going further, he provoked a war with Honduras and intervened to place a friend and sympathizer of his policies in the Honduran presidency. Zelaya next sought to foment revolution in El Salvador. At this point Guatemalan mobilization seemed to make another general Central American conflict inevitable.

Mexico and the United States then interposed their good offices. All five republics met at Washington in 1907, where several treaties were drawn up to stabilize Central American relations. A new era of peace seemed promised by the creation of a court of arbitration, for which Andrew Carnegie provided a building in San José, Costa Rica. Honduras was neutralized; all nations pledged to abstain from fomenting revolutionary movements, agreed to restrict the activities of political refugees, and pledged by treaty, in accordance with the principle advanced by the Ecuadorian Carlos R. Tobar, not to recognize governments headed by the leader of a *golpe de estado* or armed rebellion. Treaties for economic and cultural cooperation pointed toward the possibility of some kind of Central American union.

However, neither Zelaya (Nicaragua) nor Cabrera (Guatemala) took the treaties seriously. Zelaya sent filibustering expeditions against El Salvador, despite joint Mexican-U.S. naval patrols. Guatemala and El Salvador were accused of aiding revolutionaries who invaded Honduras. The threat of a new war brought representations from Mexico and the United States, urging referral of the disputes to the new Central American Court. When that tribunal ruled in favor of Guatemala, it virtually destroyed itself by what was seen to be the partisanship of the decision, although the final blow to its prestige came later.

Then, in 1909, a new political factor in international relations entered the Central American scene. The United States, having had relative political and financial success with its customs collectorship in Santo Domingo, decided under the Taft administration that a similar policy might be applied with equal success in other Caribbean states. The purpose of the policy was to break the cycle in which political instability produced economic instability and vice versa. Moreover, the policy would permit the governments to secure funds in the form of loans for commercial and economic development. The policy of substituting dollars for bullets in the maintenance of order came to be known as dollar diplomacy, understood by its critics to mean economic imperialism. Thus, what was intended for the good became inextricably associated with the bad.

Since the weakness of Honduras seemed to be the political vacuum into which the political ambition of Central American politicians rushed, the first of the new dollar diplomacy agreements was negotiated with that country, offsetting thereby British insistence on the resumption of service on two loans made in 1867 and 1870. Under the pressure and persuasion of the State Department, some U.S. bankers proved cooperative, as did the British holders of the debt, but only on the condition that the American loan be secured by a customs collectorship. A treaty to this effect was signed on January 10, 1911; but the plan came to naught, because both the Honduran congress and the U.S. Senate refused to approve the treaty.

While this Honduran treaty was being negotiated, a change in the internal political situation in Nicaragua led to the extension of the policy of dollar diplomacy to that republic. A revolution had erupted in October, 1909, against President Zelaya, who in the aftermath made the mistake of ordering the execution of two United States citizens who had served with the rebels. Diplomatic relations were broken by the United States and were not resumed until after Zelaya's resignation. The victorious revolution which followed could not have maintained the Conservative party in power without outside assistance, and part of that assistance was a loan secured by a United States customs collectorship. The loan was to be used for public works and for the payment of foreign claims. A treaty similar to that with Honduras was negotiated and signed on June 6, 1911. Banking and currency reforms were undertaken under U.S. supervision. As with the case of Honduras, refusal of the U.S. Senate to approve this treaty made the original loan arrangement impossible, but the customs collectorship continued.

A deteriorating political situation produced revolution by mid-1912, and the Nicaraguan president asked for United States assistance. The U.S. reply was to send marines to protect U.S. lives and property. Initially, the original contingent of some one hundred men did not take part in the civil war; but the presence of the marines, together with the emphatic public condemnation of the rebels, caused most of the revolutionaries to surrender their arms. Those who did not were defeated by the marine contingent. For the next thirteen years a legation guard of about one hundred marines was stationed in Managua, incidentally assisting the Conservative party to stay in power.

The efficient customs collectorship did not produce quite the same results in Nicaragua as in Santo Domingo. Although the currency was stabilized and the service on the outstanding British debt was resumed, the government continued in financial difficulties. World War I, which so adversely affected the national economies of Latin America at its outbreak, compelled both British bondholders and U.S. bankers to accept suspension of payment.

The financial crisis produced by the world war led the United States to take another diplomatic step in its attempt to rescue Nicaragua. The Bryan-Chamorro Treaty of 1916 provided for the payment of three million dollars to be used to meet the foreign debt payments, in exchange for the exclusive right to construct an inter-ocean canal across the country, using the San Juan River route. The treaty also provided rights for U.S. naval bases on the Corn Islands, off the east coast of Nicaragua, and in the Gulf of Fonseca on the west coast. To the embarrassment of the United States, this portion of the treaty brought protests from both El Salvador and Costa Rica, two states to which dollar diplomacy had not been applied. Costa Rica asserted that her riparian rights were violated by Nicaragua's granting use of the San Juan River. El Salvador felt that the construction of naval bases on the Corn Islands or in Fonseca Bay violated her rights. Both countries brought suit before the Central American Court of Justice, an action that sounded the court's definitive death knell by criticizing Nicaragua for entering into the treaty, even though not declaring it invalid, since it lacked the jurisdiction to do so. Nicaragua withdrew from the court because of the decision. Thus, in a sense, the United States had assisted in the administration of the coup de grace to one of its own efforts to establish a legal basis in international relations.

The distribution of the treaty payment also encountered difficulties, chiefly in the definition of priorities of claims payments under its terms. British bondholders and U.S. bankers sought first-priority payment. The State Department sought and secured equal consideration for other U.S. creditors and for holders of the internal debt. The increasing degree of United States involvement in the internal affairs of Nicaragua is shown by the financial plan of 1917, which fixed monthly levels of government expenditure. The balance of national revenues was applied to the payment of foreign debts. This plan and its successor (1920) became operative under a High Commission, appointed by the United States, insuring for some years direct United States supervision of national finances.

By 1924, not only had the Nicaraguan government paid its debts to U.S. bankers, it had also bought back the 51 percent share that the bankers had purchased in the national railroad and in the central bank. But dollar diplomacy was not the only U.S. policy that involved the international relations of Central America and the Caribbean during the early decades of the present century. The subregion was to experience the complexities of the Wilsonian policy of nonrecognition and the direct intervention of the United States by force for presumed national security reasons.[9]

We have previously noted the New World principle in interna-

9. Isaac Joslin Cox, *Nicaragua and the United States, 1909–1927* (Boston: World Peace Foundation, 1927); for the agreement on the dispersal of the "Canal Fund," see p. 845. See also Ryan, *et al.*, *Handbook for Nicaragua*, and Roscoe R. Hill, *Fiscal Intervention in Nicaragua* (New York: Columbia University Press, 1933).

tional relations that found controversial expression in the present century in the so-called Tobar principle of the nonrecognition of governments that have come to power by force: that is, through internal revolt, through invasion by rebels from outside the national territory, or through the direct intervention of neighboring states. This policy of nonrecognition, employed by President Rutherford B. Hayes against Porfirio Díaz in Mexico as early as 1876, became firmly established as U.S. policy under President Woodrow Wilson and continued until reversed in the course of the Latin American revolutionary wave of 1930. However, it was again applied to Peru in 1962 and to Honduras and the Dominican Republic in 1963 by the Kennedy administration, and experienced a kind of rebirth in Venezuelan policy in the form of the Rómulo Betancourt doctrine of nonrecognition of dictatorships in the 1950s.[10]

Central American Conference of 1922–1923

A new stage in the Central American search for unity had occurred in 1906 when Mexico offered her good offices to settle a war between Guatemala, Honduras, and El Salvador. In 1907, as we have seen, all the Central American states met in Washington under the joint sponsorship of Mexico and the United States. There they drew up a series of treaties providing for a Central American court, neutralizing Honduras, and including other measures for peace, including an agreement not to recognize new governments set up by revolution until elections had been held. The Central American nations convened in Washington again in 1922–1923, drawing up treaties to restore the Central American Court (unsuccessfully) but also retaining the Tobar principle of withholding recognition from governments originating in armed rebellion and headed by the leader of the revolt. This latter provision remained in effect, in general, until the revolts of the 1930s and the adoption of the Inter-American Treaty on the Rights and Duties of States in 1934.[11]

10. On the Tobar principle see Leonidas García, "La Doctrina de Tobar," *Revista de la Sociedad Jurídico-literaria* (Quito), n.s. I (January–February, 1913), 24–71. See also, Bemis, *Latin American Policy of the United States*, 161, 173 n.

11. On the Central American Conference see Bemis, *Latin American Policy of the United States*, 204–206.

Costa Rica

The Central American saga would not be complete without some mention of Costa Rica, the traditional haven of calm and neutrality in most Central American conflicts. Costa Ricans played a major role in organizing the defeat of the filibuster William Walker in the Guerra Nacional de Centroamérica; but her relations with her neighbors, while generally friendly, were usually uninvolved. The location of the Central American Court of Justice in San José, under the Central American treaty of 1907, was a recognition of this Costa Rican neutrality in subregional disputes. However, an ancient boundary dispute with Panama nearly erupted into armed conflict in the 1920s. An arbitral decision by the United States in 1914 had given the town of Coto to Costa Rica. Panama's refusal to abide by the decision and to surrender the town led to its occupation by Costa Rica in 1921. United States diplomatic pressure prevented any overt Panamanian reaction, but the quarrel was not finally settled until 1941.[12]

Although Costa Rica is a producer of bananas, the international image of the banana republic has not been applied to her. A producer of coffee, Costa Rica became involved in the international relations related to that commodity. Perhaps ironically, the first major test of Woodrow Wilson's policy of withholding recognition from governments coming to power by force came with Costa Rica in 1917, when an unpopular minority president of Costa Rica was overthrown. The "usurpation" was denounced by the United States government, and diplomatic recognition was withheld. U.S. citizens were warned against the regime. Fortunately, the matter was settled by a counter-coup in 1919, at which time the earlier Wilsonian policy was simply ignored.

In a recent study, Richard V. Salisbury has pointed out that while Costa Rica was the first Central American state to sponsor the recognition policy incorporated in the treaty of 1923, she "came full circle and led the abandonment of that very same policy" in the 1930s, in the light of the unfortunate experience in withholding recognition

12. Marco A. Soto V., *Guerra Nacional de Centroamérica* (Guatemala: Ministerio de Educación Pública, 1957).

from the dictator Maximiliano Hernández Martínez, in El Salvador.[13]

Panama and the Canal

Another factor in the international relations of Latin America of far-reaching effect in the Caribbean subregion during the decades under study was the creation of the Republic of Panama and the construction of the Panama Canal. The concept of such a canal was ancient, and the problem of its control had led, as we have seen, to the diplomatic conflict between Great Britain and the United States that was resolved by the Clayton-Bulwer Treaty of 1850.

Colombia's granting of a concession to the French company of De Lesseps in 1878 aroused considerable opposition within the U.S. government, but the opposition was short lived. By 1888 the French company had lost out against tropical disease and geography, and was bankrupt. A company chartered by the U.S. government in 1889 to construct a canal in Nicaragua had failed even to begin work. Modest United States interest in an Isthmian canal continued, however, until the Spanish-American War.[14]

That war underscored the canal as a vital interest in U.S. national defense. The obstacle of the Clayton-Bulwer Treaty to U.S. construction of the canal was eliminated by a new treaty with Great Britain, the Hay-Pauncefote Treaty of 1901, replacing the 1850 treaty. The U.S. Congress appointed a commission to study routes in Nicaragua and in Panama. Following the submission of the commission's report, Congress authorized the president on June 28, 1902, to build the canal through the Isthmus of Panama, if Colombia consented, or through Nicaragua, if no agreement could be reached with Colombia. The implementing agreement between Colombia and the United States, known as the Hay-Herrán Treaty, was signed in January, 1903. But the Colombian congress refused to ratify the treaty. The reasons for the Colombian refusal are rooted in the internal political

13. Richard V. Salisbury, "Domestic Politics and Foreign Policy, Costa Rica's Stand in Recognition, 1923–1934," *Hispanic American Historical Review*, LIV (August, 1974), 453–78.

14. On the French–U.S. canal rivalry see Stanley J. Thompson, "The French 'Challenge' in the Isthmus of Panama in the Context of American Expansionism" (Ph.D. dissertation, The American University, 1974).

situation of a country just beginning to recover from three years of disastrous civil war, the presence in office of an ineffective president, and the hope of the Colombians for more generous terms from the French company, whose franchise was about to expire, or from the United States.

The Colombian refusal provoked a revolution in Panama, whose leaders saw their economic future threatened, should the canal be constructed in Nicaragua. Whether the revolution was directly stimulated by the United States is not clear, although the actions of Philippe Bunau Varilla, both as agent of the French company and as the principal Panamanian spokesman in negotiating the subsequent treaty with the United States, suggest a U.S. role. In any case, the United States effectively prevented Colombia from suppressing the revolt by the presence of U.S. warships and by denying use of the Panama railroad to Colombian troops. United States recognition was extended to the government of the new state of Panama four days after the revolt, and a treaty with Panama was signed at Washington on November 18, 1903. The treaty guaranteed the independence of the new republic and contained an agreement for the construction of the canal. From that date on, U.S. concern for the protection of the canal increasingly came to influence U.S. policies in the Central American and Caribbean region until World War I apparently removed all extra-hemispheric threats to the vital lifeline, and U.S. policies could effectively be modified.[15]

The Inter-American System: Causes and Concerns, 1889–1910

An international conference of American states convened in Washington in 1889 to inaugurate the modern Inter-American System. Although the idea of inter-American cooperation can be traced back to Simón Bolívar and the series of regional congresses held between

15. On the canal negotiations see Philippe Bunau Varilla, *Panama, the Creation, Destruction, and Resurrection* (London: Constable, 1913); Diogenes A. Arosemena G., *Documentary Diplomatic History of the Panama Canal* (Panama: University of Panama, 1961); Dwight Caroll Miner, *The Fight for the Panama Route* (New York: Columbia University Press, 1940); and Miles P. Duval, *Cadiz to Cathay: The Story of the Long Diplomatic Struggle for the Panama Canal* (2nd ed.; Stanford: Stanford University Press, 1947), 191–92.

1826 and 1865, these early conferences were basically Spanish American. The Washington conference was an outgrowth of Secretary of State James G. Blaine's earlier attempt at peacemaking in the War of the Pacific, which introduced the concept of U.S.-Latin American collaboration for peace. Two main objectives motivated the Blaine policy: the promotion of peace throughout the Americas and the cultivation of friendly commercial relations between the United States and the Latin American states. By the first he hoped to eliminate the opportunities for European intervention and by the second he hoped to supplant European nations in the trade of Latin America.

Seizing on the War of the Pacific as an opportunity to advance his peace policy, Blaine in November, 1881, had invited all of the Latin American states except Haiti to attend a conference for the purpose of considering methods to prevent war between the nations of America. However, the assassination of President Garfield and the subsequent appointment of Frederick J. Frelinghuysen as secretary of state by President Arthur resulted in a reversal of Blaine's policy and the withdrawal of the invitations. Nevertheless, the idea of the conference survived, and in May, 1888, the U.S. Congress adopted a resolution authorizing President Cleveland to convene a conference of American states in Washington to discuss, among other things, a plan of arbitration for the settlement of disputes and questions relating to the improvement of trade, including the possibility of a customs union. Acquiescing in the desires of Congress, Cleveland allowed the resolution to become effective without his signature. Then in July, Thomas F. Bayard, as secretary of state, sent out the invitations.

Ironically, it fell to Blaine, reinstated as secretary of state in the administration of President Benjamin Harrison, to preside over the first Pan-American conference. From that first meeting all subsequent meetings of hemispheric consequence have sprung, and from it have grown the organizational instruments that evolved into the present Organization of American States.

The agenda of the first meeting and the resolutions adopted show a variety of concerns, including most of the questions to appear in the agenda of subsequent conferences. The item which engendered the greatest interest was the project for the compulsory arbitration of international disputes. The clash of national interests over this question, especially between Chile on the one hand and Peru and Bolivia on the other, due to the unsettled Tacna-Arica dispute, resulted in a stalemate at the conference. To the relief of Chile, the conference accepted a watered-down arbitration treaty, exempting from compulsory arbitration disputes already settled by treaty agreements. This treaty, signed by eleven of the states, never came into effect since none of the signatories ratified it.

Other matters dealt with at the (1889–1890) Washington conference were: extradition and citizenship, monetary and exchange controls, uniform customs and commercial regulations, health and sanitation problems, and (most important) a draft convention for the settlement of pecuniary claims, both public and private. As the patterns of future agenda and resolutions adopted would substantiate, the agreements reached had little direct impact upon the evolving Inter-American System, because only a few of the contracting parties were sufficiently interested to ratify the treaties. A study of the meetings does, however, reveal matters of concern to the Latin American states. It also shows the differences of opinion among the states on such matters as obligatory arbitration (especially in the case of Chile) and the protection of aliens, both of which became issues of contention in the hemisphere. Indicative of the area of most common concern, of trust, and of interest was the action in 1889–1890 charging the Commercial Office of the American Republics with the responsibility of collecting and disseminating information on the commercial regulations and tariffs of the members.

The second Pan-American conference, at Mexico City (1901–1902), developed from a different dimension in international relations. A protocol of adherence to the Permanent Court of Arbitration, set up by the Hague Conference in 1899, was open for signatures of the Latin American governments. To this end Mexico, the only Latin American state to take part in the first Hague Conference, endorsed the suggestion of the United States that a second Pan-American conference convene at Mexico City in October, 1901. The specific purpose was to secure as many signatures on the protocol of adherence to the Hague Court as possible. At the Mexico City conference the issue of arbitration of international disputes thus once again became a central issue of concern. The division between advocates of compulsory arbitration and of voluntary arbitration became and remained deep and sharp. Chile's opposition to any plan that might be construed as requiring the submission to arbitration of its dispute with Peru was so strong that the Chilean delegation threatened to withdraw from the conference if a compulsory arbitration agreement were submitted to the delegates for signature. After a heated debate, the conference produced a compromise plan which called for voluntary arbitrations among those American states that had not already accepted adherence to the Hague Court. A separate treaty was to be drawn up outside the conference by those delegates that would be satisfied with nothing less than an obligatory instrument. Because of this latter treaty's numerous exceptions, however, it was somewhat less than compulsory. Moreover, of the nine nations whose delegations signed the treaty, only six ratified it.

The agenda of this second conference was not concerned solely with matters of arbitration. A convention on the rights of aliens reflected the influence of the noted Argentine international lawyer Carlos Calvo, whose doctrine was then in the process of development, his work on the subject having been recently published in Paris. The issue of the rights of aliens had been raised in the first Pan-American conference in 1889 and continued to be an issue of concern in international law even after Latin American adherence to the Second Hague Protocol of 1907. The convention proposal submitted to the second (Mexico) conference on the rights of aliens reflected the Calvo Doctrine. It provided that a state might not accord privileges to aliens that it did not accord its own nationals, that the state was not responsible for damages sustained by aliens during civil conflict, that the competent national court should be the court of first instance for adjudication of the claims of aliens, and that such claims should be presented through accepted diplomatic channels. As was to become traditional, the United States alone refused to sign. On the other hand, the United States did sign, along with all of the other delegations, a treaty providing for the arbitration of pecuniary claims. The pecuniary claims convention was later ratified by ten countries, including the United States. But given the Latin Americans' hearty endorsement of the Calvo Doctrine, this treaty on pecuniary claims never became an effective feature of the Inter-American System.

The third Pan-American conference met at Rio de Janeiro, Brazil, in 1906. Between Mexico City (1901) and Rio de Janeiro, the international relations of the hemisphere had changed rather drastically. The trauma of the Spanish-American War and the Panamanian Revolution had reached its height, and the consequent power change in both hemispheric and global relations had become clearer. The vital national interests of the United States in the Caribbean and in the Isthmian canal had taken form in concrete policy. These new forms were, among others, U.S. policy in the Venezuelan Crisis (1902), the Panamanian Revolution and canal treaty (1903), and the application of the Roosevelt Corollary to Santo Domingo (1905). Most repugnant to the Latin Americans had been the creation of protectorates by the United States over Panama and Cuba, suggesting a practice of intervention that was defined as hemisphere-wide in the Roosevelt Corollary.

By 1906, attitudes that had begun to appear in the Mexico City conference had become increasingly embittered. Aware of these sentiments, the United States had sought to expunge from the third conference politically sensitive items. One such item, however, could not be got rid of, because it concerned the attendance of Latin American states at the Second Hague Conference in 1907. The resolution that recommended attendance at the Hague Conference included wording about the use of force for the collection of public debts. It suggested that the Drago Doctrine, under New World sponsorship, might hopefully receive international recognition. Such recognition would have been a triumph for a unique principle of inter-American international law. Unfortunately, the consideration of the proposal at the Hague Conference, as previously noted, proved more negative than positive. Even tacit recognition of the doctrine as an international law principle had to wait for a later day.

From the beginning of their foreign relations as independent states, the Latin American states, especially the Spanish American states, demonstrated a preoccupation with two issues: the respect for national sovereignty (nonintervention) and arbitration of international disputes, whether voluntary or compulsory. From the first decade of the present century until the cold war, the main issues were usually related to problems arising from the protection of the property rights of aliens and from the management of foreign debt. On the question of arbitration of international disputes the staunch and tireless advocates of compulsory arbitration found that they were faced with two major sources of opposition. First, Chile refused to consider any treaty or convention that might threaten her position with regard to the Tacna-Arica issue; second, the U.S. Senate refused to consent to any treaty of compulsory arbitration that did not provide for certain major exceptions affecting national interest. Consequently, voluntary arbitration became the operative pattern within the Inter-American System; surprisingly, the achievements of such arbitrations in the settlements of international disputes were impressive.

That the Rio conference of 1906 was not a disaster for the Inter-American System must be attributed in part to the prior preparations and to the presence of Elihu Root, U.S. secretary of state, who managed to convince the conference of the sincerity of the United States in its self-denial of interest in conquest or occupation and in its support of the juridical equality of states. Politically, at least, this Root effort helped to allay the suspicions that had become the grist for the mills of anti-Yankee intellectuals. Root's success, in turn, was due in large measure to the good offices of the Brazilian ambassador to the United States, Joaquim Nabuco, whose advice Root followed in preparing for the conference and who presided with great effectiveness over the conference sessions.

The experience of the Rio conference led a new administration in the United States to examine any subsequent agenda even more closely for sensitive items. Such an examination led in 1910 to an agenda for the Buenos Aires conference that produced little except further ill will and a resolution changing the name of the administrative structure to the Pan-American Union. The spirit of Pan-Americanism, which had never been hardy, almost expired in this conference. [16]

The Second Hague Conference

A year later, however, at the Second Hague Conference (1907) most Latin American states were disappointed at their failure to secure complete endorsement of the Drago Doctrine, despite the fact that the Hague Conference did in the Porter resolution, as we have seen, outlaw the use of force for the collection of debts, *provided* that the state accepted arbitration and the decision of the arbitration. Thereafter, Latin America became increasingly intolerant of any form of intervention whatsoever.

The Second Hague Conference calls for some further comments beyond the previous reference to the Drago principle. It marked the entry of Latin American states onto the international stage. Only Mexico had attended the First Hague Conference. This participation on a world scale was later furthered by World War I and membership in the League of Nations; this latter experience proved to be not entirely satisfactory. The reason for Latin America's small participation is not hard to understand; it lay in the Latin American preoccupation with internal national affairs and a consequent lack of opportunity and desire to participate in matters outside the hemisphere. At Mexican and United States urging the Latin American states had been asked to

16. On the inter-American conferences, consult Francisco Cuevas Cancino, *Del Congreso de Panamá a la Conferencia de Caracas, 1826–1954* (2 vols; Caracas: Tenth Inter-American Conference, 1954) II, 1–95; J. M. Yepes, *Del Congreso de Panamá a la Conferencia de Caracas, 1826–1954* (2 vols.; Caracas: Tenth Inter-American Conference, 1954), II, 1–78; Samuel Guy Inman, *Inter-American Conferences, 1826–1954* (Washington: University Press of Washington, D.C., 1965), Chaps. 3–10. See also, A. Curtis Wilgus, "James G. Blaine and the Pan American Movement," *Hispanic American Historical Review*, V (November, 1922), 662–708; his "The Second International American Conference at Mexico City," *Hispanic American Historical Review*, XI (February, 1931), 27 ff. and his "The Third International Conference at Rio de Janeiro," *Hispanic American Historical Review*, XII (November, 1932), 420–56; see also James B. Scott, (ed.), *The International Conferences of American States* (2 vols.; New York: Carnegie Endowment for International Peace, Oxford Press, 1931). On the special importance of Chilean-Argentine relations in these conferences see Robert N. Burr, *By Reason or Force: Chile and the Balance of Power in South America, 1830–1905* (Berkeley: University of California Press, 1965), especially 240–46.

send delegates to the second conference. Those from Honduras arrived too late to take part; Costa Rica sent none at all.

Latin American policy positions expressed at this Hague conference were indicative of certain positions taken in their international relations that are still in evidence. They gave support to the legal bulwarks that might be erected for the protection of weak states. The views of their spokesmen, such as Ruy Barbosa of Brazil, on the control of warfare were progressive and humane. Their views on arbitration reflected the diversity that had already become characteristic in hemispheric discussions. Obligatory arbitration was supported in principle, but with reservations in practice. A proposal for voluntary arbitration, however, was supported unanimously. The creation of a Court of Arbitral Justice and a Prize Court were also supported, provided that the justices were chosen on the basis of the equality of states. The main interest of the Latin American states centered upon the limitation of the use of force in the collection of damage claims and contract debts (the Drago principle). No system seemed to go far enough in the protection of debtor states against coercion by the powers on behalf of such claims of their nationals. Brazil differed with Argentina in this matter in degree, if not in substance, and even the United States attempted to support the Drago position, but with indifferent success, as already noted.[17]

The Wilson Proposal

In 1914 President Woodrow Wilson proposed to the republics of Argentina, Brazil, and Chile a project for a Pan-American pact by which the territorial integrity, the independence, and the republican forms of government of the states of the hemisphere would be mutually guaranteed. The proposed pact also contained a provision to settle all pending territorial disputes by amicable methods, including arbitration. Wilson's purpose was to continentalize the hitherto jealously guarded Monroe Doctrine, creating a system of regional security in America. Contrary to his expectations, however, the Pan-American pact encountered staunch opposition.

17. On the Second Hague Conference, see William I. Hull, "The United States and Latin America at the Hague," *International Conciliation*, No. 44 (July, 1911).

Chile, fearful that such a covenant might bind her to the arbitration of the Tacna-Arica dispute, was the principal objector. Because of Chile's opposition no headway was made in gaining acceptance of the Wilson proposal. Meanwhile, Argentina and Brazil lost interest in the project. With the entrance of the United States into the World War, President Wilson, now preoccupied with that crisis, finally dropped the project, only to resurrect it in another form, in 1919, when he presented the idea to the Paris Peace Conference as Article 10 of the League of Nations.[18]

Mexican Revolutionary Foreign Policy

In many respects the most significant development in the foreign relations of Latin America emanated from the Mexican Revolution which began in 1910. It was a popular uprising, led by Francisco Madero; but it was supported by a group of young intellectuals and such popular leaders as "Pancho" Villa and the agrarian leader Emiliano Zapata that drove Porfirio Díaz from power and installed Madero in the presidency. In February, 1913, the overthrow and assassination of President Madero and his vice president, José M. Pino Suárez, initiated a period of violent civil warfare. Aimed originally at overthrowing Victoriano Huerta, leader of the uprising against Madero, the ensuing civil war soon became a power struggle among rival revolutionary forces; but it was also a nationalist and socialist movement of radical social, political, and economic reform. Ultimately it produced the Mexican constitution of 1917, the model of many subsequent reform constitutions. The Mexican Revolution provides a good illustration of the linkage between domestic and foreign policy.

The United States withheld recognition from the Huerta government and persuaded the British and other governments to do likewise. This application of Wilson's doctrine of nonrecognition of nonconstitutional governments (akin to the Tobar Doctrine) soon encountered the opposition of Venustiano Carranza, titular leader of the "Constitutionalist" forces in rebellion against Huerta. Carranza's opposition came to a head when United States forces occupied the port of Vera Cruz in 1914, partly because the Mexicans had refused an

18. Inman, *Inter-American Conferences*, 89–90.

apology and salute to the U.S. flag after arresting and then releasing U.S. marines in Tampico, partly to prevent the unloading of a German shipment of arms for the Huerta government. While this action had a major influence in bringing the defeat of Huerta, Carranza patriotically insisted upon opposing it (even though directed against his enemy) as an intervention in Mexico. The ABC powers (Argentina, Brazil, and Chile), who had recently developed an entente under Brazilian influence, offered their good offices to effect a general settlement of the Mexican problems, meeting for this purpose at Niagara Falls, with representatives from the United States and from the various revolutionary groups in Mexico. Carranza politely accepted the ABC good offices, but insisted that they be limited strictly to ending the occupation of Vera Cruz, whereas the U.S. and the ABC nations wished to help settle the internal civil war.

Carranza then refused to send delegates to the Niagara conference. The conference ended by rejecting recognition of Huerta (or any of the rebel leaders) and suggesting that after Huerta's overthrow the various leaders meet and choose an interim president. Carranza rejected the whole Niagara procedure and its conclusions as intervention in the domestic affairs of Mexico. He held firmly to this principle of unlimited national sovereignty in several subsequent tests, giving Mexico a Carranza "Constitutionalist" foreign policy with several new aspects, subsequently adopted elsewhere in Latin America. When a raid across the U.S. border by Pancho Villa brought a "punitive expedition" into Mexico in pursuit of Villa, Carranza rejected the tentative approval of the expedition, given by his lieutenant, Alvaro Obregón, and stubbornly refused any political agreement with the United States, even though the U.S. forces were pursuing a leader in rebellion against his (Carranza's) authority. The United States withdrew the Pershing force when they virtually had Villa within their grasp, rather than risk open conflict with Carranza's forces which stood in the way of their capturing the popular guerrilla leader.

As the programs of agrarian reform (land distribution) and regulation of the petroleum industry developed, programs of reform soon to be incorporated in the new constitution, the Carranza government evolved a policy sometimes called the Carranza Doctrine. This was the policy that damage claims by foreigners, whether arising from these reforms or from the ravages of the civil war, should be treated exactly like those of Mexicans. In essence this was the Calvo principle, but Carranza gave the stand against diplomatic intervention for the protection of alien rights the strongest statement it had received from a Latin American government. No longer was it a mere theory.

Mexico, like Argentina, Chile, and several other states, maintained a policy of strict neutrality during World War I. The "punitive expedition" had been withdrawn before the U.S. entrance into the war, but the Carranza policy continued to be hostile to the United States. German agents in Mexico fostered this hostility, which went so far as to produce the ill-advised German offer contained in the "Zimmerman Note," which offered to support Mexican efforts to recapture the territory ceded to the United States at the end of the Mexican War in return for a Mexican attack on the United States. Carranza was shrewd enough not to be taken in by what was rather obviously a German propaganda move, but the revelation of this correspondence with Germany created problems for his government, not only in relations with the United States, but with the other Allied powers as well. At the same time Mexican petroleum was extremely valuable to the Allies, so much so that some German authorities have gone so far as to say that the Allies rode to victory on a flood of Mexican oil.

During the postwar years the increased application of the land and petroleum measures provided for in the new constitution of 1917 involved Mexico in serious clashes with foreign interests, particularly the British and U.S. owners of the petroleum industry. When the United States withheld recognition of the government of Alvaro Obregón after his overthrow of Carranza in 1920 and his subsequent election, a new crisis arose in these relations. It was temporarily resolved by an informal arrangement, known as the Bucareli Agreement, from the building in which the negotiations took place, and again temporarily during the presidency of Plutarco Elías Calles by the adroit diplomacy of U.S. Ambassador Dwight Morrow. The basic settlement came only later, however, during the presidency of Lázaro Cárdenas, and after the expropriation of the foreign oil companies. Meanwhile, Mexico had set an example, soon to be followed by other countries, of treating the petroleum industry as a national enterprise. Among other things, the controversial relations with the United States brought the statement of the Estrada principle of recognition, named for the Mexican secretary of foreign relations, Vicente Estrada. This principle may be defined as calling for immediate recognition, or more accurately, as simply denying the right either to grant or to withhold recognition.[19]

World War I

Latin America was totally unprepared for the outbreak of the First World War, economically, politically, and psychologically. Strong European ties and the predilections of their citizens created internal political tensions for the nations as the conflict lengthened. The carnage and destruction produced horror and revulsion. The barbarity in warfare of nations formerly considered the epitome of civilization caused a turning inward that did much to strengthen what was to become the Indo-American political movement, an ideological movement that sought new models of national and international behavior in the indigenous cultures and in other aspects of the historical heritage of the Americas. Sympathy for the Allied Powers was more widespread than for the Central Powers, but the popular feeling was by no means uniform; hence the policy of several of the major states was to maintain the strictest neutrality throughout the conflict. The positions adopted by the various nations in relation to the Central Powers were as follows:

Declared war: Brazil, Cuba, Costa Rica, Guatemala, Haiti, Honduras, Nicaragua, Panama.
Broke Diplomatic Relations: Bolivia, Dominican Republic, Ecuador, Peru, Uruguay.
Declared neutrality: Argentina, Chile, Colombia, Mexico, Paraguay, El Salvador, Venezuela.

19. On Mexican relations during these years Isidro Fabela, *Historia Diplomática de la Revolución Constitucionalista* (Mexico: Instituto Nacional de Estudios Históricos, 1957), is good, especially for international aspects of the Pershing expedition. On the Estrada Doctrine see Charles G. Fenwick, "The Problem of the Recognition of De Facto Governments," in *Inter-American Juridical Yearbook* (Washington: Organization of American States, 1948), 18–39.

Since the formation of the Inter-American System in 1889 the American republics had not raised among themselves the issues of neutrality, of mutual defense against aggression, or of economic cooperation to offset dislocations of international trade and commerce. Consequently, with the exception of the First Pan-American Financial Conference, which met in Washington in May, 1915, to discuss dislocation in transportation, commerce, and finance, agreements for defense were entirely bilateral. Multilateral security conventions did not exist and were not considered. The declarations of war, the ruptures of diplomatic relations, and the declarations of neutrality were accomplished without consultation and agreement. The war did, however, produce one very significant action. The government of Uruguay announced that "no American country which, in defense of its rights, is in a state of war with nations of other continents shall be treated as a belligerent."[20] This meant that in its neutrality Uruguay would treat the United States and other American nations at war as nonbelligerents. This Brum principle, proposed by the Uruguayan foreign minister, was destined to become an American principle of international law, forming the basis of the policy adopted by the American nations at Rio de Janeiro in 1942 for their conduct during World War II.

The disruption of the normal patterns of trade, the scarcity of shipping, and the intitial collapse of markets were keenly, if variously, felt. By May, 1915, sufficient economic dislocation existed to lead, as indicated, to the holding of the First Pan-American Financial Conference at Washington. Although its accomplishments were small, this conference may be said to mark the shift to Latin American economic and financial dependence upon the United States instead of on Europe. This transfer of dependence was thus one of the direct policy consequences of the war for the nations of Latin America.

Among the neutrals, Mexico and Argentina were actively anti-United States, if not pro-German, each for internal political reasons and in part because of the personalities of their presidents, Venustiano Carranza and Hipólito Irigoyen, and because of special conflicts

20. Baltazar Brum, *La Paz de América* (Montevideo: Imprenta Nacional, 1923), 25–26. See also, Inman, *Inter-American Conferences*, 91.

with the United States. Argentina went so far as to try to organize an inter-American conference against the United States, while Mexico, as noted, did her international image no good by receiving the inept Zimmerman proposal. This Argentine-Mexican attitude was compounded by a proposed economic boycott against *all* belligerents. In general, the actions and policies of the Latin American states during World War I demonstrate little in the way of a community of hemispheric interests, with the notable exception of the Brum principle, noted above. While the concept of "continental solidarity" was sometimes referred to, no steps were taken during or immediately after the war to strengthen the Inter-American System. The time had not yet come to consider multilateral defense or, for that matter, multilateral economic effort.[21]

Latin America and the League of Nations

World War I changed the environment in which Latin American international relations were conducted in at least four fundamental ways. First, for a seemingly indefinite future it removed the threat of any extra-hemisphere aggression, especially from traditional European sources. Second, it confirmed the New World as a sphere of United States predominance. Third, after the war the League of Nations presented new opportunities for Latin American participation in both regional and global power and collective security systems. Fourth, the American regional system, through its institutional structure, came to realize more fully its capacities for cooperation and self-development.

Eventually, all Latin American states became members of the League of Nations. As a consequence of the ratification of the Treaty of Versailles as belligerents during World War I, nine states became original members: Bolivia, Brazil, Cuba, Guatemala, Haiti, Honduras, Panama, Peru, and Uruguay. Argentina, Chile, Colombia, El Salvador, Paraguay, and Venezuela also became original members by signing and constitutionally ratifying the covenant of the league, as a document separate from the Versailles treaty, within the sixty-day

21. On Latin America in World War I, see Bemis, *Latin American Policy of the United States*, Chaps. 10 and 11.

grace period after its coming into force. Chile's endorsement of the league, however, was initially tempered with certain doubts. Expressing concern that the league maintain a scrupulous respect for existing treaties, Chile did not wish to see the Treaty of Ancón, out of which the Tacna-Arica controversy developed, subject to a review by this new world organization. Ecuador signed in 1919 but did not ratify until 1934; consequently, Ecuador was one of the two states not directly concerned with the league during the period now being considered. Nicaragua, which by right of belligerent status was an original member, did not ratify with the first nine states, but did act in time to be represented at the first assembly. Costa Rica, also a belligerent, was excluded from the original membership because Great Britain and the United States strongly disapproved of the government then in power. After a change in her government, Costa Rica became a member in December, 1920, but was never really happy in the league, feeling that the cost exceeded the benefit. The case of the Dominican Republic was complicated by the United States military occupation; consequently, it was not until September, 1924, that this state joined. Like Ecuador, Mexico did not participate in the league during the first decade of its work. Unlike Ecuador, however, and rather like Costa Rica, the Mexican relationship with the league was complicated by other factors of her international relations.

The character of Mexico's government and her attitude toward the Allied cause during World War I were what caused Mexico to be excluded from original membership. Because Great Britain and the United States disapproved of it, Mexico was not invited. Even later, when she knew the league would approve her membership, Mexico refused to apply for admission, the official reason being the continued nonrecognition of her government by Great Britain. In 1931, largely on the initiative of the republican government of Spain, the assembly of the league made the agreeable first overture, unanimously approving a resolution inviting Mexico to membership. The league invitation was accepted and Mexico became thereafter the most active supporter of the covenant from among the Latin American states.

Once members of the league, the New World states had to face a general policy question which arose from their prior participation in the Inter-American System. The question was the extent to which the league might intervene to settle problems between states of the hemisphere, in accordance with the provision of the charter, which, incidentally, mentioned the Monroe Doctrine (Article XXI), although the doctrine would seem to preclude such action. A general consensus developed within the league to the effect that purely hemispheric problems should be considered and resolved within the Inter-American System. While Latin American delegates were quick to point to the hemispheric system as a model for world order, individual national interests often tended to outweigh these broader considerations of cooperation, prestige, and idealism.

At the first assembly of the league, Argentina proposed an amendment to the league covenant eliminating the reference to the Monroe Doctrine. When this proposed amendment was set aside, Argentina announced that her mission was at an end and her delegates left Geneva. Although she did not officially withdraw, Argentina took no effective part in the political decisions of the league for the remainder of the decade, not resuming full membership until 1933. Questions of finance were also worrisome from the start, leading to repeated demands for a more favorable reallocation of the budget; failure to deal with this question led to the eventual withdrawal of several Latin American states. The first of these was Costa Rica, which presented its notification of withdrawal in January, 1925. Although her withdrawal did not become effective for two years, Costa Rica ceased all participation at that time. By 1936, Guatemala, Honduras, and Nicaragua also withdrew because of their unwillingness to pay the established contributions.

Peru and Bolivia ceased to participate in 1921 when the league declined to consider the Tacna-Arica dispute. Both states had hoped that the league would rectify what they believed to be injustices in the treaties adopted after the War of the Pacific. They did not return to the league until the Tacna-Arica dispute had been finally resolved in 1929.

Brazil gave notice of her withdrawal in June, 1926, because she had

not received a permanent seat on the council of the league, an early
example of Brazil's insistence on her status as a world power. Despite
this notification, however, Brazil continued to take part in the
league's work. She cooperated with the International Labor Organization and supported the Permanent Court of International Justice. Her
insistence upon the permanent seat had not been supported by other
Latin American members; rather, after her defeat, they unanimously
urged her to reconsider her decision to withdraw. The Brazilian action did, however, secure from the seventh assembly the designation
of three nonpermanent seats to Latin American states at the time of
the reorganization of the council. Election to the nonpermanent seats
was for three years. The system was designed so that one changed
every year, being replaced by the state chosen at a private, unofficial
caucus of Latin American delegates.

The Brazilian action produced an unexpected renewal of the special
hemispheric pattern related to the Monroe Doctrine, the status of the
Latin American states as members of the league, and the relationship
between the world and the regional organizations. When the league,
after appealing to Brazil to return, also invited Costa Rica to do the
same, that government asked the league to explain its interpretation
of the Monroe Doctrine and the scope and meaning given to the doctrine by Article 21 of the covenant. The query was made shortly after
the Havana Conference (1928) at which the United States had been
severely criticized for its interventions in Cuba, Panama, Haiti, the
Dominican Republic, and Nicaragua. As usual, the criticism of United
States policy had been led by Argentina. Her delegate pointed out
that the covenant was in error in referring to the doctrine as an example of a regional understanding, when in reality it was not more than a
unilateral assertion of policy that had never been explicitly approved
by any of the states of the region. When it became known that a
diplomatic and noncommittal reply to the Argentine charge was being
considered, the delegates of Chile, Colombia, and Cuba warned that
such a reply would have disastrous consequences for the future of the
league, as well as for Latin American adherence to the Kellogg-Briand
Pact. Consequently, the reply took a much stronger position than

might otherwise have been diplomatically wished. Costa Rica was assured that the covenant conferred equal rights and equal responsibilities on all members and that Article 21 was intended neither to extend the scope of, nor confirm the validity of, the Monroe Doctrine. Anticlimactically, the congress of Costa Rica declined to appropriate the necessary funds for Costa Rica's readmission.

This position adopted by the league on the Monroe Doctrine helped make possible the league's interposition into hemispheric affairs when fighting broke out between Bolivia and Paraguay in the Chaco Boreal in 1928. Both states were members of the league, but neither used the procedures prescribed by the covenant to bring the matter to the council. Moreover, a conference of American states, then meeting in Washington, was attempting conciliation and arbitration. Consequently, when the secretary-general placed the Chaco conflict before the council of the League of Nations, a heated debate ensued. Venezuela warned the council that the situation constituted a test of the genuine status of New World members and that failure to act would end the league in Latin America. This warning led the council to remind both parties of their responsibilities and to warn sternly against military aggression. The most effective device adopted was to advise all other league members of the situation and of the council's action with regard to it. World attention was focused, for once, on a New World conflict. The effects were salubrious, leading to an armistice and an effort at league mediation in the conflict, though unfortunately this was only temporary.

For Latin America it seemed that the league might provide something of a counterweight to the ever-expanding power and influence of the United States; but the European powers failed to realize or to act to consolidate the leadership that decisions of this kind might have given them diplomatically. Perhaps they, too, like many Latin American states, were really more concerned with their bilateral relations with the American colossus than they were with the management of world order.[22]

22. See W. H. Kelchner, *Latin American Relations with the League of Nations* (Boston: World Peace Foundation, 1930).

The Inter-American System: The Consequences of
Interventionism, 1923–1928

The fifth Inter-American Conference, originally scheduled to be held in 1914 but postponed because of the war, convened in Santiago, Chile, in March, 1923. It was attended by delegations from all of the American republics except Mexico, Bolivia, and Peru. Mexico refused to participate because her government, that of President Alvaro Obregón, was not recognized by the United States and consequently could not be represented on the governing board of the Pan American Union. Peru and Bolivia did not send delegations because of the critical nature of their relations with Chile over the Tacna-Arica controversy.

A proposal by President Baltazar Brum of Uruguay for the creation of an American league of nations afforded some of the delegates at Santiago an opportunity to launch a bitter attack on the Monroe Doctrine. The Brum plan, similar to Wilson's proposal for a Pan-American pact, included a proposal that each American state bind itself to support any American state attacked by a non-American country. In view of the United States repudiation of the League of Nations because of the obligation to defend the territory of member states, her failure to approve the Brum proposal was understandable. In reply to a number of delegates who took this opportunity to ask for a definition of the Monroe Doctrine, the head of the United States delegation firmly stated that his country viewed the doctrine as essentially a national policy. The Brum plan was finally disposed of by referring it for study to the governing board of the Pan American Union.

The centenary of the Monroe Doctrine in 1923 gave the United States secretary of state, Charles Evans Hughes, a chance to redefine national policies, including the doctrine, strictly in terms of self-defense; but he did not renounce the right of intervention. However, as the reaction to the J. Reuben Clark *Memorandum on the Monroe Doctrine* a few years later was to show, no amount of interpretation of the Monroe Doctrine by United States officials could quiet Latin American fears of United States intervention. The refusal of the United States to join the League of Nations had further increased these fears. The United States refusal meant that the provisions of Article 10, which guaranteed the political and territorial integrity of member states, rendered the league ineffectual as a counterbalance to United States power in the Americas. Consequently, Latin American states continued to seek from the United States some form of self-limitation on the latter's claim of the right to protect the interests of her nationals. By this they meant some further recognition by the United States of the inviolability of national sovereignty and a unilateral renunciation of the right of intervention, whether economic, political, or, above all, military. Since the United States did not seek to expunge political matters from the agenda of the Fifth International Conference of American States in Santiago (1923), the discussion of the Monroe Doctrine was unusually frank and open in the political context; but it was fruitless.

There was one positive result of this Santiago conference, however. This was the adoption of the Treaty to Avoid or Prevent Conflicts between the American States, popularly known as the Gondra Treaty, after its sponsor Manuel Gondra of Paraguay. This treaty embodied the principle of the Bryan cooling-off formula; it provided for submitting to a commission of inquiry all controversies not settled through diplomatic channels or through arbitration under existing treaties. Under its terms, the signatories were not to mobilize or commit any hostile acts until six months after the commission made its report. The treaty also provided for two permanent commissions, one in Montevideo and one in Washington, to receive and transmit requests for invoking commissions of inquiry. The Gondra Treaty marked a first, though limited, step towards the establishment of effective inter-American peace-keeping machinery.

The Gondra Treaty was ratified by most countries, but it is important to note that both Chile and Peru refused to ratify it. Their refusal rendered it inapplicable to the Tacna-Arica controversy, which continued to hang like a dark cloud over the inter-American movement and to effectively impede the efforts to establish an inter-American system for the pacific settlement of disputes. The Peruvian government withheld its ratification of the treaty until December, 1928, shortly after the resumption of diplomatic relations with Chile. The

definitive settlement of the Tacna-Arica question by direct negotiations the following year removed Chilean and Peruvian objections; it
also opened the door for other multilateral treaties that were destined
to become basic elements of the inter-American peace system.

The Santiago conference did modify somewhat the predominant
position of the United States in the Inter-American System by assigning many new duties to its organ, the Pan American Union. As has
been indicated, the Uruguayan proposal for the creation of an American league of nations, with its implications for regional defense and
security arrangements, died from lack of interest and through the device of "further study." Comment in the Latin American press and
other publications (and in much of the United States press and among
United States scholars) was singularly unfavorable toward the Latin
American policies of the United States at this time; nor was it favorable to the proposals of any other Latin American state. It may be true,
as Samuel Flagg Bemis remarked, that we may see the beginning of
the "liquidation of American imperialism" at this point (1923). But
criticism both in the United States and in Latin America continued to
mount throughout the decade, up until the public announcement of a
"Good Neighbor policy," early in the 1930s, reversed the trend.[23]

Both private investment and public debt were mounting in Latin
America in these postwar years of economic growth and incipient
modernization. Accompanying this growth, the old problems of the
rights of foreign ownership and of the control of foreign investment, of
debt payment, and of the treatment of foreigners in general, arose
time and again to trouble the international relations of the region. A
United States university group's attempt in the 1920s to reorganize
Ecuador's finances was matched by a banker's consortium that sought
to steer the finances of the Bolivian ship of state. Moreover, the
strong anticlerical legislation of successive revolutionary Mexican
governments during these years, coupled with moves to extend national control over the petroleum industry and to apply the land reform called for by Mexico's revolutionary constitution, caused that

23. Bemis, *The Latin American Policy of the United States*, 202; also J. Lloyd Mecham, *The
United States and Inter-American Security, 1869–1960* (Austin: University of Texas Press,
1961), 94–100. See also works of Inman, Cuevas Cancino, and Yepes cited in footnote 16 above.

nation to face a noisy, public campaign by Roman Catholics and others in the United States for intervention in the domestic conflict. This "war scare" did nothing to improve the image of United States policy in the rest of Latin America even where governments were unsympathetic toward the Mexican Revolution.

Yet, what most Latin American governments failed to realize, or refused to believe, was that United States policy was, indeed, in the slow process of major political change during the Hoover administration (1929–1933). But, even before President Hoover's tour of Latin America just after his election won grudging recognition of a change in United States policy, dollar diplomacy and the protective and preventive diplomacy of the Theodore Roosevelt and Taft eras, as well as the singular recognition policy of Woodrow Wilson, were in the process of liquidation.

Intervention in Cuba came to a halt and attention was given to negotiations looking to the abolishment of the Platt Amendment. Elsewhere, the liquidation of the responsibilities of protective and preventive diplomacy—in Haiti, the Dominican Republic, Panama, and Nicaragua—was being initiated. A United States isolation in the years following World War I was seeming to have definite, if indistinct, ameliorating impact upon United States policy towards Latin America.

Yet confusion and misunderstanding of political trends and national policies in the Americas appeared in the Inter-American Conference that assembled at Havana in 1928. This conference became something of a showdown between Latin America and the United States. But its detailed story, much too complex to be elaborated here, also reveals changing policy positions and changes in the wishes and in the political realities of the states of the Inter-American System, as 1928 closed a decade of remarkable development within the hemisphere. The conference is in many ways a prelude to the changed relationships that the next few years were to provide in the Good Neighbor era. Not the least of these indications is the fact that President Coolidge attended the conference—the first United States president to do so.

During the Havana conference the Argentine delegation tried unsuccessfully to link the freedom of hemispheric trade, in which the

United States was interested, to the judicial equality of states and to mutual respect for the complete sovereignty of states. Nonintervention in the form of the Drago and Calvo concepts supported the Latin American views in new forms of rhetoric. A reorganization of the Pan American Union, designed to restrict United States influence, was proposed in a treaty embodying a charter that, fortunately, was never ratified; ratification would have committed the organization to a much narrower role than that under the subsequent 1948 charter. A resolution condemning acts of aggression had the support of the United States delegation. But, as usual, the efforts to define aggression ran into so many snags that it was not achieved. The definition of aggression and aggressor was destined to elude the statesmen of the New World for years as completely as it did those of the League of Nations.

A number of proposals to strengthen inter-American peace machinery were presented at the Havana conference. The most important of these was a project for a treaty for the pacific settlement of international disputes presented by the Commission of Jurists, meeting in Rio de Janeiro. Although the views of Chile and Peru, whose dispute over Tacna and Arica was then in the hands of the United States as arbitrator, clashed once again over the issue of obligatory arbitration, there were signs that a friendlier atmosphere had come to prevail between the two countries. The arbitration question was resolved by the adoption of a resolution calling for the holding of a special conference on conciliation and arbitration at Washington within the period of a year.

The conference convened in Washington on December 10, 1928, and lasted until January 5, 1929. It produced two significant contributions to the inter-American peace structure, a general treaty of arbitration with a protocol on progressive arbitration, and a general convention on conciliation, extending the scope of the Gondra Treaty of 1923. The new treaties became the central part of the inter-American system for the pacific settlement of international disputes. These treaties were eventually signed and ratified by most members of the Inter-American System; but their application in the conflicts of the next decade served only to underscore the relative ineffectiveness of the peace-keeping structure of the system. Nonetheless, the search for the means to preserve the peace within the hemisphere, as well as within the world, continued.[24]

Settlement of the Tacna-Arica Question

One factor contributing significantly to the success of the Washington conference was the progress made in settlement of the Tacna-Arica dispute. Chile was still interested in maintaining a balance of power in the southern cone of the continent, but her days of expansionism were over. The years after World War I were also a time of internal difficulty for her. In December, 1921, Chile approached Peru regarding the possibility of a settlement. After an exchange of notes, the two powers, in January, 1922, agreed to send representatives to Washington to thresh out the question under the good offices of the United States. Not invited to participate in the negotiations, Bolivia issued a vigorous protest; but Chile and Peru were not willing to extend the scope of the conference to include Bolivian claims to an outlet to the sea. By July the negotiations in Washington produced a protocol whereby Chile and Peru agreed to submit to the president of the United States for arbitration the question of whether or not the plebiscite should be held. Both sides then chose their counsels and prepared their cases, which were submitted to the arbitrator in November, 1923.

On March 4, 1925, President Coolidge handed down an award stating that the provisions of the Treaty of Ancón were still in effect and that the plebiscite should be held. A commission composed of a Chilean representative, a Peruvian representative, and a United States representative, the latter to serve as presiding officer, was to supervise the holding of the plebiscite. In the previous negotiations the Peruvian government had argued that since conditions had changed completely in the disputed territory, a fair plebiscite could not be held, but that Peru should be confirmed as undisputed owner of Tacna and Arica. She protested against the award after it was made, but accepted it, demanding certain guarantees in the conduct of the plebiscite; to this the United States replied that the award was final and without appeal.

24. See works cited in footnote 23 above.

With U.S. General John J. Pershing as chairman, the plebiscite commission began its work in August, 1925. The old bitterness between Chile and Peru soon flared up, ultimately making it impossible for the commission to function effectively. In the middle of June, 1926, General William Lassiter, who had replaced General Pershing as the United States commissioner, reported that suitable conditions for a plebiscite did not exist, placing the blame for the situation on the Chilean authorities. The plebiscite was never held.

By the time the sixth Inter-American Conference convened in Havana in January, 1928, tensions between Chile and Peru had eased, and discussions by the Chilean and Peruvian delegations at the conference set in motion informal negotiations which resulted in a proposal in June by United States Secretary of State Kellogg that the two countries resume diplomatic relations. The Chilean and Peruvian governments agreed, and direct negotiations for a settlement of the Tacna-Arica dispute began in Lima shortly thereafter. These negotiations finally bore fruit, and in May, 1929, President Herbert Hoover, at the suggestion of Chile and Peru, agreed to submit a proposal which had been carefully prepared by the two governments, giving Tacna to Peru and leaving Arica to Chile. Under the agreement Peru was also to receive a money indemnity equivalent to six million U.S. dollars, together with free port privileges, a customs house, and a railway station at Arica. This agreement was quickly transformed into the Treaty of Lima, signed on June 3, 1929. At the same time the two governments signed a secret protocol not to cede any part of the territory to a third party, a provision destined to be the object of serious Bolivian objection. Ratifications of the treaty were exchanged a month later, thereby ending the most long standing and thorniest dispute in Latin American diplomatic history.[25]

25. On the Tacna-Arica dispute see William J. Dennis, *A Documentary History of the Tacna-Arica Dispute* (Iowa City: University of Iowa Press, 1927); Robert N. Burr, *By Reason or Force*; Ossa Cruchaga, *Estudios de Historia Diplomática Chilena* (Santiago: Editorial Andrés Bello, 1962); also John P. Soder, "The Impact of the Tacna-Arica Dispute on the Pan-American Movement" (Ph.D. dissertation, Georgetown University, 1970), and Jorge Basadre, *Historia de la República del Perú* (5th ed., 10 vols.; Lima: Editoria "Historia," 1961–1964).

8 Foreign Relations in the 1930s: Effects of the Great Depression

JOHN J. FINAN

In the 1930s, for the first time in half a century, a major war broke out in Latin America. The Chaco War between Bolivia and Paraguay, lasting from 1932 to 1935, had an impact not only on the two countries in conflict but on several other nations in the hemisphere as well, when they attempted to bring it to an end.

This period was also one of important change in the relations of Latin America with the United States and nonhemispheric countries. The treaty rights to intervention which the United States held in Cuba and Panama were revoked. Also, the threat of military intervention by the United States, which hovered over Latin America in general for several decades of the century, was alleviated by new policies in Washington. The stabilization of the Russian Revolution, the breakdown of the European system of states as established after World War I, and in a very particular sense the Spanish Civil War, introduced new elements and tensions in foreign relations.

The Power Politics of the Chaco War

The war between Bolivia and Paraguay that began on a full scale in 1932 was a major event in Latin American international relations of the 1930s. It concerned possession of the Chaco Boreal, a region of some 150,000 square miles between the two countries in which a definite boundary had never been clearly established. The area had been considered of little importance during the Spanish colonial period, and since provincial boundaries had never been defined clearly it was difficult, if not impossible, to apply the principle of *uti possidetis*. However, having suffered severe defeats and loss of significant territory during the nineteenth century, both Paraguay and Bolivia considered this potential source of petroleum or other resources sufficiently important to fight for.[1]

A number of attempts had been made, beginning in the last quarter of the nineteenth century and continuing down to the 1930s, to work out an agreement concerning the boundary, but although treaties had been drawn up, none of them was adhered to. Both countries accepted the principle of *uti possidetis* as of 1810, but each interpreted the principle in a different way. Paraguay, which had carried on extensive colonization in the region, interpreted the principle more like the Brazilian interpretation—the area actually occupied. Bolivia, on the other hand, interpreted the principle as applying to the boundaries as defined in the colonial period.

Because the area of the Chaco which was in dispute was that between the Paraguay and Pilcomayo rivers, this region became more important to Bolivia after she lost her sea coast to Chile in the War of the Pacific (1879–1882); the Chaco river system offered an entry to the Río de la Plata and thereby an outlet to the Atlantic. For Paraguay, on the other hand, the disputed territory, which was much closer to her population centers than to those of Bolivia, was a potentially important area for further settlements and colonization as her population expanded, as well as a possible source of petroleum. Several agreements were signed toward settlement between the two countries in the years following the War of the Pacific, but none of them was ratified. In the 1920s both countries sought outside assistance in the training of military forces, Bolivia from Germany, and

1. On the Chaco dispute see David Zook, *The Conduct of the Chaco War* (New York: Bookman Associates, 1960); Leslie B. Rout, *Politics of the Chaco Peace Conference, 1935–39* (Austin: University of Texas Press, 1970); Bryce Wood, *The U.S. and Latin America's Wars* (New York: Columbia University Press, 1966); William R. Garner, *The Chaco Dispute: A Study of Prestige Diplomacy* (Washington, D.C.: Public Affairs Press, 1966); Spruille Braden, *Diplomats and Demogogues* (New Rochelle, N.Y.: Arlington House, 1971), especially the sections on his role as U.S. representative to the Chaco Peace Conference; and E. James Holland, "An Historical Study of Bolivian Foreign Relations, 1935–1946" (Ph.D. dissertation, The American University, 1967), where important documents from the Bolivian diplomatic archives are drawn upon. See also Gordon Ireland, *Boundaries, Possessions, and Conflicts in South America* (Cambridge: Harvard University Press, 1938).

Paraguay from France. Bolivia also began fortifying the portion of the Chaco she held, and Paraguay launched colonization projects in her section. When fighting broke out between the two sides in 1928, the hostilities were stopped by the mediation of other hemispheric nations. A five-member conciliation commission, comprising representatives from Colombia, Cuba, Mexico, the United States, and Uruguay, was created, but it succeeded only in restoring the *status quo ante* and the renewal of diplomatic relations between the two countries. The fundamental dispute remained unresolved and both sides continued preparing for war.

Hostilities broke out again in June, 1932, when Bolivian forces attacked and seized a Paraguayan fort. When the Paraguayan forces recovered it shortly afterwards the president of Bolivia proclaimed that the national honor was besmirched and called for Bolivian seizure of other Paraguayan citadels. In the face of this renewal of hostilities the other republics of the hemisphere immediately called upon the two countries to desist and announced that they would not recognize the validity of territorial acquisition by force.

Later in 1932 and into 1933, several other moves were made by third parties toward settling the conflict. A "Commission of Neutrals" was created, comprising representatives of several Latin American countries and presided over by U.S. Assistant Secretary of State Francis White. This commission proposed a settlement plan, including troop withdrawal and an agreement to accept arbitration; but the two belligerents rejected it. The foreign ministers of Chile and Argentina then offered a peace formula that also had the support of Brazil and Peru. This plan recommended a cease-fire, demilitarization of the area in dispute, reduction of military forces on both sides, and submission of the conflict to arbitration. Neither Bolivia nor Paraguay was willing to accept this formula without amendment, and Paraguay formally declared war in May, 1933.

The League of Nations also tried, unsuccessfully, to stop the fighting. In late 1933 it created a Commission of Inquiry. This commission gave up after only about three weeks. A second group, a Commission of Conciliation, appointed by the league in September, 1934, partly as a result of attention given to the question at the

Seventh (Montevideo) Inter American Conference (1933–1934), produced a proposal for a truce. Paraguay rejected this proposal because she was by then in almost total military control of the Chaco Boreal, and her forces were advancing to the foothills of the Andes. Angered by the sanctions that the league then imposed because of her noncooperation, Paraguay withdrew from the league.

Neighboring countries then renewed their efforts to settle the conflict. Fearing that the war would spread, President Arturo Alessandri of Chile, in early 1935, called upon Argentine President Agustín Justo to cooperate in a move to make peace. His concern stemmed partly from the growing Chilean support for Bolivia (in whom Chile had a traditional interest), following the expulsion from Santiago of the Paraguayan minister, who was charged with spying on the Chilean army. Argentina had apparently backed Paraguay in the war to the extent of supplying arms, offering military advice, and providing information on Bolivian military maneuvers. But Argentina feared that Brazil would also be drawn into the war in accord with the nineteenth century strategic concept of a diagonal axis allying Brazil, Bolivia, and Chile in the event of an expansion of Argentine power.[2] In response to the Alessandri-Justo correspondence a mediating group, composed of representatives from Argentina, Chile, Brazil, Peru, the United States, and (later) Uruguay, was established. Meeting in Buenos Aires in May, 1935, this group called upon the foreign ministers of the warring countries to join in a discussion of their differences. The invitation was accepted and the discussions that followed produced an agreement upon a truce, the creation of a neutral security zone, and a ninety-day period of demobilization supervised by a neutral military commission. If the dispute was not settled during this period of time, it was to be submitted to arbitration.

Execution of the truce agreement proved difficult. The first issue raised was the basic one of achieving the cease-fire. Bolivia rejected the cease-fire at first because her forces had been pushed almost entirely out of the Chaco Boreal and because, before agreeing, she wanted a commitment from Paraguay to submit the disputed territory

2. Spruille Braden, in *Diplomats and Demagogues*, 149, mentions his possession of copies of this Alessandri-Justo correspondence, which is unpublished as of 1976.

now under Paraguayan control to arbitration. Paraguay, negotiating from strength, favored an immediate end to the fighting and a mutual reduction in forces before addressing the territorial dispute. Bolivia finally accepted the proposed cease-fire, however, because, as her foreign minister realistically confided to the Bolivian delegation, there was a very real chance that Paraguayan forces would soon enter the oil-rich Bolivian provinces of Santa Cruz and Tarija; these, as well as the Chaco, might thus be lost to Paraguay.[3] Bolivia, in agreeing to the armistice, obtained a guarantee from the mediating powers that after the cease-fire the dispute would be submitted, if necessary, to arbitration. A protocol for a truce was then signed by Bolivia and Paraguay on June 12, 1935. The subsequent peace conference opened in Buenos Aires on July 1, 1935, and was to last for over three years.

A second issue of the truce related to the proposed security zone between the opposing lines. Paraguay understood this to mean a single line separating its advanced occupation forces from the Bolivian troops. Bolivia, on the defensive, wanted a separation area of many meters between its forces and those of Paraguay. She therefore interpreted the security zone as two lines (rather than one), a long distance apart. This difference in definition of the security zone was important for Bolivian-Argentine relations. Paraguay's interpretation, if accepted, would have left Paraguay in control of the road connecting Argentina with the oil-rich province of Santa Cruz. If the Bolivian view was accepted, this road would lie within a neutral security zone controlled by the mediatory countries.[4] Despite intensive discussion, this question was not resolved during the ninety-day truce period.

A third issue was that of prisoners of war. Paraguay had captured over 17,000 Bolivians; the Bolivians had taken about 2,500 Paraguayan prisoners. This disproportion in numbers raised a question as to how an exchange should proceed. Paraguay, fearing that a wholesale transfer would lead to renewed fighting, argued for a one-to-one rank exchange, leaving the remaining Bolivians to be exchanged after a final peace treaty was signed. Bolivia called for a complete exchange of prisoners by the end of the ninety-day demobili-

3. Holland, "An Historical Study of Bolivian Foreign Relations, 1935–1946," 75.
4. Braden, *Diplomats and Demagogues*, 156.

zation period. At the suggestion of the United States delegate, Spruille Braden, the issue was ultimately resolved in monetary terms. Paraguay agreed to turn over all the Bolivian prisoners of war if Bolivia agreed to pay Paraguay £132,231 sterling for the prisoners' support. The money for this purpose, according to Braden,[5] was provided by the three tin magnates in Bolivia: Mauricio Hochschild, Simón Patiño, and Carlos Victor Aramayo, who wanted an early end to the war. This arrangement, acceptable to both sides, laid the foundation for a new agreement of January 21, 1936, by which the truce was extended and the simultaneous exchange of all prisoners approved.

Another issue in the negotiations was that of control of transit in the neutral zone. Paraguay had by 1935 achieved military control of an important route in the zone, the Villa Montes-Boyuibe road, and was reluctant to weaken her position by yielding control of it to the Commission of Neutrals. In order to pressure the mediators to compel Paraguay to yield control of the road to the neutral military commission, Bolivia threatened to propose their censure at the Inter-American Conference for the Maintenance of Peace meeting in Buenos Aires, December 1–23, 1936. To avoid this action by Bolivia, the Chaco Peace Conference appointed a special committee to deal with the question. This group proved to be ineffective, however, and during ensuing months, even though governments in both Bolivia and Paraguay were toppled, the issue of neutral zone transit control remained unsettled.

Despite unresolved issues, by 1938 the conference decided to move directly to a negotiation of the fundamental territorial question. As a minimum, Bolivia sought in these negotiations a port or port rights on the Paraguay River, thus gaining access to the Atlantic by way of the Río de la Plata system. For domestic and political reasons she also wanted the final territorial decision to be made by an arbitration commission, so that the almost inevitable cession of most of the Chaco to victorious Paraguay would appear to be an action of third parties and not the result of her own military failure. Thus Bolivia, adopting a realistic and flexible policy in the negotiations, was es-

5. *Ibid.*, 161.

chewing the rigidity of a strategy based entirely on the principle of not yielding territory that Paraguay had acquired by force. At the same time, Bolivia was strengthening her hand at the conference table by rearmament. She admitted, for example, in May, 1938, that during the truce she had acquired armaments valued at $25 million (U.S.) and that she was retraining her armies for possible future action in the Chaco terrain.

Bolivia also built diplomatic bridges to Argentina and Brazil with a view to obtaining their support in the negotiations, holding out to both the bait of Bolivian oil. Her overture to Argentina manifested unusual diplomatic flexibility, because it was widely believed that Argentina had supported Paraguay during the war and because the Argentine foreign minister, Carlos Saavedra Lamas, had often appeared unfriendly during the Chaco Peace Conference. In December, 1936, the two countries created a binational economic study group and in September they also agreed to study the feasibility of railroad construction from Yacuiba, on the Argentine-Bolivian border, to Bolivia's oil-rich Santa Cruz, passing through a region then under Paraguayan military control.

Another aspect of the power politics of the Chaco war settlement appeared about the same time when Bolivia signed with Brazil agreements for similar feasibility studies of railroad construction from Brazil to Bolivia's eastern lowland area and for joint development of new oil fields in the Chaco region. After these accords were formalized in treaties early in 1938, Brazil announced she would not recognize any territorial settlement of the Chaco War that did not have Bolivia's acquiescence.

Paraguay had three goals in the territorial settlement negotiations. First, she sought to retain as much as possible of the Chaco territory she had occupied in the course of the war. Second, she hoped to block Bolivian direct access to the strategic Paraguay River and thereby reduce the vulnerability of Asunción to attack. Third, in view of her battlefield gains, she understandably opposed a territorial settlement by arbitration.

The Treaty of Peace that was finally signed between the two countries in Buenos Aires on July 21, 1938, was a compromise between the demands of the two warring sides. The boundary line defined by the mediatory powers did not include for Bolivia a major port of the Paraguay River, but it did give to Bolivia a significant amount of territory then under Paraguayan military control. The line drawn gave Bolivia a comfortable buffer of about sixty miles, separating Paraguay from the Bolivian oil-rich Camiri region and from the important Villa Montes-Boyuibe road. Also, as a sop to public opinion in both countries, it was agreed that the decision of the boundary should not be made known until after the mediatory countries "arbitrated" it, that is, until it was announced publicly as an arbitral decision, rather than as a commitment that representatives of both sides at the peace conference had approved. The treaty was ratified by both Bolivia and Paraguay on August 10, 1938, and diplomatic relations between the two countries were resumed in November of that year.

New Relations with the United States

A major change in the relations of the Latin American countries with the United States took place during the 1930s. The hostility which most of them had felt toward the United States was significantly reduced. A major factor in this transformation was the imaginative and eloquently articulated "Good Neighbor Policy" toward Latin America initiated by President Franklin D. Roosevelt and his secretary of state, Cordell Hull. Some of the elements of this policy were already in existence in the closing years of the Hoover administration.[6] Events in Europe and the Far East also contributed to its enunciation, but it was the bold and well-publicized initiative of the Roosevelt administration that captured the imagination of most of the Latin American countries and encouraged them to participate, as World War II loomed, in multilateral programs for hemisphere defense.

What were the factors contributing to the creation of the Good Neighbor Policy?[7] Certainly an overwhelming element was the resentment of many Latin American nations toward United States mili-

6. See Alexander de Conde, *Herbert Hoover's Latin American Policy* (Stanford: Stanford University Press, 1951).
7. An excellent study of this question is Bryce Wood's *The Making of the Good Neighbor Policy* (New York: Columbia University Press, 1961).

tary interventions in the Caribbean and in Central America. During preceding decades, the United States had intervened militarily in Cuba, Panama, the Dominican Republic, Haiti, Nicaragua, and Mexico. Argentina, very early in the century, in the principle enunciated by Foreign Minister Luis Drago, stated the Latin American opposition to the use of military force by large states to achieve objectives in relation to smaller states. Chile had launched a campaign, beginning about 1910, for acceptance of an "American international law" which included the principle of nonintervention.

During the last years of the Hoover administration and the first years of that of Franklin Roosevelt, it was becoming clear that the interests of the United States in Latin America as a whole could no longer be served by a continuation of the interventionist policies of a more limited vision that had developed during the preceding three decades. Another factor contributing to the change of policy by the United States transcended this hemisphere, involving U.S. relations with Japan and China. An obvious ambiguity existed between word and deed in the stated concern of the United States with Japanese interventions and expansion in the Far East and the record of U.S. interventions in Latin America. The "Open Door" in China contradicted the Roosevelt Corollary.

The Good Neighbor Policy was made up of three separate but related policy changes. Each was a drastic reversal of stance on the part of the United States as represented by actions and policy statements less than a decade before. The first and most important of these new positions was that of nonintervention; this was a policy commitment not to use the armed forces of the United States to intervene in the Latin American countries. The second element of the Good Neighbor Policy was, to use Bryce Wood's term, noninterference, a commitment not to use the policy of recognition or other diplomatic pressures to assure the coming to power of Latin American governments acceptable to the United States. It will be recalled in this connection that a notable use of the recognition power was the constitutional criterion imposed on Mexican governments as a basis of recognition by President Woodrow Wilson. A third part of the Good Neighbor Policy was a trade policy of tariff reciprocity. The U.S. Congress adopted, on the urging of Cordell Hull, a policy that permitted the reduction by bilateral agreement of tariffs on many of the goods imported from Latin America, in exchange for similar reduction in Latin American customs.

This chapter will focus attention on the application of the first of these policy positions, to which the United States first formally committed itself at the inter-American conference held at Montevideo in 1933, and to the Latin American policy reaction to it. The United States delegation at Montevideo, headed by Secretary of State Cordell Hull, along with other participants signed a Convention on the Rights and Duties of States, the most significant provision of which was its Article 8: "No state has the right to intervene in the internal affairs of another." While noting a reservation that might be required by existing treaty obligations toward Cuba and Panama, Secretary Hull told the conference firmly: "I feel safe in undertaking to say that under our support of the general principle of nonintervention as has been suggested, no government need fear any intervention on the part of the United States under the Roosevelt administration."[8] A few days later, President Roosevelt, in the United States, declared, "The definite policy of the United States from now on is one opposed to armed intervention." The United States pledge to nonintervention was ratified after the approval of the U.S. Senate, and was reiterated at the special Inter-American Conference in Buenos Aires in 1936. In the following pages of this chapter the policies of four countries in testing this commitment are examined.

Cuba

Cuba emerged as a major issue in inter-American relations again in the early 1930s. The island republic was experiencing a severe depression, owing to an extreme drop in the international price of sugar, her most important export product. In 1932, for example, Cuban sugar was selling at an all-time low of about one-half cent per pound as compared with a price about four times higher in 1928. Further, the

8. An interesting, behind-the-scenes account of the conference where the principles of nonintervention were enunciated may be read in Samuel G. Inman, *Inter-American Conferences, 1826–1954: History and Problems* (Washington: University Press of Washington, D.C., 1965), Chap. 11.

country was under the control of a president, Gerardo Machado, who was governing dictatorially; he had extended his term arbitrarily and was using harsh measures to quash a growing opposition.[9] Although he had promised when elected to negotiate an end to the Platt Amendment, and not to borrow money in the United States, he had failed in the first and had to resort to the second.

The special relationship of the island to the United States, which reserved by treaty the right to intervene to maintain constitutional government and the right to supervise Cuba's foreign financial and political relations, raised a serious question about United States policy toward and responsibility for a political and economic crisis the country was undergoing. Machado's movement toward dictatorship developed momentum in 1928 when he secured approval, from a rigged constituent assembly, to extend his term six years. Desiring to maintain good relations with the United States and to forestall U.S. intervention despite earlier vows against reelection, he cleared the additional term with the Coolidge administration. The United States posed no objection, on the grounds that the question of the presidential tenure was entirely a Cuban matter. Economic problems had been serious since a bust (1921) in the sugar boom that followed the First World War; the sugar crisis had become intensified by the world depression beginning in 1929, and was further exacerbated by the Hawley-Smoot tariff (1931), which increased import duties on sugar, among other commodities, going into the United States. This tariff vitiated much of the advantage which Cuba had previously enjoyed in the U.S. market by virtue of a previous Treaty of Reciprocity (1903) granting a 20 percent duty reduction on Cuban sugar.

Despite significant opposition and discontent within Cuba, Machado was able through repressive measures to control the country. He was encouraged because the Hoover administration, as enunciated by Secretary of State Henry Stimson, followed a policy of strict

9. An excellent account of Cuban foreign relations in this period may be seen in Luis E. Aguilar, *Cuba 1933: Prologue to Revolution* (Ithaca: Cornell University Press, 1972); see also Irwin F. Gellman, *Roosevelt and Batista: Good Neighbor Diplomacy in Cuba, 1933–1945* (Albuquerque: University of New Mexico Press, 1973); Wood, *The Making of the Good Neighbor Policy*, esp. Chaps. 2 and 3; and Louis A. Pérez, Jr., "Army, Politics, Diplomacy and the Collapse of the Cuban Officer Corps: The 'Sergeants' Revolt of 1933," *Journal of Inter-American Studies*, VI (May, 1974), 59–76.

avoidance of "meddling" in Cuban affairs; thus, Machado could, for a time, count on a continuation of his government without opposition or threat of Platt Amendment intervention by the United States.

The Cuban regime found an entirely different United States policy position after the Roosevelt administration came to power in March, 1933. Uneasy about a situation in Cuba where there was repressive dictatorship, widespread poverty, and the general perception common throughout Latin America that the United States gave its blessing to a tyrannical dictatorship, Roosevelt dispatched Sumner Welles to Cuba in May, 1933, with broad authority to deal with the crisis. Welles, a Latin American specialist in the diplomatic service who was a close personal friend of President Roosevelt, had instructions to persuade Machado to end the represssion and to pave the way for a new trade agreement that would alleviate the country's economic plight. When it became clear to Machado, after Welles' arrival, that the new ambassador was urging his resignation and the creation of a caretaker government to preside over new elections, Machado sought to discredit Welles and effect his recall. Welles, on his part, by his very presence, was offering hope to Machado's opposition. He helped to bring about a defection from Machado of the chief of staff of the Cuban army. Soon after, as a general strike spread, Machado fled the country. A caretaker government was formed in August, 1933, to plan for new elections.

Unexpectedly, in September, 1933, the enlisted men of the Cuban army and navy overthrew their officers and, under the leadership of Sergeant Fulgencio Batista, proclaimed a *golpe* in association with students and faculty of the national university who had opposed Machado. In place of the transitory government that Welles had espoused, the revolutionaries called to the presidency a member of the university medical faculty, Dr. Ramón Grau San Martín. Almost immediately after taking office the new president decreed a number of radical reforms, including the abrogation of the Platt Amendment, the eight-hour day for workers, land distribution to tenant farmers, and limitations on the employment of foreigners.

Scorning Grau as "impractical and visionary," Welles called unsuccessfully for military intervention by the United States, but his call was denied by President Roosevelt, on the advice of Ambassador Josephus Daniels of Mexico. Welles then urged nonrecognition, a policy that was to contribute to Grau's downfall in January, 1934. Only two Latin American countries, Mexico and Uruguay, had recognized the revolutionary government.

The new provisional government of Carlos Mendieta was recognized by the United States eight days after Grau's fall. Although the political crisis was thus temporarily relieved, immediate as well as more long-term economic problems remained serious. To deal with the short-term problem, the Mendieta government accepted, in April, 1933, a loan from the new Export-Import Bank of the United States to help finance, through the purchase of U.S. silver, the back pay of Cuban government employees.

The more fundamental problem of increasing the U.S. market for Cuban sugar, and thereby renovating the country's sugar industry, was addressed by Mendieta in a direct request to President Roosevelt for a definite sugar quota in the United States and for tariff reduction. The appeal was granted in May, 1934, when Cuban sugar was assigned a quota in the U.S. market and the general import duty was lowered 25 percent. A new commercial treaty with the United States, the first of Secretary Hull's reciprocal trade agreements, was signed in August, 1934, continuing special customs treatment as provided in the old commercial treaty of 1903. Sugar and tobacco, the most important Cuban commodities sold in the U.S. market, received a preferential tariff reduction of 20 percent. The treaty would remain in effect until the rupture of Cuban-U.S. relations in 1960.

The Mendieta government also achieved a revision of the treaty of 1903 with the United States which contained in Article III the infamous Platt Amendment. Article III was not only vexatious to the Cubans but an embarrassment to the Roosevelt administration, especially after Secretary of State Hull had supported at the inter-American meeting in Montevideo, in December, 1933, the principle of nonintervention. Mendieta's ambassador in Washington, Manuel Márquez Sterling, pressed Sumner Welles, now assistant secretary of state for Latin American relations, for treaty renegotiations. Together, they composed a revised draft which, with only minor changes, was ultimately ratified by both governments. The new treaty canceled the old one, thereby abrogating the Platt Amendment. It did, however, specifically affirm U.S. retention of the Guantánamo naval base. In the Cuban view, the Platt Amendment was erased not just through ratification of the new treaty but through the withdrawal from Cuban waters, by September, 1934, of U.S. warships that had been stationed there during the turbulent events of the preceding thirteen months.

Despite the termination of the legal basis of political dependence upon the United States, as embodied in the Platt Amendment, Cuban relations with the United States during the next two decades continued close. The fact that about 40 percent of the Cuban sugar industry was under the capital control of U.S. firms and that a preferential customs schedule and sugar market quota had been granted to Cuba affirmed a close trade relationship that was maintained between the two countries until the government of Fidel Castro after 1959 replaced it with a similarly intimate relationship with the Soviet Union.

Revision of the Panama Treaty

Just as the original treaty of Cuba with the United States presented a major problem in inter-American relations, so the Panama-U.S. treaty of 1903, also containing provisions impairing full sovereignty, had to be reexamined in the 1930s. But while the revision of the treaty with Cuba was drafted and ratified within a few months, the revision of the Panama treaty, worked out in 1936, took over three years of consideration before it was ratified by the U.S. Senate. Meanwhile, a large body of Latin American public opinion, as exemplified in the program of the Peruvian APRA party, began to support the position of Panama. The revised treaty aimed to remove from the original treaty the commercial provisions that were most objectionable or offensive to Panamanian sovereignty.[10] As later developments were to show, it was far from a permanent solution to the U.S.-Panamanian relationship.

10. See Sheldon B. Liss, *The Canal* (Notre Dame, Ind.: University of Notre Dame Press, 1967), Chap. 2; also William D. McCain, *The United States and the Republic of Panama* (Durham, N.C.: Duke University Press, 1937), Chap. 11.

The original treaty of 1903 was vexing to the Panamanians on two major counts. First, and most immediate, were the commercial tensions created by the commissaries of the Isthmian Canal Commission, established in the Canal Zone to the competitive disadvantage of merchants in Colón and Panama. Second, the fact that Panama was a protectorate of the United States granted the right to intervene in the event of disorder. This proved embarrassing and offensive to Panamanian nationalists who called for a return of the full rights of a sovereign state in the Canal Zone.

The commercial disagreements emerged early. Shortly after the United States took possession of the Canal Zone and established ports of entry, customhouses, and U.S. standard tariffs there, businessmen of Panama City protested that such state-within-a-state trade practices would mean their ruin. Supporting their position, the Panamanian government argued that only such activities as were essential to the protection of the canal should be carried on in the Zone. As one Panamanian official said, "But it has never entered the mind of either party that the United States should turn the Canal Zone into a source of revenue by enforcing high customs tariffs, even against the Republic of Panama, which is the lord of the territory and still holds over it rights that it has not relinquished."[11]

When the United States agreed in 1904 to remove the objectionable tariffs on trade between the Canal Zone and Panama, the commercial complaint of the Panamanians continued to center on the Zone commissaries and their sales of luxury goods and tobacco. Rigid restrictions on commissary sales were included in a treaty signed between the United States and Panama in 1926 but never ratified. The issue was partially resolved in the 1936 treaty revision by a limitation of purchases of U.S. goods in the Zone to residents who were rigidly defined. Also, imports into Panama, from the Zone as well as elsewhere, were to be taxed, while imports into the Zone from Panama were to enter free of tariff.

In addition to the commercial grievances, the treaty articles impairing Panamanian sovereignty were also addressed in the treaty revi-

11. See McCain, *United States and the Republic of Panama,* 32.

sion. The United States protectorate over Panama, which was provided in Article I of the treaty, in the "guarantee" of Panamanian independence, was canceled, as was Article VI, which gave the United States the right to intervene to maintain order. The United States also renounced the right, specified in the earlier treaty, to claim additional territory in Panama outside of the Canal Zone, as might be needed in connection with canal operation and protection. This last change created tensions in Panamanian-U.S. relations during World War II, as the United States encountered Panamanian resistance when it sought permission to establish military bases there. Finally, the annuity paid by the United States for rights over the Zone was increased from $250,000 to $430,000 as a means of compensating for the depreciation of the gold content of the dollar.

The ratification in 1939 of these treaty revisions did not by any means signify that issues between the United States and Panama concerning the canal had been resolved. The treaty changes were significant in eliminating commercial frictions, and in settling the question of Panama's international position as an independent sovereign state. They did not, however, address the issue of Panamanian sovereignty over the Zone itself. This area the United States continued to control, in the words of the 1903 treaty, "as if it were sovereign."

Bolivia: The Oil Expropriation Issue

It was during the Chaco peace negotiations that the Bolivian government, in March, 1937, canceled the Standard Oil Company concession and expropriated its properties without an offer of compensation. It was an issue clearly illustrating the effect of domestic politics—in this case revolutionary nationalism following Bolivian defeat in the Chaco War—on international policy. This Bolivian action was the first test of United States commitments to a policy of nonintervention made in the Treaty on the Rights and Duties of States in 1933 and in the protocol of 1936.[12]

12. See Wood, *The Making of the Good Neighbor Policy*, Chap. 7 and Holland, *An Historical Study of Bolivian Foreign Relations, 1935–1946*, especially Chap. 4, which cites unpublished documents from the Bolivian foreign relations archives.

The circumstances surrounding the expropriation are complex. Standard Oil entered Bolivia in 1922 and, according to Bolivian accounts, followed a policy of maintaining the Bolivian oil resources as an inactive reserve supply for Standard Oil properties elsewhere. In the view of the Bolivian government, the Standard Oil Company had not pursued an aggressive policy of extracting and marketing Bolivian resources, not even to the extent of supplying Bolivia's relatively negligible oil requirements. That there was some substance to this view appears in the company's putting such a low priority on its Bolivian holdings as to enter into negotiations in 1936 for their sale to the Bolivian government. The Bolivian government also charged, and this turned out to be an especially sensitive point on the part of both Bolivia and the company, that Standard Oil had not served national requirements during the Chaco War, refusing monetary loans and forcing the Bolivian government to look elsewhere for its oil supplies. Apart from the merits of the case, the expropriation probably served domestic political purposes in helping to bolster an unstable government presided over by the field commander of Bolivia's defeated forces in the Chaco War, David Toro (president 1936–1937). The Bolivian government also viewed the country's oil as means of redressing the imbalance of trade with her neighbors, especially Argentina and Brazil. In addition, she perceived it as a lever to gain Argentine support in a Chaco settlement that would be less harsh than the defeat on the battlefield would suggest.[13]

Bolivia's relations with Argentina in connection with the expropriation are still not entirely clear. But they were important for a number of reasons, indirect or direct. First of all, one of the grounds alleged by Bolivia for the uncompensated expropriation was that the company had secretly exported oil to Argentina in 1925/26 without a payment of the prescribed export taxes. Second, while the Bolivian government seemed to have been considering expropriation of the Standard Oil properties as early as August, 1936, other evidence suggests that

13. See Holland, *Historical Study of Bolivian Foreign Relations, 1935–1946*, 199, who cites a Bolivian foreign ministry document mentioning that the Brazilian government was told that a Bolivian action against the Standard Oil Company was contemplated.

she may have been subjected to pressure from the Argentine government of President Agustín P. Justo to expropriate when she did.

Argentina sent a delegation to La Paz in October, 1936, to discuss economic collaboration between the two countries. According to a report from the United States legation in La Paz, Argentina sought control of all Bolivian oil, offering the Bolivian government a 14 percent return, rather than the 11 percent paid by Standard Oil in taxes and royalties. Argentina is said to have offered in return her backing of Bolivia at the Chaco Peace Conference. The subject of Bolivian oil was also discussed in Buenos Aires in December, 1936, in conversations between the Bolivian and Argentine foreign ministers. The outcome of these conversations was an agreement to create a Bolivian-Argentine economic commission and an Argentine commitment to construct a railroad from the Argentine border to the oil-rich area of Santa Cruz, in exchange for the acceptance of joint development rights in Bolivian oil fields. Further evidence of Argentine influences appears in a guidance paper to Bolivian diplomatic missions issued a few days after the petroleum expropriation by the Bolivian foreign minister. The guidance paper announced support of a program of collaboration of Bolivia with Argentina in oil development, and a reversal of former policy positions of opposition to "Argentine imperialism."[14]

Whatever may have been the influences on her action to expropriate the Standard Oil Company properties, Bolivia confronted, after the action to this effect, serious tensions in her relations with the United States. During the previous year, Bolivia had sought to increase the market for her crude tin in the United States. This would be in competition with the refined tin imported there from Great Britain, whose smelters were refining Bolivian tin as well as that of Malaya.[15] After the oil expropriation, Bolivia noticed a distinct cooling of interest in the United States for cultivation of a market for her crude tin. There developed quickly, thereafter, a realization in the Bolivian foreign ministry that some accommodation with the United

14. Circular Dispatch from Bolivian Foreign Minister Enrique Finot, March 20, 1937, cited *ibid.*, 215.

15. For the proposal, see R. Henry Norweb to the Secretary of State, La Paz, Sept. 25, 1936, in *U.S. Foreign Relations* (Washington: Government Printing Office, 1954), V, 237–40.

States would be necessary. The possibility was that the U.S tin market would disappear, especially in light of the slow industrial recovery in the United States and the competition of the higher grade ore coming from British Malaya.

This view was confirmed in May, 1937, when United States Under Secretary Sumner Welles told the Bolivian minister in Washington, Fernando Guachalla, that all trade discussions with Bolivia were suspended until after a settlement of the oil question. The Bolivian government rejected any suggestion of diplomatic discussion of the legality of its expropriation decree, as well as any recourse to arbitration. The Standard Oil Company challenged the Bolivian decree in the courts; but the Bolivian supreme court, after a year of consideration, ruled on appeal, in March of 1939, that the company's demands were inadmissible.

In response to the resulting impasse, Secretary of State Hull advised Minister Guachalla in Washington that strategic considerations should be taken into account by Bolivia to fend off "lawless nations, hungry as wolves for vast territory with rich undeveloped natural resources such as South America possesses."[16] Taking the hint, Minister Guachalla pursued the goal of widening the market in the United States for Bolivian tin which, by 1940, became a critical strategic material, because the European refining sources were cut off and tin supplies from Malaya and Indonesia were threatened. In November, 1940, Bolivian tin producers signed an agreement for the export to the United States of tin ore in an amount sufficient to produce the sizable supply of eighteen thousand smelted tons. In other agreements, Bolivia contracted in 1941 to sell to the United States her entire tungsten production for three years, thereby ending important sales of this strategic mineral to Japan. Contracts supplying United States needs for zinc and lead followed. Bolivia also ousted an Italian military mission at this time in favor of one from the United States, and nationalized German financial holdings in the Bolivian national airline to allow control by U.S.-owned Pan-American Grace Air Lines.

Bolivian cooperation with the United States in these many ways, as

16. Quoted in Wood, *The Making of the Good Neighbor Policy*, 182.

the war in Europe was going on, provided a friendlier climate for reconsideration of the Standard Oil Company expropriation case. Both the United States and Bolivia were concerned about Axis activity in the country. This concern was brought to a head as a result of the exposure by the United States of a purported "Nazi Putsch" in Bolivia in July, 1941. A copy of a letter, supposedly from the Bolivian military attaché in Berlin to the German minister in La Paz calling for a German-supported overthrow of the Bolivian government was revealed by the United States minister there. A day later, the German minister was expelled from the country, several publications sympathetic to the Axis were closed, and a number of military officers and civilian political leaders charged with an Axis orientation were arrested. Three decades later the incriminating letter, which caused such an important shift in Bolivian policy, was proved to be a falsification contrived by British intelligence.[17]

Bolivia's need for economic assistance from the United States, increased by wartime trade disruptions but blocked by the Standard Oil dispute, to some extent explains why an agreement between the two countries was finally worked out in January, 1942 (immediately after Pearl Harbor) during the consultation of American foreign ministers at Rio de Janeiro. Bolivian Foreign Minister Eduardo Arze Matienzo appeared at the conference ready to sign an agreement with Standard Oil, offering the company $1 million (U.S.) as, according to the Bolivians, an "indemnity." The company asked for $3 million and insisted that the settlement be clearly a sale, so as not to jeopardize its properties elsewhere. A compromise was reached, whereby the Standard Oil Company properties were sold to Bolivia for $1,500,000 (U.S.), payable within ninety days. This settlement of the dispute opened the way shortly afterwards for an award of economic assistance to Bolivia from the United States in the form of $25 million for an economic development program.

The Mexican Oil Expropriation Case

About a year after Bolivia expropriated the Standard Oil properties in

17. Cole Blasier, "The United States, Germany, and the Bolivian Revolutionaries (1941–1946)," *Hispanic American Historical Review*, LII (February, 1972), 26–54.

1937, the Mexican government, under President Lázaro Cárdenas, expropriated the oil holdings of the major United States and British companies. The reasons for the Mexican move are complex, involving two and a half decades of controversy over the relative rights of the Mexican government and the companies, as well as several labor questions which were coming to a head in Mexico after 1935. Although frequently forgotten by the oil companies, the issue of the Mexican constitutional provision reasserting the right of the national government to direct the use of all sub-soil resources was the basic question. This issue had been partially resolved in the 1920s, under President Alvaro Obregón, when the Mexican government affirmed a position that the provision of the constitution of 1917 affirming state ownership of sub-soil resources were not, in effect to be applied retroactively. [18]

In 1935, all Mexican oil workers were organized into a National Petroleum Workers Union. This union became a major affiliate of the country's burgeoning national labor association, the Confederation of Mexican Workers, organized under the leadership of Vicente Lombardo Toledano. When their demand for increased wages and selected additional benefits were rejected by the companies in November, 1936, the oil workers union called for a strike. President Cárdenas stepped into the dispute, as Mexican law required, and called for a six-month truce, during which negotiations should continue. At the end of this period, the union declared a strike. The government then stepped in again, insisting that the dispute be submitted for decision to the Federal Board of Arbitration and Conciliation. The board met the union's demands more than half way, in August, 1937, ordering the companies to increase wages by 27 percent and to provide most of the fringe benefits demanded. The companies

18. On the issues raised by the Mexican expropriation of foreign-owned oil companies, see Howard F. Cline, *The United States and Mexico* (Cambridge: Harvard University Press, 1953), esp. Chap. 12; Wood, *The Making of the Good Neighbor Policy*, Chaps. 8 and 9; E. David Cronon, *Josephus Daniels in Mexico* (Madison: University of Wisconsin Press, 1960), Chaps. 7–10; Josephus Daniels, *Shirt-Sleeve Diplomat* (Chapel Hill: University of North Carolina Press, 1947); Harlow S. Person, *Mexican Oil* (New York: Harper and Brothers, 1942); from the Mexican point of view, Francisco Castillo Nájera, *El Petróleo en la Industria Moderna* (Mexico: Cámara Nacional de la Industria de Transformación, 1949); Lorenzo Meyer, *México y Estados Unidos en el Conflicto Petróleo (1917–1942)* (Mexico: El Colegio de México, 1968), Chap. 8.

then appealed the case to the Mexican supreme court, which upheld the decision of the Federal Board of Arbitration and Conciliation.

Confronted with the official support for the workers' demands, the companies at first agreed to a wage increase, which President Cárdenas accepted on behalf of the workers. The companies thereafter became dilatory, however, demanding that President Cárdenas certify in writing his acceptance of the reduced wage offer. In expectation of further conciliation, the companies then notified the arbitration board on March 15, 1938, of their noncompliance. When President Cárdenas received word of this position of the companies, he decided to expropriate the companies' holdings, making a public announcement of the action on national radio on the very evening the companies' note of noncompliance was issued. The expropriation decree was formally issued on March 18.

The diplomatic negotiations that ensued must be viewed in the larger context of the 1933–1936 commitment of the United States to nonintervention, as well as in the concern of the United States for good relations with its Latin neighbors in the developing of World War II. In notifying U.S. Ambassador Josephus Daniels of the expropriation, President Cárdenas said that Mexico planned to compensate the companies. The United States was dissatisfied, however, by this merely oral commitment to compensate, and sent Mexico a formal note calling for compensation. To back up its demand, it suspended the regular monthly purchases of Mexican silver. The Mexican foreign minister refused to accept the note demanding compensation until it was amended to include a note acknowledging President Cárdenas' oral commitment to compensation. The United States government refused to amend the note, but Ambassador Daniels took the liberty of telling the Mexican foreign minister, without consulting or informing his superiors in Washington, that the Mexican minister might consider the note as "not received." Few United States ambassadors to Latin America have exercised such discretion, but Ambassador Daniels relied upon his personal confidential relationship with President Roosevelt. The diplomatic impasse was resolved when the United States agreed not to publish the note, merely saying that it was "delivered."

As for the suspension of silver purchases, the United States was attempting to exert major economic pressure at a time when Mexico relied heavily on its export of this metal to its most important silver market, the United States, for much needed foreign exchange. In 1936, the United States had agreed to purchase five million ounces per month at prices somewhat higher than the international market price. The silver purchase suspension lasted only about three weeks, however; U.S. firms which produced 70 percent of the Mexican silver export protested. The realization in the United States that the consequent decline in Mexico's foreign exchange would reduce the market there for U.S. goods further influenced a subsequent U.S. decision to resume silver purchases at the world market price.

Another pressure on Mexico came from the United States and British oil companies, who attempted to stop sales abroad of Mexican oil by blocking Mexican use of foreign-owned oil tankers and by preventing the sale of drilling equipment to Mexico. Instituting legal suits, both in the United States and in Europe, they attached oil cargoes from Mexico on the alleged grounds that the Mexican seizure was illegal. The U.S. government, however, took no action to block the entrance of Mexican oil into the United States, thus limiting its official pressure to a denial of Export-Import Bank loans to Mexico.

One effect of the harassment by the oil companies was to push Mexico into close commercial relations with the Axis powers, as noted. At the same time, paradoxically, an American oil man, William Rhodes Davis, assisted the Mexican government in obtaining tankers for transporting its oil to Germany. By 1939, especially through these oil sales to Germany, Mexico reported it was exporting oil at full capacity.

Attempts at settlements of the dispute between the companies and the Mexican government were unsuccessful during the first two years after expropriation. With the exception of the Sinclair Company, which negotiated and settled independently, the companies were unsuccessful in effecting an agreement. In 1940 the U.S. government then stepped in, calling upon the companies and the Mexican government to agree to submit the dispute to arbitration. The Mexicans refused on the grounds that the issue was "of a domestic character."

Arbitration, they insisted, was intervention, coercive when dealing with an issue involving foreign nationals, unless a denial of justice was evident. This denial of justice, they insisted, was not evident.

After the fall of France in 1940, however, four factors contributed to a softening of the United States insistence on arbitration. First was the worsening of the Allies' situation in the war in Europe. The United States was now beginning to give more weight, especially after the blossoming of the Mexican-German oil trade, to U.S. strategic and security interests as distinct from those relating to the protection of properties of U.S. nationals in Latin America. A second factor was the settlement worked out in 1940 between one of the U.S. oil companies, Sinclair, and the Mexican government; the Sinclair agreement was sufficiently amicable to enable Mexico to claim she was not denying justice. A third factor was the settlement in 1941 of the claims of United States citizens for lands that had been expropriated under the agrarian reform programs of the Mexican Revolution. Mexico now promised to pay a total of $40 million (U.S.), thereby affirming in deed her earlier commitment to compensation following expropriation. A final factor was the psychological effect of the anticipated settlement, without arbitration, of the United States dispute with Bolivia over the latter's expropriation of Standard Oil Company holdings.

Therefore, instead of submitting the petroleum dispute to arbitration, the two governments, in accord with an earlier Mexican proposal, agreed to create a joint commission of two experts to evaluate the expropriated holdings and recommend the amount of compensation to be paid. The commission made its report in April, 1942, setting a value of $24 million (U.S.) on the expropriated properties of U.S. companies. This compensation, plus about $5 million in interest, was paid to the companies in installments over the next seven years.

The dispute between the British companies and Mexico continued much longer, however. The British government had followed the lead of the United States, but was less ready to reach a settlement. Finally, through U.S. good offices, Mexico settled with the affected British companies in 1947. Diplomatic relations between Mexico and Great Britain, ruptured after the expropriation action of 1938, were resumed during World War II. At the end of the war, an agreement was reached getting compensation for the expropriated British holdings in the amount of $81,250,000 (U.S.). This sum was payable in fifteen installments. With the addition of interest calculated from 1938, the total compensation was about $130 million.

In summary, Mexico made it clear from the beginning that she was willing to compensate for the expropriated oil holdings. She was adamant, however, in resisting the demands of the United States for submission of the dispute to arbitration. Mexico insisted that it was essentially a domestic question and that in offering the opportunity of judicial appeal within Mexico to the affected companies, as well as in her amicable settlement with the Sinclair Oil Company, she had made it clear that denial of justice was not applicable grounds for arbitration. She insisted she had never refused to offer compensation. Mexico had suffered temporary economic reprisal by the United States government when silver sales were suspended for a three-week period immediately after the expropriation. The United States oil companies had also attempted reprisals in their efforts to deny Mexico access to tankers and drilling equipment. Mexico had also turned to Germany temporarily for tankers, equipment, and the sale of her oil. But the shadows of World War II, as well as other factors, soon influenced the United States to accept an early Mexican proposal for final settlement of the dispute through a joint commission of experts, rather than through arbitration. The success of Mexico after the war in coming to terms with British companies was something of an anti-climax.

Ecuador-Peruvian Dispute

The boundary conflict between Peru and Ecuador over the "Oriente" resulted from a confusion in border definition of the colonial units and the emergence of wild rubber as an important resource in the disputed area. After many years of discussions of the border problem, the two countries had agreed in 1887 to submit the dispute to the king of Spain, who accepted the task in the following year but made it clear that other arbitral questions submitted earlier from Spanish America would take priority. Given the delay, Peru and Ecuador decided to address the boundary question through direct negotiations. Acting with extraordinary dispatch, Arturo García, the Peruvian minister, and Pablo Herrera, Ecuador's representative, signed at Quito in 1890 a treaty defining the boundaries in a way that granted Ecuador direct access to the Marañón River, which leads to the Amazon. The Peruvian congress refused to ratify the treaty when in the early 1890s an export demand for rubber increased, and areas assigned to Ecuador in the treaty were found to be rubber rich. When Ecuador refused to accept the Peruvian modifications of the treaty it was aborted.

Meanwhile, the arbitration process of the Spanish crown continued; it handed down in 1909 a decision that was essentially a compromise between the more generous limits assigned to Ecuador in the treaty of 1890 and the modifications insisted upon by the Peruvian congress in 1893. Ecuador refused, however, to accept the modest changes in favor of Peru, and the Spanish royal arbitration was nullified. When war between the two nations became imminent in 1910, the United States, Argentina, and Brazil stepped in to mediate. No agreement was reached, but war was avoided.

In the years following 1910, the disputed region became more and more occupied by Peruvian settlers and military groups. Ecuador showed little concern for asserting her interest by settlement or by a strong military presence. Both countries submitted the dispute in 1924 to the president of the United States for mediation. It was not, however, until twelve years later that serious consideration of the dispute in Washington took place. In 1936, under United States goading, the two countries signed an agreement to retain a territorial status quo while the investigation by the United States was going on. In September, 1938, the Washington talks were broken off at Peruvian initiative, probably because of her de facto control of much of the area. Bargaining from strength, she favored direct talks with Ecuador to resolve the problem. Ecuador, on the other hand, with no more than a legal claim to the disputed area, continued to seek a solution through mediation.

Armed fighting between the two countries broke out in July, 1941. Peruvian troops moved rapidly in control of most of the disputed area and advanced even into undisputed Ecuadorian territory. Several

Latin American countries, including Brazil and Argentina, and also the United States, called unsuccessfully upon the two countries to end the fighting. Peru's forces continued to move ahead during the next month. In September, she proposed a boundary essentially at the line of her troop advance. In October, defeated Eduador accepted a truce.

Peace was ultimately restored when representatives of the two countries met at the Rio de Janeiro conference of foreign ministers in January of 1942, shortly after the attack at Pearl Harbor brought the United States into the Second World War. Realizing that because of the war situation there was little further hope for mediation by the United States or by a powerful neighboring country like Brazil, Ecuador reluctantly agreed to sign with Peru a "Protocol of Peace, Friendship and Boundaries," often termed the "Rio Protocol of 1942." Under the protocol, Ecuador lost a significant portion of the Oriente, especially lands along the Marañón River that she had claimed, and, indeed, had been acknowledged as hers in the unratified treaty of 1890.

Since the end of World War II, Ecuador has expressed open resentment at what she feels was wartime pressure put upon her to sign the Rio Protocol of 1942. Beginning in 1960, she made it clear she looked upon the protocol as invalid and appealed without avail to the United States for support. As of 1976, the issue continues to be a major source of tension between the two countries.[19]

Peruvian-Colombian Dispute over Leticia

The origins of this dispute lay in the confusion of the boundaries of the colonial viceroyalties of New Granada and Peru and in the emergence in the twentieth century of the territory around the Putamayo River in southeastern Colombia and northeastern Peru as an important source of raw rubber. It had been exploited by a Peruvian company which had consigned the Indians of the region to virtual slavery in the gathering of wild rubber. The Peruvian company turned over its en-

19. See Ireland, *Boundaries, Possessions, and Conflicts in South America*, 219–30; the author is also indebted to an unpublished paper written at The American University by Stanley S. Houston, U.S.M.C., in 1969, entitled "The Oriente in Dispute."

terprise to British capital control in 1907, occasioning a British investigation of the charges of Indian abuse.

The territorial dispute was legally resolved in 1922 by a treaty between Colombia and Peru in which the disputed area of about four
thousand square miles between the Putumayo and Amazon rivers was
assigned to Colombia. The territory, trapezoid in shape, and having at
its southeast corner the small town of Leticia, became known as the
Leticia Trapezium. Both countries ratified the treaty, and Peru formally transferred the territory, which it had formerly claimed as a
part of its Department of Loreto, to Colombia in August, 1930. In
return, Colombia acknowledged Peruvian sovereignty over a small
parcel at the west end of the boundary line.[20]

Peruvian resentment at the loss of territory was felt nationally in
the downfall, shortly after the transfer, of President Augusto Leguía,
who had long ruled the country as a dictator. The tensions were expressed locally in Loreto, on September 1, 1932, when an irregular
armed group of three hundred Peruvians invaded Leticia and took
control of the town, raising the Peruvian flag. At first the Peruvian
government disapproved of the aggression; but as popular sentiment
in support of the action grew stronger, it shifted its position and asked
for inter-American conciliation. Colombia, understandably, rejected
the conciliation proposal, pointing out that she held treaty
sovereignty over Leticia. Both countries sent regular forces to the
area and armed clashes took place in early 1933. Unilateral attempts
were made on the part of third countries, such as Brazil and the
United States to effect peace; but ultimately it was the League of
Nations that was successful. First, the league council created in
January, 1933, a three-member committee to study the problem; it
recommended the appointment of a league commission to take charge
of the Trapezium, the assignment to it of Colombian forces as an
"international" police force in the area, during conciliatory negotiations, and the entire withdrawal of Peruvian forces. When Peru refused to accept this recommendation, the council condemned her and
appointed a thirteen-member advisory committee which invited

20. See Ireland, *Boundaries, Possessions, and Conflicts in South America*, 196–206.

Brazil and the United States, both non-league members, to participate in the committee's task of monitoring the conflict.

Three factors soon contributed to a change of position on the part of
Peru and acceptance of league intervention. First, Colombian forces
were successful in taking back control of a large part of the area. Second, Peruvian President Luis Sánchez Cerro, who had assumed a
militant stand on his country's regaining the trapezium, was assassi-
nated at the end of April, 1933, and the door was thereby opened to a
more conciliatory position. Third, the new Peruvian president, Oscar
Benavides, agreed to receive for talks a Colombian representative,
Alfonso López, an old friend from mutual diplomatic service in London, who became president of Colombia the following year.

Both Colombia and Peru agreed in May to accept the league plan.
A league commission, headed by a United States army colonel and
including a Brazilian navy captain, a Spanish air officer, with a Cuban
civilian as secretary, formally assumed control of the trapezium in
June. As Peruvian forces withdrew, a league flag was temporarily
raised over the area.

Direct negotiations between Colombia and Peru began four
months later in Rio de Janeiro, and an agreement was signed in May,
1934, reaffirming the boundary treaty of 1922. A month later, the
league commission formally transferred the trapezium to Colombia.

The Lauca River Question

The Lauca River, about 150 miles long, rises in the northern Chilean
Andes, and, following an S-shaped curve, one third of which is in
Chilean territory and the remainder in Bolivia, empties into Bolivian
Lake Coipasa. Tensions between Chile and Bolivia have existed for
over two decades concerning Chile's use of the river in her territory
for irrigation and hydroelectric purposes. The tensions are related to
the whole question of Bolivia's desire for an outlet to the sea.

The issue was created in June, 1939, when Chile announced that
she was planning to divert water from the Lauca for irrigation purposes. At that time Bolivia acknowledged Chile's right, under a general inter-American river-use agreement signed in 1933, to take such

an action provided the "natural regime" of the river were not modified. When Chile began executing her plan in 1947, a mixed commission of technicians reviewed and approved Chile's engineering projects for damming the river in her territory for irrigation and, additionally, for a hydroelectric plant in the dry Department of Arica. Bolivia at that time raised no objection.

It was in 1953 that the revolutionary government of Bolivia protested the entire Chilean project: Chile responded by citing the report of the mixed commission four years earlier. Bolivia protested again in 1959, seeking a progress report on the Chilean project and a re-creation of the commission of technicians, which was indeed again constituted, and again reported approvingly of the Chilean projects.

When Bolivia learned that an experimental diversion of water would actually begin in late 1961, she protested again, and, for the first time, tied the dispute to its concern for an outlet to the sea. She also charged Chile, before the OAS, with "geographic aggression" and "disturbance of the peace" and asked that sanctions be imposed on Chile under the Rio treaty of 1947. The OAS Council, holding that the Rio pact was not applicable, called upon the two countries to settle the matter between them peaceably. Bolivia proposed mediation of the dispute by five Latin American countries; Chile refused, but agreed to submit the matter to international arbitration on the grounds that the issues were legal and juridical rather than diplomatic and political. In the resulting impasse, Bolivia withdrew for about three years from the OAS Council and broke off relations with Chile. Relations between the two countries were later resumed but the dispute has continued unresolved. Final resolution may ultimately be related to a larger possible settlement between the two countries of the question of a Bolivian sea outlet.[21]

Colombian-Venezuelan Dispute

This controversy, like so many others relating to boundary problems

21. Useful summaries are in M. I. Glassner, "The Rio Lauca: Dispute over an International River," *Geographical Review* LX (1970), 192–207 and in R. D. Tomasek, "The Chilean Lauca River Dispute and the OAS," *Journal of Inter-American Studies*, IX (1967), 351–66. See also J. Valerie Fifer, *Bolivia: Land, Location and Politics Since 1825* (Cambridge: Cambridge University Press, 1972).

of the states of Spanish America, had its origin in an uncertain colonial border. During much of the nineteenth century, Colombia favored a settlement of the problem by arbitration, but Venezuela refused. Because of this disagreement, diplomatic relations between the two countries were broken off during most of the decade of the 1870s.

In September, 1881, Colombia and Venezuela agreed to submit the disputed boundary to the arbitration of the Spanish crown. Although King Alfonso XII died before the royal investigation was completed, both countries agreed to accept the intervention of Queen Regent María Cristina, whose government continued the case. She signed an arbitration award in 1891 defining the boundaries between the two countries, the most important aspect of which, from the point of view of the present, was the granting to Colombia of the entire Guajira peninsula. However, Colombia and Venezuela agreed to modify the terms of the award in 1894 when Colombia ceded to Venezuela ownership of an eastern portion of the Guajira peninsula; surprisingly, the Venezuelan congress refused to ratify this and other aspects of the very generous modifying accord. So the 1891 award of the Spanish government remained without execution.

In ensuing years, an issue arose whether the award could be partially executed. Colombia affirmed that she had a right to take possession of those boundary areas that were undisputed; Venezuela argued that the entire boundary question should be settled before any partial acquisition of territory on either side. They decided in 1916 to submit the issue to arbitration, by the government of Switzerland. The Swiss arbitral decision was handed down in 1921, favoring the Colombian position. As a result of this decision, the work of partial boundary marking went forward. Down to the present, however, final boundary demarcation, especially that relating to the Guajira peninsula and offshore waters continues in dispute.[22]

22. The major aspects of the dispute down to 1922 are discussed in Ireland, *Boundaries, Possessions, and Conflicts in South America*, 206–19. The Swiss award is discussed in James Brown Scott, "The Swiss Decision in the Boundary Dispute Between Colombia and Venezuela," *American Journal of International Law*, XVI (July, 1922), 428–31.

9 Latin America and World War II

Although all the nations felt the effect in their international relations, the complex story of the role of the Latin American countries in the Second World War may be best related from the vantage points of five major countries: Brazil, Argentina, Mexico, Chile, and Colombia. The policies and experiences of these countries are examined in this chapter against a background of the developing defense policy of the United States and of the multilateral actions of the hemisphere nations with reference to the war.

Strategic and Policy Background

The evolving hemisphere defense policy of the United States found expression in a series of strategic plans which, by the time the United States entered the war in late 1941, focused on the importance to United States security of the Panama Canal and the "bulge" of Brazil. In the United States defense view, the strategic significance of the canal made the entire Caribbean area important. Mexico, for example, was viewed as valuable not only because of its location on the United States border, but also to provide landing rights to U.S. military planes traveling to and from the Canal Zone. The Brazilian "bulge" was deemed vital because of its proximity to Africa; United States defense planners feared, on the one hand, the entry of Axis forces into the Western Hemisphere through this region and early recognized on the other hand the value of the "bulge" as a base for ferrying Allied troops by air across the Atlantic. With respect to the

222

war role of Latin America as a whole, the United States, after it entered the war, encouraged the Latin American countries to break off relations with the Axis, but not necessarily to become more directly involved through declarations of war.[1]

Certain multilateral actions of the hemisphere countries before and during the war provided important foundations for hemispheric cooperation afterward. Thus, at the inter-American conference in Lima, in 1938, it was agreed by resolution that the American states should consult with each other in the event of any threat to the peace, security, or territorial integrity of any one of them. The instrument agreed upon for consultation was a meeting of ministers of foreign affairs. Hence, after war broke out in Europe in September, 1939, a meeting was held in Panama, the first meeting of consultation of ministers of foreign affairs in keeping with the Lima declaration. At this meeting it was agreed to establish a neutrality belt around the hemisphere, consisting of an area of three hundred miles of offshore sea. The following year, at a second meeting of consultation of foreign ministers in Havana, the Lima agreement was reaffirmed that the American states would consult in the event of an extra-hemispheric attack on any one of them and that an attack on one was to be viewed as an attack on all. Here, more concretely than at Lima, the germ of multilateral defense consultation was established, to be formalized later in the Rio Treaty of Reciprocal Assistance (1947). Although it was viewed as less important at the time, another action taken at the Havana conference was to be of longer-range significance. This was the creation of the Inter-American Peace Committee, consisting of elected representatives of five American states who were given authority to mediate the peaceful settlement of disputes among American states.

Following the Japanese attack on the United States at Pearl Harbor in December, 1941, a meeting of American foreign ministers was held in Rio de Janeiro in January, 1942. The major decision of this meeting was a resolution recommending the rupture of diplomatic and other

1. A good summary of U.S. strategic policy at this time may be found in Stetson Conn and Byron Fairchild, *The Western Hemisphere: The Framework of Hemisphere Defense* (Washington: Government Printing Office, 1960).

relations with the Axis countries. Only Argentina and Chile delayed significantly in complying with the resolution, the latter complying a year later, and the former, in a token fashion, in January, 1944. Other measures adapted at the Rio conference included the creation of the Emergency Advisory Committee for Political Defense, based in Montevideo, to study and report on espionage and subversion. To coordinate military policies and actions, the Inter-American Defense Board was established, with a seat in Washington. It consisted of military representatives of all the American republics.[2]

Brazil

No Latin American country had a more active role in World War II or received more military and other wartime assistance from the United States than Brazil. Her nearness to Africa raised, on the one hand, the specter of possible invasion by Axis forces. On the other hand, it suggested the country's usefulness as a potential Brazil-Africa-Europe base for shipment of arms and troops. Both considerations made Brazilian involvement in the war virtually inevitable.[3]

Brazil's foreign policy toward the events in Europe that were to bring on World War II was at first by no means clear. In 1937 the Brazilian president, Getulio Vargas, proclaimed a new constitution, establishing the *Estado Novo*, with corporative ("fascist") provisions that generated speculation about Axis influence on the regime. We now know that Vargas was clearly influenced by the model and ideology of the Salazar regime in Portugal.[4] Vargas denied any close connection of his government with the Axis powers, despite the trade agreements he had entered into, and reasserted the traditional policy position of Brazil as one of close association with the United States.

2. Volumes dealing with this period in addition to that of Conn and Fairchild include John L. Mecham, *The United States and Inter-American Security, 1889–1960* (Austin: University of Texas Press, 1961), and Donald Dozer, *Are We Good Neighbors? Three Decades of Inter-American Relations, 1930–1960* (Gainesville: University of Florida Press, 1959).

3. For Brazil's foreign relations during World War II, see Frank D. McCann, Jr., *The Brazilian-American Alliance, 1937–45* (Princeton: Princeton University Press, 1973), and Conn and Fairchild, *The Western Hemisphere.*

4. The foregoing statement is supported in Elmer R. Broxson, "Plinio Salgado and Brazilian Integralism," (Ph.D. dissertation, Catholic University of America, 1972).

But his early record made it difficult for his ambassador in Washington, Oswaldo Aranha, to persuade U.S. public opinion of this change. When Aranha returned to Brazil in early 1938, he was appointed foreign minister and announced that the goal of his foreign policy was Brazilian economic development through close ties with the United States. On a scale that he could not have anticipated at the time, this goal was to be significantly advanced later as the United States introduced massive economic assistance to Brazil in exchange for wartime cooperation.

What was the extent of Axis sympathy and influence in Brazil? About one million Brazilians were of German ancestry and about one-fifth of these in 1938 were German-born. Almost all were concentrated in the southern portion of the country. There were over two thousand German social organizations in the country, and the Nazis controlled most of them. Hitler himself had expressed an interest in Brazil, declaring, "We shall create a new Germany there."[5] Moreover, in the 1930s, Brazil depended heavily on Europe, rather than on the United States, for military equipment. She was especially dependent on Germany for artillery purchases, sending the Krupp Company in March, 1938, an order in the amount of $55 million. After 1935, Brazil, shielding her gold reserves, also entered into special trade arrangements with Germany by which she sold her primary products advantageously in exchange for German-subsidized manufactured goods. By 1938, Brazil ranked in sixth place among all countries buying German goods; on the other side of the ledger, Brazil was selling Germany about one-sixth of her exports, a volume almost one-half of that going to her largest trading partner, the United States.

Many forces, however, worked to turn Brazil toward the Allies after the outbreak of World War II in September, 1939. First, the Brazilian government began to realize that the Germans would not be able during the war to continue indefinitely their end of the trading relationship. Indeed, by the middle of September, 1939, Brazil had German credits more than five time those held against Brazil in Ger-

5. McCann, *The Brazilian-American Alliance*, 80, quoting Hermann Rauschning.

many. Second, the leaders of the Brazilian military feared understandably that wartime obstacles would prevent German military supplies reaching Brazil. Third, the economic advantages offered by the United States were becoming clear and appealing. True, the United States had reneged, in the face of Argentine protests, on its offer of three old destroyers to the Brazilian navy. But a reciprocal trade agreement had been worked out between the two countries in 1935, and the United States had not taken any hostile action toward Brazil when in 1937 payments on her foreign debt were suspended, although by the end of 1938 she owed over $350 million on United States bonds.

The economic benefits dangled before Brazilian eyes by the United States were attractive. In early 1939, the Export-Import Bank offered Brazil almost $20 million to pay back obligations and offered additional credits for purchases in the United States. Too, the strategic importance of Brazil to U.S. military planning—the undefended Brazilian "bulge" was only about 1,400 miles and eight air hours from Dakar, French West Africa—held out a hope of greater economic assistance in the event the United States was drawn into World War II. In September, 1940, the Export-Import Bank lent Brazil $10 million and promised $20 million toward the construction of a steel mill at Volta Redonda, near Rio de Janeiro. The Volta Redonda mill was a major step toward Brazilian long-range industrialization.

Military cooperation with the United States had some limitations in the Brazilian view, however. The United States plan to dispatch 100,000 troops to Brazil to prevent an Axis invasion, following the possible fall of Britain, was rejected by the Brazilian government; Brazilian-U.S. cooperation never extended to include the landing of U.S. troops in the country. On the other hand, the United States was so anxious to assure Brazilian cooperation that in August, 1940, she offered arms to Brazil on acceptable terms.

After the United States entered the war, in December, 1941, Brazil realized that her only available source of material was the United States. At the end of January, 1942, Brazil announced at the inter-American meeting in Rio, then her capital city, her break with the

Axis. Two months later, the United States agreed to lend Brazil $100 million for the production of strategic items, $14 million for iron exploration and production and railroad development, $5 million for rubber production, and $5 million for health programs. This was the most important United States commitment made to a Latin American country during the Second World War.

What military measures were taken by Brazil during the war? First of all, President Vargas secretly asked U.S. Vice Admiral Jonas Ingram to assume responsibility for protection of Brazilian ships and opened all Brazilian facilities to the U.S. navy. Despite these measures, Brazil, by the end of June, 1942, had lost ten vessels to Axis torpedoes. These losses, together with the victories of the Germans against Russia and the inability of the United States to satisfy Brazilian gasoline and coal needs, raised questions in Brazil about the direction and outcome of the war. When in August seven more Brazilian vessels were attacked by German U-boats, one vessel being sunk with over 250 men aboard, the Brazilian reaction was different from what the Germans probably expected. Rather than retreating to neutrality, in the face of German intimidation, Brazil entered the war on August 22, 1942. In a remarkable move, President Vargas granted Admiral Ingram temporary authority over the Brazilian navy and air force. The Brazilians were not so willing to cooperate with the U.S. army, however, fearing the presence of a large number of U.S. troops in Brazil. Yet, eventually, Brazil granted the U.S. army the right to create two commands there, one at Natal and one at Recife. But these commands were limited to ferrying forces across the Atlantic.

Brazil also mounted an expeditionary force for combat in Europe, the only Latin American country to do so. The group took as its symbol a smoking cobra, because it was rumored that Hitler had doubted the seriousness of Brazilian desire to enter combat and had remarked that Brazilian forces would be in battle when Brazilian snakes started smoking pipes. The expedition was dispatched to Italy, arriving in Naples in July, 1944, where the force was further trained. Other detachments were sent in succeeding months. Despite problems of inadequate clothing (the group were forced to wear U.S. uniforms because their own dress proved inadequate) and hygiene, the Brazilians served bravely and effectively. Their most famous victory was the capture, under heavy fire, of Monte Castello in 1944.

The arms and economic assistance extended to Brazil by the United States during the war was far greater than that to any other Latin American country. It provided a base for Brazilian economic development as well as enhancing the strength of Brazil's armed forces. In March, 1942, Brazil signed an agreement with the United States by which she should receive $100 million (U.S.) in credit from the Export-Import Bank for the development of strategic material production. Brazil also was to receive, from the U.S., through a lend-lease agreement, military equipment in the amount of $200 million. By the end of the war, through its wartime role, Brazil had been able to develop a foundation for further industrialization. She had also created the most powerful armed force in Latin America.

Argentina

Of all the Latin American countries, Argentina's policy position toward World War II was the most independent; she was the last, by far, of all to break off relations with the Axis powers and did so under such pressure and so begrudgingly as to raise serious questions at the time about the authenticity of her commitment.[6]

When the Second World War began, the presidency of the country was in the hands of a civilian, Roberto M. Ortiz, who had come to power, as did his predecessor, supposedly through rigged elections, and who relied for support primarily on the military and landowning establishments. The country had an historically close economic link with Great Britain, to whom Argentina sold most of her agricultural products during the war; she was precluded from the markets of Axis-dominated Europe by the Allied blockade.

6. On Argentina's role see Robert Potash, *The Army and Politics in Argentina, 1928–1968* (Stanford: Stanford University Press, 1969), importantly drawn upon here; see also Arthur P. Whitaker, *The United States and Argentina* (Cambridge: Harvard University Press, 1955); Ray Josephs, *Argentine Diary* (New York: Random House, 1944); Harold Peterson, *Argentina and the United States, 1810–1960* (Albany: State University of New York Press, 1964); Spruille Braden, *Diplomats and Demagogues* (New Rochelle, N.Y., Arlington House, 1971), especially Chaps. 30–32.

The fall of France to Axis forces in May, 1940, was also influential in shaping Argentine war policy. Argentina had earlier affirmed a position of neutrality in the war, in keeping with her strong tradition of noninvolvement in the conflicts of the great powers (Argentina was neutral during World War I). For many Argentines, especially the Argentine military, the Axis victories in Europe tended to confirm the wisdom of this position. On the other hand, in 1940, the ailing President Ortiz, as he turned his powers over to his vice-president, expressed the sympathy for the Allies held by many Argentines. This sympathy was especially strong among the landowning class, many of whom viewed France as their spiritual home. "We are neutrals," Ortiz said in a message to the congress in May, 1940, "but Argentine neutrality is not, nor can it signify, absolute indifference and insensitivity."

Most of the leading officers in the politically powerful army, however, expressed their antipathy toward Britain, favoring an authoritarian political structure for the country. Their attitudes had been significantly shaped, not only by growing nationalistic sentiments, but by Nazi propaganda circulated widely among the officer corps, by the experience of several Argentine officers trained in Germany, and by the presence in Argentina of a six-man German military mission that advised the Argentine general staff and also taught in the Argentine military institutions.

The anti-British nationalism of many high army leaders was consonant with the sentiments of Vice-President Ramón Castillo, who succeeded Ortiz in July, 1940, as noted. Castillo tended to rely more and more heavily on the army for political support and to adopt their foreign policy postures as the war in Europe progressed. By mid-1941, however, the very success of the German military machine in Europe was causing significant division in war attitudes within the army. At the highest military levels there was growing concern that a victorious Germany might pose a threat to Argentina, as already shown by the extensive German espionage, infiltration, and propaganda activity going on in the country. Middle- and junior-level officers, on the other hand, appeared to have their nationalism and alienation from inter-American solidarity hardened by the German military successes in Europe; they showed little or no concern over Nazi spying or subversive activity in the country.

Because of this policy division within the army, Castillo's course became increasingly tortuous and contradictory. For example, despite his affirmation of staunch neutrality, he decided in November, 1941, to send an army-navy mission to the United States to discuss Argentine defense procurements under the United States Lend Lease Act. Also, following the Japanese attack on Pearl Harbor and the United States entry into the war in December, 1941, the Castillo government, while reaffirming Argentine neutrality, declared that in terms of military cooperation the United States would not be deemed a belligerent, perhaps following the Baltazar Brum principle set forth at the time of World War I.[7] On the other hand, through state-of-siege powers, Castillo cracked down firmly on pro-Allied demonstrations in Buenos Aires and, at the Rio conference in January, 1942, which was called to address hemispheric security issues following the United States entry into the war, the Argentine delegation insisted successfully that the conference resolution calling for a rupture with the Axis be not obligatory but only recommendatory. In short, Argentina was adamant in maintaining diplomatic ties with the Axis powers.

Such ambiguity in policy understandably created tensions in Argentina's relations with the United States, and a diplomatic tug-of-war began. Argentina, jealous of the U.S. military aid flowing to Brazil, hoped to purchase in the United States needed modern equipment for its army and navy. Emphasizing her treatment of the United States as a nonbelligerent, in accordance with the Brum principle, she notified the United States that as her contribution to continental defense and protection of her long coast, she had doubled the size of her army. The United States insisted, however, on an Argentine diplomatic rupture with the Axis as a condition for furnishing war material, pointing out that the military assistance being granted to Argentina's neighbors, especially strategically important Brazil, as well as to Uruguay, was justified by the fact that they had broken Axis relations.

Instead of yielding to pressures from the United States to terminate

7. See Baltasar Brum, *La Paz de América* (Montevideo: Imprenta Nacional, 1923), 25–26.

Axis relations, the Castillo government approached Germany with a request for military assistance. The hard-pressed German government rejected the request on the grounds of the insufficiency of such materials for the German war effort, even though, as the Spanish government seems to have suggested, the German armaments could be transferred to Argentina via Spain. As a result of this German rebuff, Argentina became more than ever concerned about her defenses, especially after her historic rival Brazil, relying on vast military assistance from the United States, entered the war on the side of the Allies in August, 1942. The question of how to gain a supply of armaments without breaking with the Axis remained unanswered through 1942 and the first part of 1943.

When in June, 1943, the Castillo government was overthrown by a military group who called themselves the Group of United Officers and the presidential chair was assumed by Castillo's minister of war, General Pedro Ramírez, a reassessment of the armaments question began. Ramírez's foreign minister, Admiral Segundo Storni, urged a rupture in relations with the Axis as a means of obtaining arms from the United States. In opposition to this position, more nationalist-minded officers argued that a break with the Axis would be an admission that Argentina was bending to pressures from neighboring Chile and Brazil who had fortified their borders. President Ramírez, consequently, worked both sides of the street in the quest for arms. He contacted the chargé of the German embassy in Buenos Aires and exacted from him a promise of arms. At the same time, Foreign Minister Storni appealed to Secretary of State Cordell Hull for armament.

This request of Storni to Hull in August, 1943, precipitated a crisis in U.S.-Argentine relations, as well as a domestic political crisis in Argentina. In the main, Storni seemed to be asking military assistance from the United States to offset the nationalistic and pro-Axis forces in the Argentine government. The tone of some sections of the letter, however, perhaps to appease the nationalists, was peremptory and provocative. Hull rejected the request bluntly, and the subsequent publication of the exchange of correspondence in Argentina precipitated Storni's resignation.

During the next month, September of 1943, President Ramírez sent a secret mission to Germany to negotiate the purchase of armaments. In charge of the mission was an Argentine naval reserve officer, Osmar Alberto Helmuth, who had apparently been in regular contact with a resident German secret agent, self-designated as a personal representative of Hitler. When Helmuth's ship arrived in Trinidad, en route to Spain, he was seized by British authorities who obtained a confession from him that he was himself a German secret agent.

These revelations, plus the information Washington received that the Argentine embassy in La Paz had been involved in the December overthrow of the government of Bolivia, toughened the United States policy position toward Argentina. The U.S. State Department threatened to publish its information concerning Argentine participation in the Bolivian *golpe*. To forestall such an embarrassing exposure of the Argentine role in Bolivia, as well as of the arms mission to Germany, the Argentine government agreed to break diplomatic relations with Germany and Japan. The rupture, announced suddenly on January 26, 1944, was justified officially on the grounds that an axis espionage group had been uncovered. The ensuing crisis created such dissension within the Argentine armed forces that General Ramírez was forced to resign as president in Febraury, 1944. The vice president, General Edelmiro Farrell assumed the presidency.

The change in government in Argentina provided an opportunity for the United States to employ the nonrecognition weapon as diplomatic pressure. Argentina's break in relations with the Axis, it was believed, was only nominal; acting on the grounds that the fall of the Ramírez regime was due to its rupture with the Axis, Washington deemed it prudent to deny recognition to the Farrell government. This policy of nonrecognition was to last for over a year.

Cut off from any possible source of armament in the United States or Britain during the remainder of 1944, Argentina sought again, even though relations were officially ruptured, to obtain arms from Germany. Towards this end, frequent meetings were held in Madrid between the Argentine military attaché there and representatives of German armament factories. Hard-pressed Germany could do little more, however, than take note of the Argentine requests; subsequently she rejected them.

Principally as a result of this lack of success in obtaining equipment from Germany, as well as Germany's declining fortunes in the war, Argentina reached a general political agreement with the United States and with other hemisphere countries in 1945. A resolution adopted by the Inter-American Conference on Problems of War and Peace (Chapultepec Conference) in Mexico City in March, 1945, called upon Argentina to declare war on the Axis and to control Axis espionage in the country. Shortly after the conference, Argentina declared war on Germany and Japan; she also agreed to institute controls over Axis espionage and subversion in the country. Later, with United States and Latin American support, she applied successfully for membership in the United Nations, when it was formed at San Francisco. By this time, also, she had reached an understanding with the United States on arms purchases under lend-lease.

By May, 1945, however, Argentina confronted a sharp reversal in the U.S. policy of conciliation. The change of United States policy was personified in the U.S. ambassador, Spruille Braden, sent to Argentina when recognition was extended after more than a year of delay. The day after his arrival, Braden held a press conference in which he indicated that he would seek to encourage constitutional democracy in military-controlled Argentina. He also met with Vice President Juan Perón and told him that the arms agreement could not be executed until Argentina acted vigorously, in accord with her commitments at the Mexico City (Chapultepec) conference, by turning over to the United States all Axis assets and agents in the country.

A personal vendetta developed thereafter between the U.S. ambassador and Perón. Braden carried out a number of maneuvers to force release of political prisoners in the country and encouraged U.S. correspondents there to report acts of political repression. For his part, Perón launched a leaflet and poster barrage against Braden, in preparation for Perón's successful campaign for election to the presidency in 1946. In August Braden was recalled to Washington, but his policy was affirmed by his appointment as Assistant Secretary of State for American Republics Affairs.

The feud between Perón and Braden continued during the next several months after Braden's departure from Argentina. In an effort to weaken Perón's political position, especially after it became clear that Perón would seek the presidency in elections planned for early 1946, Braden effected a postponement of an inter-American conference to negotiate a mutual assistance treaty, scheduled for the fall of 1945 in Rio de Janeiro. The justification for the postponement, in Braden's view, was that an Argentine power group that had flirted with the Axis during the war still existed there, making Argentine participation in any postwar mutual security agreement uncertain. Braden's strategy for defeating Perón in the presidential elections was to use the conference postponement as an occasion for exposing Argentine complicity in Nazi espionage and other activity during the war. Toward this end, Braden organized a special task force within the Department of State to comb the captured German archives and other information gathered by the Inter-American Committee on Political Defense in Montevideo for incriminating information. The findings were published by the Department of State in February, 1946, about two weeks before the election, in a "Blue Book" leadenly entitled *Consultation Among the American Republics with Respect to the Argentine Situation.* Perón's consequent stunning electoral victory, in spite of the "Blue Book" (Perón exploited the Braden harassment politically as an electoral choice of "Braden or Perón"), forced a change in U.S. policy. Two days after the election, the United States sent as ambassador to Argentina, George Messersmith, who shortly after his arrival in Buenos Aires announced a reversal of the Braden policy, even though Braden himself was to continue as assistant secretary until June, 1947. In accord with the change in U.S. policy, Argentina began to receive armaments from the United States, with a view to redressing the military imbalance with Brazil.

Mexico

Mexico's policy toward the increasing tensions in Europe was at first ambiguous. On the one hand, because of her problem in selling oil abroad following her expropriation in 1938 of United States and British oil properties, Mexico had turned to Axis markets, since the

United States and British markets were closed to her. The Axis powers were desperately eager to receive the oil, and Mexico worked out a trade arrangement by which she received manufactured goods from Axis countries in exchange for oil. On the other hand, Mexico had been the firmest of all the Latin American countries in supporting the republican side in the Spanish Civil War and had refused to recognize the Franco regime, in part because it had received German and Italian support against the republicans.[8]

As conversations between Mexico and the United States concerning the expropriation question began in 1939, Mexican policy toward trade with the Axis started to shift. At the same time, political antipathy in Mexico toward the Axis increased. For example, many partisans of President Lázaro Cárdenas, who had supported successfully the election of Manuel Ávila Camacho as his successor, resented politically damaging rumors against them, which they claimed were spread by Nazi sympathizers. According to these rumors, Cárdenas, Ávila Camacho, and some U.S. army officers had signed a "treaty" by which Mexico, in exchange for U.S. recognition of Ávila Camacho's government, would cede to the United States Lower California, the use of all Mexican ports as naval bases, a monopoly on the country's minerals, and permission for the U.S. army to occupy Mexico.[9]

By 1941, Mexico's opposition to the Axis was clear and vocal. During the early months of the year several officials of the Mexican government, including President Ávila Camacho, made speeches attacking Axis policies and conquests in Europe. Mexico began seizing Axis ships that entered her waters and cooperated with the United States in controlling persons and firms on a blacklist of Axis agents and supporters. In August, 1941, Mexico ended commerce with Germany and closed its consulates there.

A political group in Mexico that the Axis apparently was using to further its ends was *Sinarquismo*, a movement led by conservative Catholics who, in the name of "order," had drawn upon pro-Spanish

8. See Howard F. Cline, *The United States and Mexico* (Cambridge, Mass,: Harvard University Press, 1953) and Conn and Fairchild, *The Western Hemisphere.*

9. See Betty Kirk, *Covering the Mexican Front* (Norman: University of Oklahoma Press, 1942).

(Hispanidad) and Fascist ideology to organize in 1937 an active opposition to the government of the revolution. The movement was disparate in its social makeup, comprising some members of the old aristocracy in opposition to the anticlerical policies of the revolution, as well as discontented peasants who had been benefited only marginally or not at all by the land reforms that were sweeping Mexico. The hierarchy of the Catholic Church in Mexico denied connection with *Sinarquismo*, although charges were made that the movement was often directed by them; some church leaders supported the movement, while others spoke out against it. The *Sinarquistas* claimed to have one million members, a great part of them calling themselves "soldiers" in the service of the movement. Many of them were organized in agrarian colonies in, from a World War II vantage point, strategically important Lower California.

The extent of Axis influence on and manipulation of *Sinarquismo* to foment subversion before and during World War II will probably never be clearly known. The Mexican government, however, was firmly of the opinion that the movement formed an Axis "fifth column," and it was directly as a means of keeping *Sinarquismo* under surveillance that an espionage law was enacted in September, 1941.[10]

The signing of an agreement in November, 1941, to deal with the question of compensation to the companies whose oil had been expropriated in 1938, coming as it did about one month before the Japanese attack on Pearl Harbor and the entry of the U.S. into the war, prevented any serious obstacle to close cooperation between the two countries during the war. The mutual security concerns of Mexico and her northern neighbor were made clear in President Ávila Camacho's hemisphere-wide radio call for support of the United States. They found expression also in the creation of a Joint Mexican-United States Defense Commission in January, 1942. This commission supervised arrangements by which the U.S. army was granted air rights over Mexico as well as landing and refueling privileges in Mexican airfields for planes on a primary route from the

---

10. Harold E. Davis, "Enigma of Mexican Sinarquism," *Free World*, V (May, 1943), 410–16; Donald J. Mabry, *Mexico's Acción Nacional* (Syracuse, N.Y.: Syracuse University Press, 1973), Chap. 2.

United States to the Panama Canal. Working out this military cooperation was a delicate task because of the sensitivity of Mexicans to the presence of army air corps technicians at designated fields. This may be seen in the Mexican request, which the United States rejected, that U.S. military personnel not wear uniforms while on duty.

In May, 1942, German submarines assaulted and sank two Mexican tankers with a loss of twenty-one men. Germany ignored Mexico's note of protest and a Mexican declaration of war on Germany followed. The security of Mexico herself in the conflict consequently became a paramount consideration of Mexican policy. As a consequence, almost all of the forty million dollars in credit which Mexico received through the lend-lease agreements with the United States was used up in the course of the war for weapons and for training Mexican military men in the United States. Especially important to Mexico in this two-ocean war was her Pacific coastal area. President Ávila Camacho called former President Cárdenas back into military service and named him commander-in-chief of the force guarding Mexico's Pacific coast. In addition, strategically significant radar stations were constructed with United States assistance in Lower California.

The most dramatic contribution of Mexico to World War II was her expeditionary air force sent to the battle front in the Philippines. Composed of three hundred volunteers, the group, after training in the United States, was ordered in March, 1945, to a base close to the Philippines. They went into action in June and continued offensive action until the Japanese surrender in August; eight of the group lost their lives in the hostilities. These Mexican airmen, together with the Brazilian infantrymen in Italy, constituted the Latin American combat contribution to World War II.

During World War II Mexico moved to reopen diplomatic relations with the Soviet Union, broken off in 1927. She had been the first nation in the Western Hemisphere to recognize the Soviet Union in 1924 but had broken off relations during the Calles administration. Following her declaration of war against the Axis, it was natural that as a wartime ally she should reestablish diplomatic relations. The Soviet Union sent to Mexico one of its most experienced and important diplomats, Constantin Oumanski, who had served in 1939 as ambassador to the United States and then rose to be deputy foreign minister. In 1943 he created a large and important embassy in Mexico City and used it as a base for the opening of diplomatic and commercial relations of the USSR with seven other Hispanic American countries. Oumanski served as ambassador only about two years before his death in an air crash in Mexico City in early 1945. But this diplomatic tie, created during the war, has remained unbroken.

Chile

Like Argentina, Chile maintained firm neutrality as the Second World War spread to the Western Hemisphere with United States entrance into the conflict in 1941. Located on the southwest coast of South America, remote from the conflict in Europe, Chile, as in World War I, did not see her interests served by involvement. She also had a long tradition of admiration for Germany, extending at least back to the 1880s, when Germany was perceived as preventing European involvement in the War of the Pacific; after the war, a German general had been invited to reorganize the Chilean army on the Prussian model.[11] Also, corporatism, in the forms of Spanish and Italian fascism, or German nazism, gained favor in Chile in the 1920s and after. A national socialist party, influenced by the German Nazi movement, but reflecting strong indigenous misgivings during the Depression about democracy and a lack of central planning, was founded in 1932; it never had a large membership but several of its leaders were distinguished and influential intellectually. These Chilean Nazis, who had nominated former President Carlos Ibáñez as their presidential candidate in 1938, launched a coup in September, 1938, in an unsuccessful attempt to take over the government by violence just before the elections. The move was quashed quickly by the national police, but their killing of sixty-two young rebels who

11. Frederick B. Pike, *Chile and the United States, 1880–1962* (Notre Dame, Ind.: University of Notre Dame Press, 1963), especially Chap. 3; also Frederick M. Nunn, "Emil Korner and the Prussianization of the Chilean Army: Origins, Process and Consequences, 1885–1920," *Hispanic American Historical Review*, L (May, 1970), 300–322; Claude Bowers, *Chile Through Embassy Windows* (New York: Simon & Schuster, 1958), and his *My Life: The Memoirs of Claude Bowers* (New York: Simon & Schuster, 1962).

had surrendered garnered a backlash of public sympathy for the movement.

After World War II began in 1939, Chile's policy toward the Nazi party and German espionage activity was ambiguous. On the one hand, the Nazis were allowed to operate freely as a political party. On the other hand, there was intermittent harassment, as, for example, when several Nazi leaders were arrested in August, 1941, on the grounds of complicity in a plot to overthrow the government. Germany, for her part, sought to keep Chile neutral by preventing any occasion for diplomatic rupture; Chilean vessels were advised to have clear identification so as to avoid German submarine attack.[12]

Although Chile took a lead, following the Japanese attack on Pearl Harbor, in calling the consultative meeting of hemisphere foreign ministers, held in Rio de Janeiro in January, 1942, at which a recommendation for rupture with the Axis was voted unanimously, she herself refused to comply with the Rio resolution. She asserted that her defense vulnerabilities, especially in relation to Japan, were too great; Japan had made clear, she said, that Chile would not be attacked if she remained neutral.

Among the conditions Chile imposed for a diplomatic break with Germany and Japan were a special defense agreement with the United States and, through United States Lend-Lease, a supply of antiaircraft weapons and reconnaissance planes. The response of the United States, anxious about German and Japanese espionage emanating from their diplomatic missions in Chile but unpersuaded that the likelihood of Axis direct attack so far south was real, was limited. President Roosevelt sent personal assurance that Chile would be fully assisted in the event of attack, along with token defense matériel in the form of trainer aircraft and cannon. These proved insufficient, however, to change Chile's policy of neutrality.[13]

The issue was brought to a head in October, 1942, when U.S. Undersecretary of State Sumner Welles publicly charged Chile, along with neutral Argentina, with permitting the other hemisphere coun-

12. For this section the author has relied on the unpublished paper by Christel Converse acknowledged in the Preface.

13. *Foreign Relations of the United States, 1942* (Washington: Government Printing Office, 1962), V, *passim*.

tries to be "stabbed in the back" by Axis operatives. Going further on the offensive, the United States sent to the Inter-American Emergency Advisory Committee for Political Defense a memorandum on Axis espionage activities in Chile. In January, 1943, shortly after publication of the memorandum, which generated a popular demand in Chile for rupture, a diplomatic break with the Axis was announced. Chile signed in March, 1943, a formal Lend-Lease Agreement with the United States, receiving in the course of the war matériel in the amount of about six million dollars. Chile formally declared war on the Axis in February, 1945.

Colombia

Colombia had a special importance in World War II because of her strategic location in relation to the Panama Canal. During World War I, she had, like Mexico and Argentina, been staunchly neutral, a position that reflected the hostility to the United States engendered by U.S. involvement in the secession of the northern province of Panama. Colombian policy toward the United States changed after World War I, however, during the administration of Marco Fidel Suárez (1918–1921), who called for a close association with the United States, which he viewed as the northern "polar star" by which the Colombian ship of state was to be guided in the international sea. The hostility toward the United States was also assuaged by the Thomson-Urrutia Treaty of 1922, by which the United States granted $25 million in implicit reparation for the loss of Panama.

Colombia's policy toward the conflict in Europe that became World War II was importantly molded during the administration of Eduardo Santos (1938–1942).[14] President Santos initiated a number of policies that placed Colombia clearly on the side of the United States. Shortly after he was inaugurated, for example, he invited a U.S. naval mission to replace a British naval group for providing training and technical assistance. This invitation was later expanded to include a U.S. air mission. In mid-1939, not long before the start of the conflict in Europe, he affirmed what became Colombia's wartime

14. See David Bushnell, *Eduardo Santos and the Good Neighbor, 1938–1942* (Gainesville: University of Florida Press, 1967).

policy toward the defense of the Canal: "No one will be allowed to menace the security of the Canal from Colombian territory, directly or indirectly, in any form."[15]

Such a position did not mean, however, that there were not Axis interests in the country which presented problems for Colombian policy. The most important of these was the German administration of the nation's major airline, many of whose pilots and technicians were German, serving in the German air force after service in Colombia. The United States perceived threats to her security in the aerial surveys of Colombia, including the approaches to the Canal that were taken by German personnel of the airline, and in its extensive radio network, which was also under German control. Beginning in 1939, the airline company was revamped, providing for eventual Colombian government and private-sector majority financial control of the organization in association with Pan American Airways of the United States. In this restructuring, German personnel were discharged and replaced by Colombians and North Americans. Colombia broke off relations with Japan and Germany very shortly after the Japanese attack on Pearl Harbor—the first South American country to do so. She did not declare war against the Axis, however, because, as President Santos explained, Colombia was "not a military power which could make the weight of its forces appreciably felt in the . . . struggle."[16]

However, in accordance with the agreement of Rio de Janeiro in 1942, Colombia granted nonbelligerent status to all hemisphere countries who had declared war. At the same Rio conference of January, 1942, Colombia took a lead in supporting a call for a collective breaking of relations with the Axis by all American nations. In addition, Colombia cracked down on German agencies and associations that were believed to be subversive, including the Bogotá office of the German-controlled Transocean news organization.

Control of Axis activity in Colombia became even more intense in 1943 after the sinking of the Colombian schooner *Resolute* by a German submarine and the reported machine gunning of survivors in the water. All assets of Axis nationals in Colombia were frozen and Axis

15. Quoted *ibid.*, 15.
16. Quoted *ibid.*, 104.

nationals were forbidden to reside in coastal or port areas. Military cooperation with the United States also became closer. U.S. military observers, disguised as consulate officers, were permitted in several Colombian ports and other cities, and the United States was granted the right to establish a fueling base on Providencia Island to aid anti-submarine operations in the Caribbean.

Colombia signed a lend-lease pact with the United States in May, 1942, providing for a supply of defense materials in the amount of $16,200,000 (U.S.) repayable without interest and at a discount of over 50 percent. Actually, during the entire course of World War II, Colombia took only $6.5 million in defense supplies from the United States. To aid the wartime rubber shortage in the United States, Colombia accelerated the collection of wild rubber and agreed to send all of her rubber exports to the United States.

In summary, Colombia's wartime role was one of full support, short of a declaration of war, for the allied cause. Because of her strategic location as the South American country closest to the Panama Canal, she contributed by her stance of wartime friendship with the United States, for whom the protection of the canal held top priority in hemisphere defense.

In general, the relationship of the Latin American countries to World War II stands out in sharp contrast to their relations to the First World War. The main difference was a much higher degree of involvement, which led all the nations, with the notable exception of Argentina, acting in concert, to break off diplomatic relations with the Axis powers, or to declare war shortly after Pearl Harbor. Even Argentina joined the consensus toward the end of the war, as we have seen, declaring war under pressure from her Latin American colleagues, in order to participate in the organization of the United Nations.

10 Latin America and the Cold War

The intense rivalry or "cold war" that developed after World War II between the Soviet Union and the United States had a great impact on Latin America. Traditionally within the power sphere of influence of the United States, the region was subject to pressures on the one hand from the Soviet bloc to bring it under Soviet influence and efforts on the other hand by the United States, often in cooperation with individual Latin governments, to insulate the area from such pressures.

Postwar Regionalism

The Latin American countries anticipated the great power tensions that were to position them in such a tug-of-war between the United States and the Soviet Union. When the question of regional organizations arose at the San Francisco Conference (1945) to draw up the Charter of the United Nations, it was the Latin American representation that insisted upon the incorporation of regionalism in the charter. Under the leadership of Alberto Lleras Camargo, former president of Colombia, and in accordance with the principle of the Act of Chapultepec,[1] they pressed for the inclusion in the charter of Article 51. They refused indeed to accept the veto in the Security Council with-

1. The "Act of Chapultepec," signed at the Inter-American Conference on Problems of War and Peace in Mexico City (February 21–March 8, 1945) recommended the negotiation of a mutual security treaty and a "regional arrangement for dealing with such matters relating to the maintenance of international peace and security as are appropriate for regional action in this Hemisphere."

out it. This Article 51, by providing for the right of individual and collective self-defense, gave a legal basis for the Rio treaty of reciprocal assistance and for the extension and development of the Organization of American States, both of which were called upon frequently later in dealing with cold war issues.

The Rio treaty of 1947 (formally known as the Inter-American Treaty of Reciprocal Assistance) was the first of several regional treaties that the United States entered into for the purpose of binding defensively most of the free world as a part of a global cold war strategy. While the main thrust of the treaty is toward joint measures in the event of *armed* attack, provision is made in Article 6 for consultation in the event a participating country "should be affected by an aggression which is not an armed attack," thus opening a legal door for multilateral action against Communist subversion.

Likewise, the Bogotá Conference (1948), which drafted the Charter of the Organization of American States, also made reference to the cold war. Secretary of State George Marshall, who was the representative of the United States at the conference in Bogotá, referred to the "determined and open opposition of the Soviet Union to world recovery and peace." The very fact that a riot broke out during the conference, on April 9 (the *"Bogotazo"*), incorrectly blamed on Communists, was conducive to the passing of a resolution by the 1948 conference condemning international communism "as incompatible with the concept of American freedom." A similar anti-Communist position was taken at a meeting of the foreign ministers of the American states in Washington in 1950 following the outbreak of the Korean War. These earlier positions culminated in the anti-Communist resolution adopted by the Tenth Inter-American Conference in Caracas in 1954, as we shall see later.

While these collective actions were being taken to gird the hemisphere to face a perceived threat of international communism, several individual countries took actions to insulate themselves officially from the Communist bloc by breaking off diplomatic relations with Eastern European countries. During most of the 1950s only three Latin American countries—Argentina, Uruguay, and Mexico—maintained relations with the Soviet Union. As anxiety spread concerning the support given Communist conspiratorial agents by Soviet diplomatic missions, Latin American countries were inclined to blame embassies of Communist countries for stimulating or exacerbating public disorder. Indeed, shortly after the rioting known as the *Bogotazo* occurred in Bogotá in 1948, the Colombian government broke off relations with the Soviet Union, blaming the disorder and destruction on Communists.

An exception to the strong anti-Communist position taken by almost all of the Latin American republics was the foreign policy stand of the regime of Juan D. Perón (1946–1955) in Argentina. He enunciated a "Third Position" and sought unsuccessfully to lead the Latin American countries in this stance.

Domestic Aspects of the Cold War

Most cold war battles, however, were not fought in the Organization of American States or even among conflicting factions in government but elsewhere within the Latin American countries. Given the fact that the Soviet Union had official diplomatic relations with only a few of the Latin American republics, the mechanism that was used to exert influence within a country was the front group. Emanating from international movements of labor, students, women, etc., the local fronts sought to gain a foothold in national labor organizations, student federations, and peasant leagues. By controlling them and using them as a base, they hoped to influence political action. The tug-of-war that thus characterized the battles of the cold war was more often than not the quiet and usually undramatic political conflict within national organizations between factions, one oriented toward the Soviet Union and another toward the "free world." In the case of Latin America, the latter usually meant a group favorable to the United States.[2]

Labor was the most important politico-social group in the cold war arena in Latin America. Two regional labor organizations, the Confederation of Workers of Latin America (CTAL) and the Inter-

2. See the careful examination of various aspects of the cold war in Robert Alexander, *Communism in Latin America* (New Brunswick, N.J.: Rutgers University Press, 1957) and Rollie E. Poppino, *International Communism in Latin America, a History of the Movement, 1917–1963* (Glencoe, Ill., Free Press, 1964).

American Regional Workers' Organization (ORIT), representing respectively the Latin American representative of the World Federation of Trade Unions (WFTU) oriented to the Soviet Union and the Free World's International Confederation of Free Trade Unions (ICFTU), competed for affiliation of the national labor confederations of the Latin American countries. In addition, Argentina under Perón (1946–1955) launched a Latin American Labor Association (ATLAS).

A lesser but also very important group was that of students, whose national federations were likewise courted by international organizations, on the one hand the International Union of Students, Communist-oriented in Czechoslovakia, and on the other hand the non-Communist World Assembly of Youth, in Holland. Meetings of each of the international organizations, frequently held in exotic places and usually attended by delegates whose expenses were paid, had important Latin American student representation. Teachers' organizations in the various Latin American countries also became involved in these ideological conflicts.

Of all the battles of the cold war, the two most important did not concern organizations within countries so much as the governments of the countries themselves. These are, of course, those occurring in Guatemala (1944–1954) and Cuba (1959–). Guatemala was a likely cold war arena. The largest Central American country, strategically close to the Panama Canal, this preponderantly Indian nation had a long history of repressive, sterile dictatorships. The overthrow in 1944 of the government of General Jorge Ubico, who had been in power for thirteen years, opened the door to social revolution and the restoration of civilian government under Juan José Arévalo (1945–1951). Communist leaders rose to control the newly organized National Labor Confederation, however, and, in various positions, both official and nonofficial, exerted great influence on Arévalo's successor, Jacobo Arbenz. Decreeing agrarian reform, Arbenz expropriated a large portion of the holdings of the United Fruit Company, a U.S. enterprise that was a target of nationalists because in addition to its large banana plantation holdings, it controlled the nation's railway system and major ports. In foreign policy, Arbenz established closer relations with the Communist bloc, especially Czechoslovakia and Poland.[3]

The Caracas Resolution and the Overthrow of Arbenz

The Tenth Inter-American Conference, held in Caracas, Venezuela (March 1–March 28, 1954), had on its agenda at the suggestion of the United States the question of "Intervention of International Communism in the American Republics." This item was clearly directed toward the situation of Guatemala's moving closer to the Communist orbit. The resolution called for the adoption of appropriate action in the event of domination or control by the international Communist movement of the political institutions of a member of the inter-American community. A modification was introduced by U.S. Secretary of State John Foster Dulles to allay fears that the resolution reopened the door to intervention closed by the treaties of 1933 and 1936. It made clear that the resolution did not impair "the inalienable right of each American state freely to choose its own form of government and economic system and to live its own social and cultural life." All the delegations present at the conference approved the resolution, except Guatemala, Argentina, and Mexico, the latter two abstaining. Costa Rica was absent in protest against the dictatorial regime in Venezuela.

Events in Guatemala shortly afterwards were to have a long-lasting effect on the country's politics and foreign policy. The arrival in Guatemala in May, 1954, of a load of arms from Eastern Europe "sharpened the contradictions between the Army and the worker elements of the Arbenz regime by precipitating the issue of arming a civilian militia."[4] The shipment brought fear to Guatemala's neighbors as well as to the Guatemalan army, which felt its own strength would be thereby diluted. Dissident elements of the Guatemalan army, with assistance from the United States, moved across the Honduran frontier and brought about the downfall of the Arbenz govern-

3. See the detailed study by Ronald M. Schneider, *Communism in Guatemala, 1944–1954* (New York: Praeger, 1958).
4. *Ibid.*, 308.

ment in late June of 1954. The leader of the rebellious forces, Carlos Castillo Armas, assumed the presidential power and Guatemala was thereafter substantially removed from the cold war.

The Cuban Revolution

Of even greater significance in the cold war was the Cuban revolution of 1959.[5] For almost three decades, since the revolution of 1933, which overturned the dictatorship of President Gerardo Machado, Cuba had been under the control, direct and indirect, of Fulgencio Batista, a sergeant who emerged as a strongman. Following Batista's overthrow of the government in 1952, corruption became rampant and it was a widespread belief throughout Latin America that the Batista regime survived because of Cuba's especially close relation to the United States. This intimate relationship stemmed from a number of circumstances. The first factor is that Cuba had achieved her independence as a result of U.S. intervention in the Cuban war for independence in 1898. The United States thereafter became an important force in Cuban national life. Before U.S. occupying forces were removed, the United States had insisted that Cuba include in its constitution stipulations granting the United States the right to intervene in the event of civil disruption, limiting the Cuban right to contract foreign debts or enter into treaties with foreign countries, and leasing to the United States a naval base at Guantánamo Bay. In accord with this "Platt Amendment," not revoked until 1934, the United States intervened several times in Cuba on occasions of political instability.

A second element in the Cuban-U.S. relationship was the large amount of U.S. private capital investment in sugar plantations. By the time of the revolution of 1959, despite some decline after World War II, about 40 percent of the plantations engaged in sugar production were owned by U.S. corporations or individuals. A third factor was the complementary trade relationship between the United States and Cuba, the most important element in which was the quota of U.S.

5. The literature on the Cuban revolution of 1959 is vast. See Theodore Draper, *Castro's Revolution: Myths and Realities* (New York: Praeger, 1962), and Andrés Suárez, *Cuba: Castroism and Communism, 1959–1966* (Cambridge, Mass.: M.I.T. Press, 1967).

sugar imports guaranteed on the other side of the ledger to Cuba; almost all of Cuban imports came from the United States. In short, Cuba, at the time of the revolution which was to bring Fidel Castro to power, had a long history of unusually close political and economic ties with the United States, ties placing Cuba in a client relationship that could not but offend widespread nationalistic sentiments on the island.

The rise of Fidel Castro was not sudden. Along with several companions, he had organized an anti-Batista revolt, attacking an army barracks as early as 1953. Although several members of the rebellious group were killed in the assault, Castro survived, and was imprisoned. Within a year he was paroled and left for Mexico. In December, 1956, he returned to Cuba with a group of followers on the famous ship *Granma*. Believed to have been killed by government forces, Castro attracted world attention when an interview by Herbert Matthews appeared in the New York *Times* in February, 1957. Discontent within Cuba, especially on the part of middle classes, who were dissatisfied with arbitrary, corrupt dictatorial government, grew as Castro assumed the heroic role of deliverer leading a guerrilla band in the Sierra Madre. When the United States government in late 1958 placed an embargo on arms exports to Cuba, it was a signal to the Cuban military establishment that the United States would do nothing to support Batista. Therefore, it was just a question of time until the Batista regime would collapse. The time came on January 1, 1959, when Castro and his group moved into Havana, as Batista fled.

It is futile to debate the question whether Fidel Castro was a Communist before the revolution of 1959, but the effect of the Castro revolution on the cold war is obvious. Soon the thrust of Cuban foreign policy in the years 1959 and 1960 was to turn Cuba away from its close relationship with the United States to an equally intimate relationship with the Soviet Union. Even before the United States broke relations with Cuba in January, 1961, the U.S. sugar quota, so important to the Cuban economy, had been discontinued. A long-range commitment for the purchase of Cuban sugar was then made by the Soviet Union, as well as an agreement for military assistance.

The problem of the relations of the other Latin American states with Communist Cuba was to prove the most critical problem of the cold war. As early as August, 1960, the United States began pressuring the Latin American states to exclude Cuba from the Inter-American System. Largely at the initiative of the United States, the Seventh Meeting of Consultation of Foreign Ministers of the OAS (San José, 1960) adopted a declaration that "The Inter-American System is incompatible with any form of totalitarianism." As a condemnation of the government of Cuba, the statement was innocuous, but the United States in the spring of 1961 unsuccessfully took unilateral action, supporting an invasion of Cuba by Cuban refugees, the infamous "Bay of Pigs" invasion, to bring down the Castro government.

Of greater, albeit still limited, success in isolating Cuba from the other American states was the action taken at the Eighth Meeting of Consultation of Foreign Ministers in January, 1962, at Punta del Este, Uruguay. At this meeting, a resolution to the effect that Cuba had excluded herself from the Inter-American System by her adherence to Marxism-Leninism, putting herself in a position of incompatibility with OAS principles and objectives, was adopted. However, six countries, among them Argentina, Brazil, Chile, and Mexico, refused to go along with the resolution, introducing a significant doubt as to the efficacy of the action.

The most important event crystallizing Latin American hostility to Cuba was the attempt on the part of the Soviet Union in October, 1962, to place offensive nuclear missiles in Cuba. The irrefragable evidence presented by the United States to the council of the United Nations of the existence of such missiles in Cuba further coalesced Latin American sentiments for the isolation of Cuba. Finally, in July, 1964, at a conference of foreign ministers, convoked by Venezuela in accord with the Rio treaty, on the grounds of Cuban armed support of insurgency in Venezuela, the mandatory severance of diplomatic and trade relations with Cuba was approved. Only Mexico, of all the American states, clinging to the Estrada position, refused to comply with this action; during the next four years she alone of the Latin American countries maintained official contact with Cuba. The mandatory application of these sanctions was lifted in 1975 by the OAS countries.

Argentina and the Cold War

Argentina's independent stance with respect to the polarization of the post–World War II world was first manifested in the "Third Position" of Juan Domingo Perón, president from 1946 to 1955, who renewed relations with the Soviet Union after almost two decades of rupture.[6] However, as a way of assuring a supply of arms from the United States, Perón indicated in August, 1946, that in the event of actual war between the United States and the Soviet Union, Argentina would be on the side of the United States. Argentina participated in the 1947 inter-American conference at Rio de Janeiro at which the Treaty of Reciprocal Assistance was signed, but delayed ratification for about three years; the ratification, in June, 1950, coincided both with a credit of $125 million from the U.S. Export-Import Bank and with the beginning of the Korean War. At first, Argentina indicated a desire to take an active role in the war, but reversed herself as the initiative proved unpopular.

Argentina took two other actions in the early 1950s that expressed her "Third Position" in relation to the cold war. At the 1951 meeting of OAS foreign ministers, she, along with Mexico, voted against a resolution for military cooperation in defense of the hemisphere. Also, on the U.S.-initiated resolution at the Caracas conference of 1954, condemning international communism with implicit reference to the Guatemalan situation, she abstained, charging that the resolution constituted intervention. She sought further to blunt the thrust of the resolution by a move to condemn all interventions whether Communist or non-Communist.

With reference to the Soviet Union, Perón's Argentina negotiated, beginning in 1952, a significant trade agreement; she was the first of the major countries of Latin America to do so. At the same time, Perón did not burn diplomatic bridges to the United States, maintaining in 1954 and 1955 a strong interest in securing U.S. capital investment.

During the administration of Arturo Frondizi (1958–1962), Argen-

6. See Harold P. Peterson, *Argentina and the United States, 1810–1960* (Albany: State University of New York Press, 1964); also Alberto Conil Paz and Gustavo Ferrari, *Argentina's Foreign Policy* (Notre Dame, Indiana: Notre Dame University Press, 1966).

tina's first civilian president since the fall of Perón in 1955, two initiatives in cold war policy were taken. The first was a rapprochement with Brazil, with a view to creating a power alliance in South America that could play a mediating or conciliatory role in the East-West struggle, especially on the issue of Cuba. This initiative was dramatically emphasized at a meeting held with Brazilian President Janio Quadros at Frondizi's request in the frontier community of Uruguaiana in April, 1961, shortly after the Bay of Pigs invasion. The move never flourished, because Quadros resigned the presidential office a few months later and Frondizi was overthrown by the Argentine military early in the following year. But it is of interest because Frondizi had apparently sought to organize a bloc of South American states that would have included Brazil, Chile, Peru, and Uruguay, and possibly also Ecuador and Bolivia.[7]

Frondizi's second cold war initiative was a direct attempt at Argentine mediation between Cuba and the United States in 1961. He met secretly in August, 1961, with Che Guevara, who flew to Argentina while attending the first Punta del Este conference and who had indicated to Frondizi that Cuba desired a detente with the United States. Frondizi arranged a secret meeting for Guevara, while in Buenos Aires, with Richard Goodwin, then deputy assistant secretary of state for inter-American affairs during the Kennedy administration. These moves apparently led to nought, for when they were disclosed they created embarrassments both in Argentina and the United States.[8]

Under Frondizi, Argentine policy toward the question of Cuba's membership in the Organization of American States was ambiguous, probably because of the behind-the-scenes tug-of-war between the president and the military establishment. On the one hand, Argentina sought in vain to postpone the Punta del Este conference of 1962, at which it was voted to exclude the government of Cuba from the organization. On the other hand, it was the Argentine delegation at the conference that came up with the formula by which Castroist

7. See F. Parkinson, *Latin America, the Cold War and the World Powers, 1945–1973* (Beverly Hills, California: Sage Publications, 1974), 96.
8. *Ibid.*, 106.

Cuba was excluded, namely that Marxism-Leninism, which Castro openly espoused in December, 1961, was incompatible with the principles of the Organization of American States.

In summary of Argentine policies during the cold war, it can be said that she maintained relations with the Soviet Union during the entire period, establishing them just as the cold war was beginning. She deferred ratifying the Rio pact for three years, being one of the last Latin American countries to do so. She established new trade relationships with the Soviet Union while seeking public economic assistance and private investment from the United States. She made unsuccessful initiatives toward organizing a bloc of Latin American states to assert a Latin American cold war position independent of both the United States and the Soviet Union.

After the military assumed power in Argentina (1966–1973), Argentine governments took a staunchly anti-Communist and anti-Castroist position in close association with the United States. But when Juan Domingo Perón resumed power in 1973, he indicated a desire to reassert Argentina's earlier more independent foreign policy stance.

Brazilian Cold War Neutralism, 1960–1964

A new direction in Brazilian foreign policy, one that was to change for over three years Brazil's traditionally close association with the United States, was initiated by President Janio Quadros after his election in 1960.[9] His travels before taking office, to Cuba, Yugoslavia, Egypt, and India, and those of his vice president elect, João Goulart, to China and the Soviet Union during the same period, made it clear that the Brazilian cold war foreign policy of close association with the United States was being reexamined. Quadros called soon after inauguration for closer ties with Africa and Asia, set in motion procedures for reopening relations with the Soviet Union as well as with several other Eastern European countries, and suggested the possibility of diplomatic recognition of the People's Republic of China. In several concrete ways he manifested a suspension of Brazil's "unwritten al-

9. *Ibid.* See also K. L. Storrs, "Brazil's Independent Foreign Policy, 1961–1974" (Ph.D. dissertation, Cornell University, 1973), T. E. Skidmore, *Politics in Brazil, 1930–1964* (New York: Oxford University Press, 1967), and W. A. Selcher, *The Afro-Asian Dimension of Brazilian Foreign Policy* (Gainesville: University of Florida Press, 1970).

liance" with the United States. First of all, he ordered an end to Brazilian military training in the United States. He also displayed coolness to United States diplomatic representatives in Brazil, while manifesting close friendship with Cuban leaders, even awarding Brazil's esteemed Southern Cross to Che Guevara, then Cuban minister of industries. Also, he carefully balanced an official invitation to visit the United States with one to visit the Soviet Union. Finally, his was a very loud Latin American voice in condemning the United States-sponsored intervention in Cuba at the Bay of Pigs.

Within South America, Quadros also indicated a change in Brazil's traditional aloofness from her rival Argentina. He met with the Argentine President Arturo Frondizi in April, 1961, shortly after the Bay of Pigs invasion; as an affirmation of a new entente between the two countries, and in reaction against United States policies toward Cuba, the two presidents pointedly enunciated their commitment to the principle of nonintervention. This entente ended when Frondizi was overthrown in 1962.

The "neutralist" cold war policy innovations of Quadros, who suddenly resigned his office in August, 1961, were continued during the administration of his successor, João Goulart. In November, 1961, Brazil reopened relations with the Soviet Union after a rupture of fourteen years. Further, Brazil's policy toward Cuba, as articulated by Goulart's first foreign minister, F. C. San Thiago Dantas, was one of opposition to the imposition of sanctions against Cuba by hemispheric countries and one of support for Cuba's continued membership in the Organization of American States. Cuba's political system, he argued, was not incompatible with the principles of the Inter-American System, and that country, therefore, merited not exclusion but a special neutral status. On the occasion of the Cuban missile crisis of October, 1962, Brazil, along with Mexico and Bolivia, abstained from supporting an OAS resolution calling for action to stop Cuba's importation of offensive weapons. In this connection, Brazil, unlike Mexico, qualified her support for a blockade of Cuba during the missile crisis, on the grounds that it violated Cuban territorial integrity and independence. As another manifestation of independence in foreign policy, the Goulart administration, in April,

1963, entered into a five-year trade agreement with the Soviet Union, raising the annual commerce between Brazil and the USSR almost one third over that of 1962. During much of 1963 and early 1964, the Goulart government sought to advance from a position of policy independence to one of leadership of the entire Third World as, for example, in her actions at the United Nations Conference on Trade and Development in Geneva in 1964. During the last months of the Goulart regime, Brazil sought in vain to prevent the holding of an OAS meeting of consultation, under the Rio pact, to impose diplomatic and economic sanctions on Cuba.

After Goulart was overthrown at the end of March, 1964, the new military government made it clear that it was returning to a more traditional policy of closer association with the United States. While the new government did not break relations with the Soviet Union, it did take a lead at the Ninth OAS Meeting of Foreign Ministers in July, 1964, during which sanctions against Cuba were voted.

Mexico and the Cold War

Mexico's cold war policy was one of affirmation of independence from the United States while, indeed, frequently showing cooperation. Mexico supported the United Nations and United States action in Korea in 1950 and received naval matériel from the United States for protection of the Mexican coast on the Pacific. At the same time, Mexico made it clear that she would not allow herself to be dragged into a fighting war by the United States. At the 1951 meeting of OAS foreign ministers in Washington, Mexico opposed any agreement for military cooperation beyond that required by the Rio pact. Although Mexico indicated in 1952 a desire for a bilateral military agreement with the United States as a means of receiving military assistance under the U.S. Mutual Security Act of 1951, domestic opposition in Mexico to such cooperation prevented it.

The question of international communism in Guatemala moved to the center of Mexican foreign policy concerns as domestic support for the government of Guatemalan President Jacobo Arbenz increased. In 1954 former Mexican President Lázaro Cárdenas considered pressures against Guatemala to be of such magnitude as to constitute a renewal of the issue of interventionism. At the inter-American conference in Caracas in 1954, Mexico was the most adamant of all the Latin American countries in opposing even a watered-down resolution of condemnation of Guatemala, on the grounds that such action constituted intervention in the internal affairs of her revolutionary neighbor.

Mexico's policies toward the Cuban revolution of 1959 were in many ways the most independent of all of the Latin American countries. She alone of all of the Latin American countries maintained relations with Cuba without interruption. At the same time she was concerned with the whole question of hemispheric peace endangered by the tensions between the United States and Cuba. However, Mexico's evident desire to serve in a mediating role between Cuba and the United States was aborted by the Bay of Pigs invasion. Mexico then took an outraged stance, insisting on adherence to the principle of nonintervention and she opposed any meeting of consultation to deal with the Cuban question.[10]

After Castro declared in December, 1961, that he was a Marxist-Leninist, a serious crisis emerged in Mexican policy toward Cuba. To resolve the crisis, President Adolfo López Mateos appointed a consultative committee of all former living presidents to advise him. Probably in the face of economic repercussions from this policy crisis, especially a decline in foreign investment, Mexican Foreign Minister Manuel Tello announced in January, 1962, Mexico's condemnation of Marxism-Leninism, reasserting her respect for private property and indicating she favored exclusion of Cuba from the OAS, albeit supporting Cuba's right to a politico-social system of her own choosing.

Other ambiguities in Mexican policy were especially evident at the Punta del Este conference in late January, 1962, on the question of exclusion of Cuba from the OAS. On this issue Mexico abstained, while at the same time supporting a resolution declaring Marxism-Leninism incompatible with the Inter-American System. A similar contradiction is evident in Mexican policy with reference to the issue of a blockade of Cuba during the missile crisis. Mexico voted at the

10. Parkinson, *Latin America, the Cold War and the World Powers*, 110–111 and *passim*.

OAS meeting of October 23, 1962, in favor of a blockade, but abstained on the question of the use of force.[11]

With reference to the Venezuelan call in November, 1963, for sanctions against Cuba, in accord with the Rio pact, following discovery of a cache of Cuban arms in the Venezuelan Paraguana Peninsula, Mexico insisted on a continuation of diplomatic relations with Cuba. Toward the issue of intervention by the United States in the Dominican Republic in 1965, Mexico expressed clear opposition; yet she assumed a role of mediator at the extraordinary OAS conference held in Rio in November of 1965.

Thus a varied foreign policy pattern was manifested by the several Latin American countries during the cold war. Each of them asserted policy positions according to individual country interests and requirements of national security. To what extent could these varied interests be served by closer association? That was the question raised by proponents of an Alliance for Progress, discussed in the following chapter.

11. *Ibid.*, 166–67.

11 A Decade of Alliance and Integration

JOHN J. FINAN

The most significant aspect of the foreign relations of the Latin American states (excluding Cuba) in the 1960s was a commitment to work within a multilateral context toward the solution of problems related to underdevelopment. This commitment has had two major thrusts: one, in association with the United States, the Alliance for Progress; the other, carried out within Latin America, has been the movements for integration. In this respect, the independence of the Caribbean commonwealth countries and their participation in the Inter-American System has presented some new dimensions to the relationship.

Origins of the Alliance for Progress

In the same way that many germs of the Good Neighbor Policy may be noted in the years prior to the Roosevelt administration, so the roots of the Alliance for Progress are to be found in the decade preceding that in which President John F. Kennedy first enunciated and named the program. At several inter-American meetings in the 1940s and 1950s the Latin American states called for cooperation for development. As early as the Mexico City (Chapultepec) conference in 1945, an "Economic Charter of the Americas" was approved, calling for the "sound economic development of the Americas through the development of natural resources, industrialization, improvement of transportation, modernization of agriculture, development of power

258

facilities and public works, the encouragement of investment of private capital, managerial capacity and technical skills, and the improvement of labor standards and working conditions, including collective bargaining, all leading to a rising level of living and increased consumption." Little was done at the time to execute such a charter of development.

Also at the Rio conference in 1947, primarily concerned with working out a multilateral defense treaty for the hemisphere, the Mexican minister of foreign affairs, Jaime Torres Bodet, bespeaking the sentiments of many of the Latin delegates, declared that raising the standard of living of the masses was as important an obligation as joint defense. Again, however, there was no significant response from the United States. Secretary of State George Marshall told the delegates that the United States must give priority aid to Europe.

In the following year (1948) at the Ninth Inter-American Conference in Bogotá, where the Charter of the Organization of American States was drawn up, an economic agreement was signed calling for cooperation for development and the convening of a special inter-American economic conference at Buenos Aires. Largely because of the opposition of the United States, whose consistent position favored free trade ("most favored nation") and private rather than public capital for development, the economic conference was not held until 1957, although a preliminary meeting took place in Rio de Janeiro in 1954. In the meantime, however, the Latin American states fruitlessly reiterated their economic development concerns at the Fourth Meeting of Consultation of Foreign Ministers in Washington in 1951,[1] at the Tenth Inter-American Conference held in Caracas in 1954, and at a meeting of ministers of finance in Rio later the same year.

At the long-delayed economic conference which convened in Buenos Aires in 1957, the Latin American delegates called for com-

---

1. At this Washington meeting the Brazilian foreign minister bespoke some of the goals later enunciated in the Alliance for Progress: "By stimulation of industrial development through technical and financial assistance, the standards of living of the inhabitants of the various parts of the Western Hemisphere could be elevated, creating an atmosphere favorable for work and for the welfare of all."

modity agreements, encouragement of greater foreign capital investment, and especially for the creation of an inter-American development bank—an institution that the United States opposed on the
grounds that "the adequacy of capital to meet the needs of sound development is not a question of additional institutions but the fuller
utilization of those in being."[2]

The hostile reception, however, which then Vice President Richard
Nixon received during his trip to Latin America in the spring of 1958
suggested a change in the Latin American policy of the United States.
Shortly after the Nixon trip, President Juscelino Kubitschek of Brazil,
taking the initiative, wrote to President Eisenhower declaring, "The
hour has come for us to undertake jointly a thorough review of the
policy of mutual understanding in this hemisphere." In subsequent
correspondence, Kubitschek put forward his *Operação panamericana*
(Operation Pan-America) calling for a high-level conference of American states to consider the "disease of underdevelopment."

At a subsequent informal meeting of foreign ministers held in
Washington in September, 1958, it was agreed that faith in democratic capitalism was in jeopardy in Latin America and, therefore, it
was necessary to "intensify action to promote the greatest economic
development." A "Committee of 21," representing the presidents of
the countries, was created to study the main points of Kubitschek's
Operation Pan-America and make recommendations. From this
group came a recommendation in April, 1959, for the establishment
of an inter-American credit institution, the purpose being "to contribute to the acceleration of the process of economic development of
the member countries, individually and collectively." Such a bank
was envisaged as handling many of the "soft loans," such as those for
housing and education, which the Export-Import Bank and other
international financial institutions would not consider, as well as hard
loans of the type provided by the World Bank. Another recommendation from the Committee of 21, made at a meeting in Bogotá in September, 1960 ("Act of Bogotá"), called for measures for social improvement as well as economic development.

2. Remarks of Secretary of the Treasury Robert B. Anderson, quoted in John L. Mecham,
The United States and Inter-American Security (Austin: University of Texas Press, 1961), 375.

The Alliance for Progress Program

Not long after he was inaugurated in 1961, President Kennedy endorsed the Act of Bogotá and obtained from the U.S. Congress, to supplement the regular U.S. contribution to the Inter-American Development Bank, $500 million for carrying forward a program which Kennedy called the "Alliance for Progress." At a meeting in Washington of ambassadors from the Latin American countries in March, 1961, Kennedy said: "I propose that the American republics begin on a vast ten-year plan for the Americas—a plan to transform the 1960s into an historic decade of democratic progress." The United States agreed to "provide a major part of the minimum $20 billion, principally in public funds, which Latin America will require over the next ten years from all external sources in order to supplement its own efforts." In the distribution of the $500 million of the congressional appropriation, $349 million was assigned to a Social Progress Trust Fund of the Inter-American Development Bank, $100 million was designated for U.S. bilateral education and health programs, and $6 million was granted to the Pan American Union for alliance technical studies.[3]

The alliance was formally established by the Charter of Punta del Este in August, 1961, and was approved by all of the American republics except Cuba. Because of its importance in providing an overarching design for the development of Latin America, the charter, although not a formal treaty, merits detailed attention. Along with a reiteration of the principle of nonintervention and asseveration of constitutional representative democracy as a political goal, it called for agrarian reform, fair wage and welfare benefits for urban labor, provision of housing and health and sanitation measures, reduction in illiteracy, tax reform, and price stabilization of major Latin American export products. Thus in essence it was an agreement by the United States to finance economic development in exchange for a Latin American promise of social reform.

Each of the Latin American signatories of the charter was called

3. See J. Warren Nystrom and Nathan A. Haverstock, *The Alliance for Progress* (Princeton, N.J.: Van Nostrand, 1966), and Jerome Levinson and Juan de Onís, *The Alliance that Lost Its Way: A Critical Report on the Alliance for Progress* (Chicago: Quadrangle Books, 1970).

upon to prepare and present a "comprehensive and well-conceived national program for the development of its own economy." These national plans were to be worked out with the advice of experts, including the staff of the recently created Inter-American Development Bank. The great significance of the requirement in the charter for the formulation of national plans was that it stimulated many Latin American countries, particularly the smallest and the poorest, to engage in national development planning for the first time in their history. Whatever the shortcomings of the Alliance for Progress, especially in the attainment of major social reform, there can be no denying the long-range importance of this introduction of systematic and sophisticated planning in parts of Latin America that had not known it or had avoided it.

Aims and Achievements of the Alliance

The basic economic goal of the Alliance for Progress was an annual increase of 2.5 percent of the combined gross national product of the participating Latin American nations, a goal hard to achieve because of the high population growth rate of several countries. Up to 1969, the participants had achieved an average annual growth of 4.5 percent but this was reduced on a per capita basis to 1.5 percent because of the high birth rates and the decline in death rates caused by advances in public health.

Likewise, the social development goals proved difficult to attain. Almost all of the member countries which had not carried out significant agrarian reform (as was already in effect in Mexico, Bolivia, and Venezuela by 1962) drafted and approved agrarian reform laws, limiting maximum size of holdings and providing for redistribution to the landless. Except for the recent exceptions in Chile and Peru, these laws have remained by and large only partially executed, at best.

It would be premature for the historian to assess the successes and failures or to attempt to weigh the factors contributing to the lack of fulfillment of the unquestionably important goals of the Alliance for Progress. Several facile explanations have been made: the United

States excessively propagandized the program to compensate for the loss of Cuba and the Bay of Pigs disaster; the government-to-government, rather than people-to-people, structure of the alliance allowed oligarchic groups within Latin American countries to impede real social transformation. Another obstacle was the unerasable image of the alliance as essentially a bilateral arrangement between the United States AID program and the individual countries rather than a multilateral program, an impression that the Inter-American Committee for the Alliance for Progress (CIAP) sought with great difficulty to modify. Finally, the continued political instability in several Latin American countries frightened off many of the investors who, it was expected, would provide the $300 million annual private capital requisite to the program.

Intervention in the Dominican Republic

Especially disconcerting to the general mood of hemisphere entente, as represented by the Alliance for Progress, was the military intervention by the United States in the Dominican Republic in 1965. The occasion for the intervention was a revolt by several middle-level Dominican officers espousing the return to power of Juan D. Bosch, who had been deposed in September, 1963. Charging that the rebel movement had come under control of "Communist and Castroite" power-seekers, the United States sent into the Dominican Republic over twenty thousand troops during the last week of April, 1965. In a move to obtain sanction of the intervention by the Organization of American States, the United States proposed the creation of an inter-American peace force which was organized under Brazilian military leadership, about one-fourth of the troops coming from Brazil, Costa Rica, Honduras, Nicaragua, and Paraguay and the rest from the United States. The force remained in the Dominican Republic until late 1966 after the election of Joaquín Balaguer to the presidency.[4]

4. See Abraham F. Lowenthal, *The Dominican Intervention* (Cambridge, Mass.: Harvard University Press, 1972), John Bartlow Martin, *Overtaken by Events: The Dominican Crisis from the Fall of Trujillo to the Civil War* (Garden City, N.Y.: Doubleday, 1966) and G. Pope Atkins and Larman C. Wilson, *The United States and the Trujillo Regime* (New Brunswick, N.J.: Rutgers University Press, 1972).

Perhaps the very lack of success of the alliance contributed to a firmer realization on the part of the Latin American countries that only by acting in concert, apart from the United States, could they best serve their own national goals. This leads to an examination of the movements for integration in Latin America.

Integration

An exciting series of movements toward greater integration of Latin America paralleled the development of the Alliance for Progress.[5] There are a number of reasons for this. Certainly the example of Europe has been important. Too, the Latin American countries have become more aware of the enormity of the challenge of building heavy industry without markets transcending the national borders. In addition, the aspirations of Latin America toward greater recognition in the world arena can be best fulfilled, it is believed, through aggregation of several individual political and economic strengths.

The obstacles to integration are, of course, very great. Intraregional trade in Latin America is still a relatively small percentage of the total. Transportation and communications systems between and among the several countries are limited. Concepts of political and economic units within Latin America transcending the nation are still not widespread. Serious discrepancies in industrial development will also have to be surmounted.

These obstacles notwithstanding, several important integrative movements have been launched. The first is the Central American Common Market, which originated in discussions in 1958 among the five Central American countries, Guatemala, Nicaragua, El Salvador, Costa Rica and Honduras. A treaty signed in 1960 provided for the gradual creation of a customs union over a five-year period. Despite an early reluctance on the part of Costa Rica to participate and the continuance of historic tensions in the region such as found expression

5. A succinct analysis of the economic implications of integration in Latin America is in George Wythe's *The United States and Inter-American Relations* (Gainesville: University of Florida Press, 1964). Many larger issues are treated in Joseph Grunwald, Miguel Wioncek, and Martin Carnoy, *Latin American Integration and the United States* (Washington, D.C.: Brookings Institution, 1972).

in the conflict between Honduras and El Salvador in 1969, trade among the member countries increased during the 1960s by almost 800 percent.

About the same time that the Central American Common Market was getting underway, the Latin American Free Trade Association (LAFTA) was created. This organization came about on the initiative of the countries of southern South America: Argentina, Brazil, Uruguay, and Chile. A treaty was signed in Montevideo in 1960 establishing a Free Trade Zone. In addition to the above four countries, Peru, Paraguay, Mexico, Colombia, and Ecuador entered into membership. Venezuela later joined (1969). Like the European Free Trade Association, which perhaps served as a model, LAFTA countries maintain tariffs on imports from outside of the zone, at the same time working to reduce duties on intrazone trade.

Toward the end of the decade of the sixties, two additional integration groups were formed. The Andean Subregional Pact, signed in 1969, had five original members, Chile, Bolivia, Colombia, Peru, and Ecuador; Venezuela entered later. A Caribbean Free Trade Association, similar in purpose, has also been organized.

SELA

As another move to further Latin American integration, and as an expression of concern about Latin America's position in the international economic arena, an association of Latin American states to address mutual economic problems was proposed. This suggestion emerged from a common concern expressed in correspondence in 1974 between President Luis Echeverría of Mexico and President Carlos Andrés Pérez of Venezuela. A joint commission was created to deal with the matter and, in March, 1975, a recommendation was made for the creation of a Latin American Economic System (SELA). A meeting of representatives of Latin American countries was held in July, 1975, in Panama, at which was approved the creation of SELA. In October, 1975, another meeting of representatives was held at which the charter of SELA was signed. It provides for a council of representatives of member states, which is to meet annually and establish general policies for the organization, approve a budget, and elect a secretary general with a four-year term. The headquarters of the organization is in Caracas, Venezuela.

The potential of the integration movements within Latin America is real. As this volume goes to press, however, it is too early to assess the extent to which the Latin American countries are able to supersede the many impediments in their path, not the least of which are historic tensions and power rivalries among them, which are the warp and woof of their diplomatic history.

Selected Bibliography

The only study comparable in scope to the work here presented is that of Vicente Quesada, the Argentine diplomat and historian, to be noted in the following bibliography. The best general guide to the subject, though lacking comprehensiveness, is Part VII of *Latin America: A Guide to the Historical Literature* (Austin and London: University of Texas Press, 1971), edited by Charles C. Griffin and J. Benedict Warren. No more general bibliography exists, but David F. Trask, Michael C. Meyer, and Roger B. Trask have published an extensive *Bibliography of United States–Latin American Relations Since 1810* (Lincoln: University of Nebraska Press, 1968), listing over eleven thousand published items. Some nations, usually through their ministries of foreign relations, have published national bibliographies of their diplomatic relations. The best of these is Daniel Cosío Villegas, *Cuestiones Internacionales de México* (Mexico: Secretaría de Relaciones Exteriores, 1966). Peru has published a less ambitious one by José Pareja Paz Soldán and José C. Mariátegui, "Para Una Bibliografía Diplomática del Perú," *Boletín Bibliográfico de la Universidad Nacional Mayor de San Marcos*, XX (1950), 335–62.

The national archives maintained by all the countries usually contain a section of documents from their ministries of foreign relations, but conditions for their use vary considerably. Permission in advance is usually required and this permission is usually not given for documents of recent years. *Memorias*, frequently annual, published by the ministries of foreign relations and the messages of presidents to congresses are valuable sources. Most governments have issued various collections of documents bearing upon specific issues, and most have published collections of treaties. Brazil has published a good guide to her diplomatic records. For a general guide to the various national archives we have Roscoe R. Hill (ed.), *The National Archives of Latin America* (Cambridge, Mass.: Harvard University Press, 1945). It may be supplemented with that of Arthur E. Gropp, *Guide to the Libraries and Archives in Central America and the West Indies, Panama, Bermuda, and British Guiana* (New Orleans: Tulane University Middle American Research Institute, 1941). The most recent, and a very useful guide to these archives is Ronald L. Seckinger, "A Guide to Selected Diplomatic Archives of South America," *Latin American Research Review* (Spring, 1975), 127–53.

The national archives of the various nations with which Latin American nations have had important relations are, of course, useful sources for research. Guides to some of these collections may be found in Griffin and Warren, *Latin America: A Guide to the Historical Literature*, mentioned above. John P. Harrison, *Guide to Materials on Latin America in the National Archives* (Washington: National Archives, 1961–), is an invaluable guide.

General Works

Alexander, Robert. *Communism in Latin America*. New Brunswick, N.J.: Rutgers University Press, 1957.

Astiz, Carlos Alberto, ed. *Latin American International Politics*. Notre Dame, Ind.: University of Notre Dame Press, 1969.

Bailey, Norman A. *Latin America in World Politics*. New York: Walker & Co., 1967.

———. *Latin America: Politics, Economics, and Hemisphere Security*. New York, Washington, London: Frederick A. Praeger, 1965.

Bemis, Samuel Flagg. *The Latin American Policy of the United States*. New York: Harcourt, Brace, and Co., 1943.

Braden, Spruille. *Diplomats and Demagogues*. New Rochelle, N.Y.: Arlington House, 1971.

Brooks, Philip C. *Diplomacy and the Borderlands*. Berkeley: University of California Press, 1939.

Brum, Baltazar. *La Paz de América*. Montevideo: Imprenta Nacional, 1923.

Callcott, Wilfrid Hardy. *The Western Hemisphere: Its Influence on United States Policies to the End of World War II*. Austin: University of Texas Press, 1968.

Connell-Smith, Gordon. *The Inter-American System.* London: Oxford University Press, 1966.

Davis, Harold Eugene, *et al. Latin American Foreign Policies: An Analysis.* Baltimore: Johns Hopkins University Press, 1975.

Fenwick, Charles G. "The Problem of the Recognition of De Facto Governments." In *Inter-American Juridical Yearbook.* Washington, D.C.: Organization of American States, 1948.

Gil, Federico. *Latin American Relations of the United States.* New York: Harcourt Brace Jovanovich, 1971.

Glauert, E. T. and L. D. Langley, eds. *The United States and Latin America.* Reading, Mass.: Addison Wesley, 1961.

Goldhamer, Herbert. *The Foreign Powers in Latin America.* Princeton: Princeton University Press, 1972.

Gómez Robledo, Antonio. *Idea y Experiencia de América.* Mexico: Fondo de Cultura Económica, 1958.

Graham, Robert A. *A Study of Church and State on the International Plane.* Princeton: Princeton University Press, 1959.

Grunwald, Joseph, Miguel Wioncek, and Martin Carnoy. *Latin American Integration and the United States.* Washington, D.C.: Brookings Institution, 1972.

Guerra y Sánchez, R. *La Expansión Territorial de los Estados Unidos a Expensas de España y de los Países Hispanoamericanos.* Havana: n.p., 1935.

Inman, Samuel Guy. *Latin America: Its Place in World Life.* New York: Harcourt, Brace, and Co., 1947.

———. *Inter-American Conferences, 1826–1954.* Washington: University Press of Washington, D.C., 1965.

Jacobini, H. B. *A Study of the Philosophy of International Law as Seen in the Works of Latin American Writers.* The Hague: Martinus Nijhoff, 1954.

de Leturia, Pedro. *Relaciones entre la Santa Sede e Hispanoamérica.* 3 vols. Rome and Caracas: Sociedad Bolivariana de Venezuela, 1959.

Mecham, John L. *A Survey of U.S.–Latin American Relations.* Boston: Houghton Mifflin, 1965.

———. *Church and State in Latin America.* Rev. ed. Chapel Hill: University of North Carolina Press, 1966.

———. *The United States and Inter-American Security, 1889–1960.* Austin: University of Texas Press, 1961.

Munro, Dana G. *Intervention and Dollar Diplomacy in the Caribbean, 1900–1921.* Princeton: Princeton University Press, 1964.

———. *The U.S. and the Caribbean Republics, 1921–1933.* Princeton: Princeton University Press, 1974.

Nabuco, Carolina. *The Life of Joaquim Nabuco.* Stanford: Stanford University Press, 1950.

Quesada, Vicente G. *Historia Diplomática Hispanoamericana.* 3 vols. Buenos Aires: La Cultura Argentina, 1918–1920.

Rippy, J. Fred. *British Investments in Latin America, 1822–1949.* Minneapolis: University of Minnesota Press, 1959.

Robertson, W. S. *Hispanic American Relations with the United States.* New York: Oxford University Press, 1923.

Stuart, Graham T. *Latin America and the United States.* Fifth edition. New York: Appleton-Century-Crofts, 1955.

Tambs, Lewis A. "Geopolitical Factors in Latin America." In Norman A. Bailey, ed. *Latin America: Politics, Economics, and Hemisphere Security.* New York, Washington, London: Frederick A. Praeger, 1965.

Ugarteche, Pedro. *Diplomacia Chilena, 1826–1926.* Lima: n.p., 1926.

Whitaker, Arthur P. *The Western Hemisphere Idea: Its Rise and Decline.* Ithaca, N.Y.: Cornell University Press, 1954.

Williams, Mary W. *Anglo-American Isthmian Diplomacy, 1815–1915.* Washington: American Historical Association, 1916.

General—Eighteenth Century

Bernstein, Harry. *Origins of Inter-American Interest, 1700–1812.* Philadelphia: University of Pennsylvania Press, 1945.

Cortesão, Jaime, ed. *Alexandre de Gusmão e o Tratado de Madrid (1750).* 8 vols. Rio de Janeiro: Ministerio das Relações Exteriores, Instituto Rio Branco, 1950–60.

Fulton, Norman. *Relaciones Diplomáticas entre España y los Estados Unidos a fines del Siglo XVIII.* Madrid: Facultad de Filosofia y Letras, 1970.

Pereira Salas, Eugenio. *Los Primeros Contactos entre Chile y los Estados Unidos (1778–1809).* Santiago: Editorial Andrés Bello, 1971.

International Aspects of Independence Movements, 1775–1825

Bosch-García, Carlos. *Problemas Diplomáticos del México Independiente.* Mexico: Colegio de México, 1947.

Calogeras, Joao Pandiá. *Política Exterior do Imperio.* 2 vols. Rio de Janeiro: Imprensa Nacional, 1927.

Griffin, Charles C. *The United States and the Disruption of the Spanish Empire, 1810–1822.* New York: Columbia University Press, 1937.

Guerra Iñiguez, Daniel. *El Pensamiento Internacional de Bolívar.* Caracas: "Ed. Ragon," 1955.

Hasbrouck, Alfred. *Foreign Legionnaires in the Independence of Spanish South America.* New York: Columbia University Press, 1928.

Humphreys, Robert A., ed. *British Consular Reports on the Trade and Politics of Latin America, 1824–26.* London: Royal Historical Society, 1940.

Kaufmann, William W. *British Policy and the Independence of Latin America.* New Haven: Yale University Press, 1951.

Lockey, J. B. *Pan Americanism: Its Beginnings.* New York: Macmillan, 1920.

Manning, W. R. *Diplomatic Correspondence of the United States Concerning the Independence of the Latin American Nations.* Washington, D.C.: Government Printing Office, 1925.

de Mendoça, Renato. *Historia da Política Exterior do Brasil, 1500–1852.* Mexico: Fondo de Cultura Económica, 1944.

Miramón, Alberto. *Diplomáticos de la Libertad.* Bogotá: Empresa Nacional de Publicaciones, 1956.

Piccirilli, Ricardo. *San Martín y la Política de los Pueblos.* Buenos Aires: Ediciones Gure, S.R.L., 1957.

Robertson, W. S. *France and Latin American Independence.* Baltimore: Johns Hopkins University Press, 1939.

Rydjord, John. *Foreign Interest in the Independence of New Spain.* Durham, N.C.: Duke University Press, 1935.

Vicuña MacKenna, Benjamin. *San Martín, la Revolución de la Independencia del Perú.* Vol. VIII of *Obras Completas.* Santiago: Universidad de Chile, 1938.

Webster, C. K., ed. *Britain and the Independence of Latin America, 1812–30.* 2 vols. London and New York: Oxford University Press, 1938.

Whitaker, Arthur P. *The United States and the Independence of Latin America.* Baltimore: Johns Hopkins University Press, 1941.

General—Nineteenth Century

Barrenechea y Raggada, Oscar. *Congresos y Conferencias Internacionales Celebradas en Lima, 1847–1894.* Buenos Aires: Peusee, 1947.

Becker, Jerónimo. *Historia de las Relaciones Exteriores de España durante el Siglo XIX.* 3 vols. Madrid: n.p., 1924–26.

Bosch-García, Carlos. *Relaciones Diplomáticos Hispanoamericanos, 1839–1898.* Mexico: Colegio de México, 1949.

Burr, Robert N. *By Reason or Force.* Berkeley, Los Angeles, London: University of California Press, 1965.

———. *The Stillborn Panama Congress: Power Politics and Chilean-Colombian Relations During the War of the Pacific.* Berkeley and Los Angeles: University of California Press, 1962.

Burr, Robert N. and H. D. Hussey. *Documents on Inter-American Cooperation, 1810–1945.* Philadelphia: University of Pennsylvania Press, 1955.

Bushnell, David. "The Religion Question in the Congress of Gran Colombia." *The Americas,* XXXI (July, 1974), 1–17.

Chávez, Julio César. *Historia de las Relaciones entre Buenos Aires y el Paraguay, 1810–1813.* Buenos Aires: n.p., 1959.

Cuevas Cancino, Francisco. *Del Congreso de Panamá a la Conferencia de Caracas, 1826–1954.* 2 vols. Caracas: n.p., 1955.

Davis, William Columbus. *The Last Conquistadores: The Spanish Intervention in Peru and Chile, 1863–66.* Athens: University of Georgia Press, 1950.

Drouet, Benigno Checa. *La Doctrina Americana de uti possidetis de 1810.* Lima: Imprenta Gil, 1936.

Frazer, R. W. "The Role of the Lima Congress in the Development of Pan Americanism." *Hispanic American Historical Review,* XXIX (August, 1949), 319–48.

Magnet, A. *Orígenes y Objetos del Panamericanismo.* Santiago: Collección de Estudios de Derecho Internacional, 1945.

Manning, W. R. *Diplomatic History of the United States: Inter-American Affairs.* 12 vols. Washington, D.C.: Government Printing Office, 1932–39.

Nuremberger, G. A. "The Continental Treaties of 1856: An American Union Exclusive of the United States." *Hispanic American Historical Review,* XX (March, 1940), 32–35.

Perkins, Dexter. *A History of the Monroe Doctrine.* Boston: Little Brown, 1955.

———. *The Monroe Doctrine, 1823–1826.* Cambridge, Mass.: Harvard University Press, 1927.

———. *Monroe Doctrine, 1826–1867.* Baltimore: Johns Hopkins University Press, 1932.

———. *Monroe Doctrine, 1867–1907.* Baltimore: Johns Hopkins University Press, 1937.

Pratt, Julius W. *Expansionists of 1898.* Baltimore: Johns Hopkins University Press, 1936.

Rippy, J. Fred. *Rivalry of the United States and Great Britain over Latin America, 1808–1830.* Baltimore: Johns Hopkins University Press, 1929.

Scroggs, William O. *Filibusters and Financiers: The Story of William Walker and His Associates.* New York: Russell and Russell, 1963.

Seckinger, Ron L. "South American Power Politics During the 1820's," *Hispanic American Historical Review,* LVI (May, 1976), 241–67.

Van Aken, J. F. *Pan-Hispanism: Its Origins and Development to 1866.* Berkeley: University of California Press, 1959.

Williams, Mary W. *Anglo-American Isthmian Diplomacy, 1815–1915.* Washington, D.C.: American Historical Association, 1916.

————. "Secessionist Diplomacy of Yucatán." *Hispanic American Historical Review*, IX (May, 1929), 132–43.

Yepes, J. M. *Del Congreso de Panamá a la Conferencia de Caracas, 1826–1954.* 2 vols. Caracas: n.p., 1955.

General—Twentieth Century

Ameringer, Charles E. D. "Philippe Bunau-Varilla: New Light on the Panama Canal Treaty." *Hispanic American Historical Review*, XLVI (February, 1966), 28–52.

Burr, Robert N. and H. D. Hussey. *Documents on Inter-American Cooperation, 1810–1945.* Philadelphia: University of Pennsylvania Press, 1955.

Conn, Stetson and Byron Fairchild. *The Framework of Hemisphere Defense.* Washington, D.C.: Government Printing Office, 1960.

Cruchaga Ossa A., Alberto. *Estudios de Historia Diplomática Chilena.* Santiago: Editorial Andrés Bello, 1962.

De Conde, Alexander. *Herbert Hoover's Latin American Policy.* Stanford, Calif.: Stanford University Press, 1951.

Dozer, Donald. *Are We Good Neighbors? Three Decades of Inter-American Relations, 1930–1960.* Gainesville: University of Florida Press, 1959.

Fenwick, Charles G. *The Organization of American States.* Washington, D.C.: n.p., 1963.

Fernández Shaw, Félix G. *La Organización de los Estados Americanos.* Madrid: Ediciones Cultura Hispánica, 1959.

Gatell, Frank O. "The Canal in Retrospect: Some Panamanian and Colombian Views." *The Americas*, XV (July, 1958), 23–36.

Ireland, Gordon. *Boundaries, Possessions, and Conflicts in Central and North America and the Caribbean.* Cambridge, Mass.: Harvard University Press, 1941.

————. *Boundaries, Possessions, and Conflicts in South America.* Cambridge, Mass.: Harvard University Press, 1938.

Kelchner, William H. *Latin American Relations with the League of Nations*, Vol. III. Boston: World Peace Foundation, 1930.

Levinson, Jerome and Juan de Onís. *The Alliance that Lost its Way: A Critical Report on the Alliance for Progress.* Chicago: Quadrangle Books, 1970.

Nystrom, J. Warren and Nathan A. Haverstock. *The Alliance for Progress.* Princeton, N.J.: Van Nostrand, 1966.

Parkinson, F. *Latin America, the Cold War, and the World Powers.* Beverly Hills, Calif.: Sage Publications, 1974.

Poppino, Rollie E. *International Communism in Latin America, a History of the Movement, 1917–1963.* Glencoe, Ill.: Free Press, 1964.

Ronning, C. Neale. *Law and Politics in Inter-American Diplomacy.* New York: John Wiley and Son, 1963.

Thomas, Ann Van Wynen and A. J. Thomas, Jr. *The Organization of American States*. Dallas: Southern Methodist University Press, 1963.

Wood, Bryce. *The Making of the Good Neighbor Policy*. New York: Columbia University Press, 1965.

———. *The United States and Latin American Wars, 1932–42*. New York: Columbia University Press, 1965.

Wythe, George. *The United States and Inter-American Relations*. Gainesville: University of Florida Press, 1964.

Yepes, J. M. *Del Congreso de Panamá a la Conferencia de Caracas, 1826–1954*. Caracas: n.p., 1955.

Zook, David. *The Conduct of the Chaco War*. New York: Bookman Associates, 1960.

Argentina

Alberdi, Juan Bautista. *Historia de la Guerra del Paraguay*. Originally published in 1865. Buenos Aires: Ediciones de la Patria Gratia, 1962.

"Argentine-Paraguay Boundary Treaty." *The Geographical Review*, XXVI (January, 1946), 153–54.

Bagú, Sergio. *Argentina en el Mundo*. Mexico: Fondo de Cultura Económica, 1961.

Barba, Enrique M. "Las Relaciones Exteriores con los Países Americanas." In *Historia de la Nación Argentina*. Edited by Ricardo Levene. Buenos Aires: Libreria y Editorial, 1951.

Caicedo Castilla, J. J. *El Panamericanismo*. Buenos Aires: R. Depalma, 1961.

Dallegri, Santiago. *El Paraguay y la Guerra de la Triple Alianza*. Buenos Aires: Instituto Amigos del Libro Argentino, 1964.

Ferns, H. S. *Britain and Argentina in the Nineteenth Century*. Oxford: Clarendon Press, 1960.

Haring, Clarence H. *Argentina and the United States*. Boston: World Peace Foundation, 1942.

Lascano, Víctor. *América y la Política Argentina: Antecedentes Diplomáticos e Históricos*. Buenos Aires: n.p., 1938.

McGann, Thomas F. *Argentina, the United States, and the Inter-American System, 1880–1914*. Cambridge: Harvard University Press, 1957.

Moreno Quintano, L. M. *Política Internacional de la República Argentina*. Buenos Aires: Universidad Nacional, Instituto de Derecho Internacional Publicación, 1948.

Peterson, Harold F. *Argentina and the United States, 1810–1960*. New York: University Publishers, Inc., 1964.

Potash, Robert. *The Army and Politics in Argentina, 1928–1968*. Stanford: Stanford University Press, 1969.

Rodríguez Araya, Raúl. "La Doctrina Monroe y la República Argentina." *Revista de Derecho Internacional* (Havana, December 31, 1951), 454–71.

Rosa, José María. "La Doctrina de Monroe y su Aplicación en la República Argentina." *Revista Científica, Jurídica y Social*, Tercera Epoca, año 9, no. 41, pp. 5–29.

Ruíz Moreno, Isidro. *Historia de las Relaciones Exteriores Argentinas, 1810–1955.* Buenos Aires: Editorial Perrot, 1961.

Whitaker, Arthur P. *The United States and Argentina.* Cambridge: Harvard University Press, 1955.

Barbados

Makinson, David H. *Barbados, A Study of North American–West Indian Relations, 1739–1789.* London: n.p., 1964.

Belize, see also Guatemala

García Bauer, Carlos. "Belize, Problema de América." *Revista Brasileira de Política Internacional*, Año IV, Núm. 13 (March, 1961), 37–60.

Humphries, Robert A. *The Diplomatic History of British Honduras, 1638–1901.* London: Oxford University Press, 1961.

Mendoza, José Luís. *Britain and Her Treaties on Belize, British Honduras.* Second edition. Trans. by Lilly de Jongh Osborne. Guatemala: Ministry for Foreign Affairs, 1959.

Bolivia

Blaiser, Cole. "The United States, Germany, and the Bolivian Revolutionaries, 1941–1946." *Hispanic American Historical Review*, LII (February, 1972), 26–54.

Fifer, J. Valerie. *Bolivia: Land, Location, and Politics Since 1825.* New York: Cambridge University Press, 1972.

Holland, E. James. "An Historical Study of Bolivian Foreign Relations, 1935–1946." Ph.D. dissertation, The American University, 1967.

Vergara Vicuña, Aquiles. *Bolivia y Chile: Lecciones del Pasado, Advertencia para el Porvenir.* La Paz: Imprenta Intendencia Gral. de Guerra, 1936.

Brazil

de Abranches, Dunshee. *Brazil and the Monroe Doctrine.* Rio de Janeiro: Imprensa Nacional, 1915.

Accioly, Hildebrando. *O Reconhecimento de Brasil pelos Estados Unidos de América.* Second edition. São Paulo: Editôra Nacional, 1945.

———. *Os Primeiros Núncios no Brasil.* São Paulo: Instituto Progresso Editorial, 1949.

————. *Limites do Brasil: A Fronteira com o Paraguai.* São Paulo: Companhia Editôra Nacional, 1938.

de Barros, Jaime. "A Diplomacia Brasileira e a Defesa da America." *Cultura Política*, III (November, 1943), 107–111.

————. *A Política Exterior do Brasil, 1930–1942.* Rio De Janeiro: Departamento de Imprensa e Propaganda, 1941.

Burnes, E. Bradford. *The Unwritten Alliance: Rio Branco and Brazilian-American Relations, 1902–1912.* New York: Columbia University Press, 1966.

Calmón, Pedro. *Brazil e América: Historia de Uma Política.* Rio de Janeiro: J. Olympio, 1943.

Calógeras, João Pandiá. *A Política Exterior do Imperio.* 2 vols. Rio De Janeiro: Imprensa Nacional, 1927.

de Carvalho, Carlos Miguel Delgado. *Historia Diplomática do Brasil.* Ser. 3, Vol. 65. São Paulo: Companhia Editôra Nacional, 1959.

Chaves, Omar Emir. "Fronteiras do Brasil. Limites com a República da Colombia. Os Tratados." *Biblica Militar*, LXIII (1943), 219.

Cortesão, Jaime, ed. *Alexandre de Gusmão e o Tratado de Madrid (1750).* 4 pts. 8 vols. Rio de Janeiro: Ministerio das Relações Exteriores, Instituto Rio Branco, 1950–60.

————. *Historia do Brasil nos Velhos Mapas.* 2 vols. Rio de Janeiro: Ministerio de Relações Exteriores, Instituto Rio Branco, 1971.

da Costa, João Frank. *Joaquím Nabuco e a Política Exterior do Brasil.* Rio de Janeiro: Graf Record, 1968.

Dantas, Santiago. *Política Externa Independente.* Rio de Janeiro: Editôra Civilização Brasileira, S.A., 1962.

Ganzert, Frederic William. "The Boundary Controversy in the Upper Amazon Between Brazil, Bolivia, and Peru." *Hispanic American Historical Review*, XIV (November, 1934), 427–49.

Graham, Richard. *Britain and the Onset of Modernization in Brazil, 1850–1914.* New York: Cambridge University Press, 1968.

Grande, Humberto. "A Doutrina do Panamericanismo Belico e o Brasil." *Cultura Política*, Ano 5, No. 48 (January, 1945), 26–42.

Haring, Clarence H. *Empire in Brazil: A New World Experiment in Monarchy.* Cambridge: Harvard University Press, 1958.

Hill, Lawrence F. *Diplomatic Relations Between the United States and Brazil.* Durham, N.C.: Duke University Press, 1932.

Hilton, Stanley E. *Brazil and the Great Powers, 1930–1939.* Austin: University of Texas Press, 1975.

de Holanda, Nestor. *Diálago Brasil–URSS.* Rio-Bahia: Editôra Civilização Brasileira, 1960.

————. *O Mundo Vermelho*. Rio de Janeiro: Irmãos Pongetti, 1961.

Leita Filho, Barreto. "Operation Pan America: Primeiro Ano de Discussões e Negociacões." *Revista Brasileira de Política Internacional*, II (March, 1959), 44–47.

Lima, Manoel de Oliveira. *O Reconhecimiento do Imperio*. Rio de Janeiro. Libraria Garnier, 1902.

Lyra, H. *Historia Diplomática e Política Internacional*. Rio de Janeiro: Editôra Civilização Brasileira, 1941.

McCann, Frank D., Jr. *The Brazilian-American Alliance: 1937–1945*. Princeton: Princeton University Press, 1974.

Manchester, Alan. *British Pre-eminence in Brazil*. Chapel Hill: University of North Carolina Press, 1933.

Ministerio das Relações Exteriores. *Archivo Diplomático da Independencia*. 5 vols. Rio de Janeiro: Ministerio das Relações Exteriores, 1923.

————. *Brasil e a Segunda Guerra Mundial*. Rio de Janeiro: Imprensa Nacional, 1945.

————. *Lista de Publicações, 1826–1950*. Rio de Janeiro: Ministerio das Relações Exteriores, 1950.

————. *O Tratado de 8 de Setembro de 1909 entre os Estados Unidos e a República do Peru*. Rio de Janeiro: Imprensa Nacional, 1910.

Napoleão, Aluizio. *Rio Branco e os Relações Entre o Brasil e os Estados Unidos*. Rio de Janeiro: Imprensa Nacional, 1947.

Quadros, Jânio. "Brazil's New Foreign Policy." *Foreign Affairs*, XL (October, 1961), 19–27.

Rodríguez, José Honório. *Brazil and Africa*. Translated from Portuguese, original title *Brasil e Africa, Outro Horizonte*. Berkeley: University of California Press, 1965.

Selcher, W. A. *The Afro-Asian Dimension of Brazilian Foreign Policy*. Gainesville: University of Florida Press, 1970.

Storrs, K. L. "Brazil's Independent Foreign Policy, 1961–1964." Ph.D. dissertation, Cornell University, 1973.

Vianna, Hélio. *Historia das Fronteiras do Brasil*. 2 vols. Rio de Janeiro: Biblioteca Militar, 1948–49.

Warren, Harris G. "Brazil's Paraguayan Policy, 1868–1876." *The Americas*, XXVII (April, 1972), 388–406.

British Commonwealth Caribbean

Augier, F. R., *et al. The Making of the West Indies*. London: n.p., 1960.

Burns, Alan C. *History of the British West Indies*. Rev. ed. New York: Barnes and Noble, 1965.

Glasgow, Roy Arthur. "The Commonwealth Caribbean Countries." In H. E.

Davis *et al.*, *Latin American Foreign Policies.* Baltimore: Johns Hopkins University Press, 1975.
Newton, Arthur P. *The European Nations in the West Indies, 1492–1700.* London: n.p., 1933.
Watt, D. C. "American Strategic Interests and Anxieties in the West Indies." *Journal of the Royal Service Institute,* CXIII (1963), 224–32.

Central America. See also individual countries

Karnes, Thomas L. *The Failure of Union: Central America, 1824–1960.* Chapel Hill: University of North Carolina Press, 1961.
————. "The Central American Republics." In H. E. Davis, *et al.*, *Latin American Foreign Policies.* Baltimore: Johns Hopkins University Press, 1975.
Ministerio de Relaciones Exteriores. *Carta de la Organización de Estados Centroamericanos (ODECA).* San José: Imprenta Nacional, 1967.
Moreno, Laudelino. *Historia de las Relaciones Interestatuales de Centro América de Rafael Altamira.* Madrid: Companía Ibero-americana de Publicaciones, 1928.
Munro, Dana G. *The Five Republics of Central America.* New York: Oxford University Press, 1918.
Rodríguez, Mario. *A Palmerstonian Diplomat in Central America: Frederick Chatfield, Esq.* Tucson: University of Arizona Press, 1964.
Soto V., Marco A. *Guerra Nacional de Centroamérica.* Guatemala: Ministerio de Educación Pública, 1957.

Chile

Álvarez, Alejandro. *La Diplomacia de Chile durante la Emancipación y la Sociedad Internacional Americana.* Madrid: Editorial América, 1916.
————. *Rasgos Generales de la Historia Diplomática de Chile, 1810–1910.* Santiago: n.p., 1911.
Barros Borgoño, Luis. *The Problem of the Pacific and the New Policies of Bolivia.* Baltimore: Baltimore Sun, 1924.
Bowers, Claude. *Chile Through Embassy Windows.* New York: Simon and Schuster, 1956.
————. *My Life: The Memoirs of Claude Bowers.* New York: Simon and Schuster, 1962.
Burr, Robert N. *The Stillborn Panama Congress and Chilean-Colombian Relations During the War of the Pacific.* Berkeley: University of California Press, 1965.
————. *By Reason or Force: Chile and the Balancing of Power in South America, 1830–1905.* Berkeley: University of California Press, 1965.

Calderón Cousino, Adolfo. *Short Diplomatic History of the Peruvian-Chilean Relations, 1819–1879*. First English edition. Santiago: Imprensa Universitaria, 1920.

Cardozo, Efraim. *El Imperio del Brasil y el Rio de la Plata: Antecedentes Y Estallido de la Guerra del Paraguay*. Buenos Aires: Librería del Plata, 1961.

Dennis, William J. *Documentary History of the Tacna-Arica Dispute*. Iowa City: University of Iowa Press, 1927.

———. *Tacna and Arica*. New Haven: Yale University Press, 1931.

Espinosa Moraga, Oscar. *El Aislamiento de Chile*. Santiago: n.p., 1961.

———. *Bolivia y el Mar, 1810–1964*. Santiago: n.p., 1964.

Evans, Henry Clay, Jr. *Chile and its Relations with the United States*. Durham, N.C.: Duke University Press, 1927.

Eyzaguirre, Jaime. *Chile y Bolivia; Esquema de un Proceso Diplomática*. Santiago: Zig-Zag, 1963.

Glassner, M. I. "The Rio Lauca: Dispute over an International River." *Geographical Review*, LX (No. 2, 1970), 192–207.

Hamburg, Roger P. "Soviet Foreign Policy. The Church, the Christian Democrats, and Chile." *Journal of Inter-American Studies*, XI (October, 1969), 605–615.

Jordán López, M. *Historia Diplomática de la Guerra del Pacífico*. Santiago: Editoria Universitaria, 1957.

Larraiu, Carlos J. "El Tratado de Paz Chileno-Boliviano de 1904 y sus Proyecciones." *Boletín de la Academia Chilena de la Historia*, XXIX (Segundo Semestre de 1962), 44–72.

Markham, C. R. *The War Between Chile and Peru*. London: S. Low, Marston, Searle and Rivington, 1882.

Ministerio de Relaciones Exteriores. *La Cuestión de Río Lauca*. Santiago: n.p., 1963.

Pike, Frederick B. *Chile and the United States, 1880–1962*. Notre Dame, Ind.: Notre Dame University Press, 1963.

Pinochet de la Barra, Oscar. *La Antártica Chilena*. Third edition. Santiago: Editorial Pacífico, S.A., 1955.

Ríos Gallardo, Conrado. *Chile y Perú: Los Pactos de 1929*. Santiago: Editorial Nascimento, 1959.

Smith, Geoffrey S. "The Role of José M. Balmaceda in Preserving Argentine Neutrality in the War of the Pacific." *Hispanic American Historical Review*, XIL (May, 1969), 254–67.

Soder, John P. "The Impact of the Tacna-Arica Dispute on the Pan American Movement." Ph.D. dissertation, Georgetown University, 1970.

Soto Cárdenas, Alejandro. *Guerra del Pacífico: Los Tribunales Arbitrales (1882–1888)*. Santiago: Universidad de Chile, 1950.

Stuart, Graham H. *Tacna Arica Dispute*. Boston: World Peace Foundation, 1927.

Talbot, Robert D. *A History of the Chilean Boundaries*. Ames, Iowa: Iowa State University Press, 1964.

————. "The Chilean Boundary in the Strait of Magellan." *Hispanic American Historical Review*, XLVII (November, 1967), 519–31.

Tomasek, R. D. "The Chilean Lauca River Dispute and the OAS." *Journal of Inter-American Studies*, IX (1967), 351–66.

Villalobos R., Sergio. *La Disputa del Beagle*. Santiago: Editorial Tradición, 1968.

Worcester, Donald E. *Sea Power and Chilean Independence*. Gainesville: University of Florida Press, 1963.

Yrigoyen, Pedro. *La Alianza Perú-Boliviano-Argentina y la Declaratoria de Guerra de Chile*. Lima: Sanmartí, 1921.

Colombia

Bushnell, David. *Eduardo Santos and the Good Neighbor, 1938–1942*. Gainesville: University of Florida, 1967.

Cadena, Pedro Ignacio. *Anales Diplomáticos de Colombia*. Bogotá: Imprenta Manuel de J. Barrera, 1878.

Cavalier, Germán. *La Política Internacional de Colombia*. 4 vols. Bogotá: Editorial Iqueima, 1959.

Córdoba, Diago Luis. *El Debate sobre el Protocolo del Rio de Janeiro*. Bogotá: Imprenta Nacional, 1936.

Forero León, L. A. *Dos Ciudades: La Iglesia y el Estado*. Bogotá: Editorial Ferrini, 1938.

García de la Parra, Pablo. *Colombia en las Conferencias Panamericanas*. Bogotá: Editorial Minerva, 1926.

García Samudio, Nicolás. *República de Colombia*. Bogotá: Imprenta Nacional, 1950.

Kitchens, John W. "Mosquera's Missions to Chile and Peru." *The Americas*, XXIX (October, 1972), 151–72.

League of Nations. *The Verdict of the League; Colombia and Peru at Leticia*. Boston: World Peace Foundation, 1933.

Miner, Dwight C. *The Fight for the Panama Route*. New York: Columbia University Press, 1940.

Ministerio de Gobierno. *El Generalísimo Trujillo y Colombia*. Bogotá: Imprenta Nacional, 1955.

Ministerio de Relaciones Exteriores. *Historia de la Cancillería de San Carlos: Pórtico*. Bogotá: Ministerio de Relaciones Exteriores, 1942.

Olarte Camacho, Vicente. *Los Convenios con el Perú*. Bogotá: Imprenta Nacional, 1911.

República de Colombia. *La Política Internacional.* Bogotá: Imprenta Nacional, 1936.

Restrepo, Juan Pablo. *La Iglesia y el Estado en Colombia.* London: Gilbert & Rivington, Ltd., 1885.

Rippy, Fred J. *The Capitalists and Colombia.* New York: Vanguard Co., 1931.

Rivas, Raimundo. *Relaciones Internacionales entre Colombia y los Estados Unidos, 1810–1850.* Bogotá: Imprenta Nacional, 1915.

———. *Historia Diplomática de Colombia, 1810–1934.* Bogotá: Imprenta Nacional, 1961.

Roosevelt, Theodore. "How the United States Acquired the Right to Dig the Panama Canal." *Outlook,* XCIX (October 7, 1911), 314–15.

Suárez, Marco Fidel. *Doctrina Internacional.* Bogotá: Imprenta Nacional, 1955.

Uribe, Antonio José. *Colombia y los Estados Unidos de América.* Bogotá: Imprenta Nacional, 1931.

———. *Colombia, Venezuela, Costa Rica, Eucador, Brasil, Nicaragua y Panama.* Bogotá: Imprenta Nacional, 1931.

Costa Rica

Cochrane, James D. "Costa Rica, Panama, and Central American Economic Integration." *Journal of Inter-American Studies,* VII (July, 1955), 331–44.

Gonzales Viques, Cleto. "Relaciones entre Costa Rica y Nicaragua." *Brecha* (San José), IV (January, 1959), 1–4.

Gutiérrez, Carlos José. "Neutralidad e Intervención. Dirección y Problemas de la Política Internacional Costarricense durante el Primer Tercio del Siglo XX." *Revista de La Universidad de Costa Rica,* XIV (November, 1956), 9–61.

Obregón Loria, Rafael. "Nuestras Relaciones Internacionales a Mediados del Siglo XIX." *Revista de la Universidad de Costa Rica,* XIV (November, 1956), 63–140.

Salisbury, Richard V. "Domestic Politics and Foreign Policy, Costa Rica's Stand on Recognition, 1923–1934." *Hispanic American Historical Review,* LIV (August, 1974), 453–78.

Cuba

Aguilar, Luís E. *Cuba 1933; Prologue to Revolution.* Ithaca: Cornell University Press, 1972.

Callahan, James M. *Cuba and International Relations: A Historical Study in American Diplomacy.* Baltimore: Johns Hopkins University Press, 1899.

Concheso, Aurelio. *Cuba en la Vida Internacional.* Jena and Leipzig: n.p., 1935.

Draper, Theodore. *Castro's Revolution: Myths and Realities.* New York: Frederick A. Praeger, 1962.

Ettinger, Amos A. *The Mission to Spain of Pierre Soule, 1853–1855: A Study in the Cuban Diplomacy of the United States.* New Haven: Yale University Press, 1932.

Fitzgibbon, Russel H. *Cuba and the United States, 1900–1935.* Menasha, Wis.: George Banta, 1935.

Gellman, Irwin F. *Roosevelt and Batista: Good Neighbor Diplomacy in Cuba, 1933–1945.* Albuquerque: University of New Mexico, 1973.

Guerra Sánchez, Ramiro. *Cuba en la Vida Internacional.* Havana: n.p., 1923.

Pérez, Louis A., Jr. "Army, Politics, Diplomacy and the Collapse of the Cuban Officer Corps: The 'Sergeants' Revolt of 1933." *Journal of Inter-American Studies,* VI, Pt. I (May, 1974), 59–74.

Portell Vilá, Herminio. *Historia de Cuba en sus Relaciones con los Estados Unidos y España.* 4 vols. Havana: Jesús Montero, 1938–41.

Realy, David F. *The United States in Cuba, 1890–1902: Generals, Politicians, and the Search for Policy.* Madison: University of Wisconsin Press, 1963.

Smith, Robert P. *The United States and Cuba: Business and Diplomacy, 1917–1960.* New York: Bookman Associates, 1960.

Suárez, Andrés. *Cuba: Castroism and Communism, 1956–1966.* Cambridge: M.I.T. Press, 1967.

Thomas, Hugh. *Cuba: The Pursuit of Freedom.* New York: Harper and Row, 1971.

Urban, Stanley C. "The Africanization of Cuba Scare 1853–1855." *Hispanic American Historical Review,* XXXIII (February, 1957), 29–45.

Dominican Republic

Atkins, G. Pope and Larman C. Wilson, *The United States and the Trujillo Regime.* New Brunswick, N.J.: Rutgers University Press, 1972.

El Tratado Trujillo-Hull y la Liberación de la República Dominicana. Bogotá: Consorcio Editorial, 1941.

Gleijeses, Piero. *La Crise Dominicaine, 1965.* Milan: A. G. Battaia, 1973.

Gómez, Remón Tamames. *La República Dominicana y la Integración Económica de América Latina.* Buenos Aires: Instituto para la Integración de América Latina, 1968.

Inchaústegui Cabral, Joaquín M. *Historia Dominicana, 1844–1941.* Ciudad Trujillo, Santo Domingo: Librería Dominicana, 1953.

Lowenthal, Abraham F. *The Dominican Intervention.* Cambridge: Harvard University Press, 1972.

Martin, John Bartlow. *Overtaken by Events: The Dominican Crisis from the Fall of Trujillo to the Civil War.* Garden City, N.Y.: Doubleday, 1966.

Peña Batlle, Manuel. *Historia de la Cuestión Fronteriza Dominican-Haitiano.* Ciudad Trujillo, Santo Domingo: Editora L. Sánchez Andujar, 1946.

Szulc, Tad. *Dominican Diary.* New York: Delacorte Press, 1965.

Welles, Sumner. *Naboth's Vineyard: The Dominican Republic, 1844–1924.* 2 vols. New York: Payson & Clarke, 1928.

Ecuador

Bustamante Muñoz, Antonio. *Lista de los Instrumentos Internacionales Concluídos por el Ecuador.* Quito: Editorial Casa de la Cultura Ecuatoriana, 1960.

Cabeza de Vaca, Manuel. *Aspectos Históricos y Jurídicos de la Cuestión Limítrofe: las negociaciones en Washington y los Desenvolvimientos Posteriores.* Quito: Talleres Gráficos Nacionales, 1956.

García, Leonidas. "La Doctrina de Tobar." *Revista de la Sociedad Jurídico-literaria* (Quito), New Series, I (January–February, 1913).

Ministerio de Relaciones Exteriores. *El Protocolo de Río de Janeiro con el Sistema Jurídico Interamericano y con el Derecho Internacional.* Quito: Case de la Cultura Ecuatoriana, 1960.

Pattee, Richard. "García Moreno y la Política Internacional Ecuatoriana." *Boletín de la Academia Nacional de Historia*, Special Edition, XVII (January–June, 1939).

Pérez Concha, Jorge. *Ensayo Histórico-crítico de las Relaciones Diplomáticos del Ecuador con los Estados Limítrofes.* 2 vols. Quito: Editorial Casa de la Cultura Ecuatoriana, 1958–1959.

Pino Ycaza, Gabriel. *Derecho Territorial Ecuatoriano.* Second edition. Guayaquil: Imprenta de la Universidad, 1953.

Scholes, W. and M. V. Scholes. "The United States and Ecuador: 1909–1913." *The Americas*, XIX (January, 1963), 276–90.

Tudela, Francisco. *The Controversy Between Peru and Ecuador.* Lima: Imprenta Torres Aguirre, 1941.

Tumbes, Jaen and Maynas Tumbes. *Estudio integral de la Controversia Limítrofe Peruano-Ecuatoriana hasta el Protocolo de Río de Janeiro y su renuncia por el País del Norte, con sinópsis histórica de las operaciones militares en 1941.* Lima: Ministerio de Relaciones Exteriores, 1961.

Vasquez, Honorato. *Memoria Histórico-Jurídica sobre los limítes Ecuatoriana-Peruanos.* Quito: Imprenta Nacional, 1904.

Zook, David H. *Zaramilla Marañón: The Ecuador-Peru Dispute.* New York: Bookman, 1964.

El Salvador

Blutstein, Howard I., *et al. Area Handbook for El Salvador.* Washington, D.C.: The American University Press, 1971.
De la Neutralidad Vigilante a la Mediacíon con Guatemala. San Salvador: Publicaciones de la Secretaría de Información de la Presidencia, 1955.

Guatemala

Arrutia-Aparicio, Carlos. *Juridical Aspects of the Anglo-Guatemala Controversy: in re Belize.* Washington, D.C.: n.p., 1951.
Grieb, Kenneth J. "Jorge Ubico and the Belize Boundary Dispute." *The Americas*, XXX (April, 1974), 445–74.
Mendoza, José Luís. *Britain and her Treaties on Belize, British Honduras.* Trans. by Lilly de Jongh Osborne; second edition. Guatemala: Ministry for Foreign Affairs, 1959.
Ministerio de Educación de Guatemala. *Límite entre Guatemala y México.* Second edition. Guatemala: Editorial del Ministerio de Educación, José Pineda Ibarra, 1964.
Ministerio de la Relaciones Exteriores, República de Guatemala. *Libro Blanco: Controversia entre Guatemala y la Gran Bretaña relativa a la Convención de 1859, Sobre Asuntos Territoriales.* Guatemala: n.p., 1938.
Schneider, Ronald M. *Communism in Guatemala, 1944–1954.* New York: Frederick A. Praeger, 1958.

Guyana

Glasgow, Roy Arthur. *Guyana.* The Hague: Martinus Nijhoff, 1970.
Millette, James. "Doctrines of Imperial Responsibility." *New World* (Georgetown, Guyana, Independence Issue), 79–85.
Mitchell, William B., *et al. Area Handbook for Guyana.* Washington, D.C.: Foreign Area Studies Division, The American University, 1969.
Newman, Peter. *British Guiana.* London: Oxford University Press, 1964.

Haiti

Davis, H. P. *Black Democracy: The Story of Haiti.* Rev. ed. New York: McVeigh, 1936.
Logan, Rayford. *Diplomatic Relations of the U.S. with Haiti 1776–1891.* Chapel Hill: University of North Carolina Press, 1941.
———. *Haiti and the Dominican Republic.* New York, London: Oxford University Press, 1968.
Millspaugh, Arthur C. *Haiti under American Control.* Boston: World Peace Foundation, 1931.
Montague, Ludwell Lee. *Haiti and the United States, 1774–1938.* Durham, N.C.: Duke University Press, 1940.

Honduras

Zelaya, Antonio, ed. *Las Conferencias de Mediación en la Controversia de Fronteras en las Repúblicas de Honduras y Nicaragua.* San José, Costa Rica: Impresión Trejos, 1938.

Jamaica. See also British Commonwealth Countries

Great Britain Colonial Office. *Report on Jamaica.* London, 1946–55, also Kingston, 1956.

Mexico

Archivo Histórico Diplomático Mexicano. 40 vols. Mexico: Secretaría de Relaciones Exteriores, 1928–.

Arnaiz, Arturo, and Freg and Claude Bataillon, eds. *La Intervención Francesa y el Imperio de México, Cien Años Después, 1862–1962.* Mexico: Associación Mexicana de Historiadores, Instituto Francesa de América Latina, 1965.

Blumberg, Arnold. *The Diplomacy of the Mexican Empire, 1863–1867.* Philadelphia: The American Philosophical Society, 1971.

Callahan, James M. *American Foreign Policy in Mexican Relations.* New York: Macmillan Company, 1932.

Carreño, Alberto María. *La Diplomacia Extraordinaria entre México y Estados Unidos, 1789–1947.* 2 vols. Mexico: Editorial Jus, 1951.

Carrillo Flores, Antonio. "La Politica Exterior de México." *Foro Internacional,* VI (July, 1965–June, 1966), 233–46.

Castañeda, Jorge. *Mexico and the United Nations.* New York: Carnegie Endowment for Peace, 1958.

Castillo Nájera, Francisco. *El Petróleo en la Indústria Moderna.* México: Cámara Nacional de la Indústria de Transformación, 1949.

Cline, Howard F. *The United States and Mexico.* Cambridge: Harvard University Press, 1953, 1963.

Comisión Nacional para la Celebración del Sesquicentenario de la . . . Independencia . . . y del Cincuentenario de la Revolución Mexicana. *Labor Internacional de la Revolución Constitucionalista de México.* Documents, 1913–1918. Mexico: 1960.

Cosío Villegas, Daniel. *Cuestiones Internacionales de México.* Mexico: Secretaría de Relaciones Exteriores, 1966.

———. 6 vols. *Historia Moderna de México,* Vols. V and VI. Mexico: Ed. Hermes, 1955–63.

Cronon, David E. *Josephus Daniels in Mexico.* University of Wisconsin Press, 1960.

Daniels, Josephus. *Shirt-Sleeve Diplomat.* Chapel Hill: University of North Carolina Press, 1947.

Delgado, Jaime. *España y México en el siglo XIX*. Madrid: Instituto Gonzalo Fernández de Oviedo, 1950.

Diáz, Lilia, ed. *Versión Francesa de México, 1864–1867*. 4 vols. Mexico: El Colegio de México, 1967.

Estrada, Genaro. *Un Siglo de Relaciones Internacionales de México (a través de los mensajes presidenciales)*. Mexico: Imprenta de la Secretaría de Relaciones Exteriores, 1935.

Fabela, Isidro. *Historia Diplomática de la Revolución Mexicana*. 2 vols. Mexico: Fondo de Cultura Económica, 1958, 1959.

García Robles, Alfonso. *Política International de México*. Mexico: Talleres Gráfico de la Nación, 1946.

Gómez Robledo, Antonio. *México y Arbitraje Internacional. El Fondo Piadoso de las Californias. La Isla de la Pasión. El Chamizal*. Mexico: Ed. Porrúa, 1965.

Kühn, Joachim. *Das Ende des Maximilianischen Kaiserreichs in Mexico*. Gottingen, Berlin, Frankfurt: Musterschmidt Verlag, 1965.

Luquín, Eduardo. *La Política Internacional de la Revolución Constitucionalista*. Mexico: Instituto Nacional de Estudios Históricas de las Revolución Mexicana, 1957.

Meyer, Lorenzo. *México y Estados Unidos en el Conflicto Petróleo 1917–1942*. Mexico: El Colegio de México, 1968.

Ojeda Gómez, Mario. "México en el Ambito Internacional." *Foro Internacional*, VI (1965–66), 247–70.

d'Olwer, Nicholau, ed. *Relaciones Hispano-Mexicanos, 1839–*. 3 vols. Mexico: El Colegio de México, 1949–.

Parson, Harlow S. *Mexico Oil*. New York: Harper, 1942.

Price, Glen W. *Origins of the War with Mexico*. Austin: University of Texas, 1967.

Rippy, J. Fred. *The United States and Mexico*. New York: Alfred A. Knopf, 1926.

Rives, George L. *The United States and Mexico, 1821–1842*. 2 vols. New York: Charles Scribner's Sons, 1913.

Shelby, Charmion. "Mexico and the Spanish American War." In *Essays in Mexican History*, edited by Thomas Cotner and Carlos Castañeda. Austin: Institute of Latin American Studies, University of Texas, 1958.

Smith, Justin H. *The War with Mexico*. 2 vols. New York: Macmillan Co., 1919.

Teja Zabre, Alfonso. *Historia de México: Una Moderna Interpretación*. Mexico: Secretaría de Relaciones Exteriores, 1935.

Turlington, Edgar Willis. *Mexico and Her Foreign Creditors*. New York: Columbia University Press, 1930.

Weckmann, Luis, ed. *Las Relaciones Franco-Mexicanas.* Vol. II. Mexico: Secretaría de Relaciones Exteriores, 1962.

Zorrilla, Luis G. *Historia de las Relaciones entre México y los Estados Unidos de América, 1800–1958.* Vols. XXIX and XXX. Mexico: Editorial Porrúa, 1965–66.

Nicaragua

Bailey, Thomas A. "Interest in a Nicaragua Canal, 1903–1931." *Hispanic American Historical Review,* XV (1936), 2–28.

Cordero Reyes, Manuel and Carlos Cuadra Pasos. *Exposición y Sugerencia de la Delegación de Nicaragua en el Litigio de Límites con Honduras.* Managua: Ministerio de Relaciones Exteriores, 1957.

Cox, Isaac Joslin. *Nicaragua and the United States 1909–1927.* Boston: World Peace Foundation, 1927.

Hill, Roscoe R. *Fiscal Intervention in Nicaragua.* New York: Columbia University Press, 1933.

Rippy, J. Fred. "Justo Rufino Barrios and the Nicaraguan Canal." *Hispanic American Historical Review,* XX (May, 1940), 190–97.

Ryan, John Morris, *et al. Handbook for Nicaragua.* Washington, D.C.: The American University, 1970.

Panama

Arosemena G., Diogenes A. *Documentary Diplomatic History of the Panama Canal.* Panama: University of Panama Press, 1961.

Bunau Varilla, Philippe. *Panama, the Creation, Destruction and Resurrection.* London: Constable, 1913.

Curtis, W. J. *The History of the Purchase by the United States of the Panama Canal: The Manner of Payment and the Distribution of the Proceeds of Sale.* Birmingham, Ala.: n.p., 1909.

DuVal, Miles P. *Cadiz to Cathay: The Story of the Long Diplomatic Struggle for the Panama Canal.* Second edition. Stanford: Stanford University Press, 1947.

Ealy, Lawrence O. *The Republic of Panama in World Affairs, 1903–1950.* Philadelphia: n.p., 1951.

Liss, Sheldon B. *The Canal.* Notre Dame, Ind.: University of Notre Dame Press, 1967.

Mack, Gerstle. *The Land Divided.* New York: Knopf, 1944.

McCain, William D. *The United States and the Republic of Panama.* Durham: Duke University Press, 1937.

Miner, Dwight Caroll. *The Fight for the Panama Route.* New York: Columbia University Press, 1940.

Paraguay

Area Handbook for Paraguay. Washington, D.C.: Foreign Area Studies Division, The American University, 1972.

Baéz, Cecilio. *Historia Diplomática del Paraguay*. 2 vols. Asunción: n.p., 1931–32.

Box, Pelham H. *The Origins of the Paraguayan War*. Urbana: University of Illinois Press, 1929.

Cooney, Jenny W. "Paraguayan Independence and Doctor Francia." *The Americas*, XXVIII (April, 1972), 407–428.

Sánchez Quell, Hipólito. *Política Internacional del Paraguay 1811–1870*. Asunción: Imprenta Nacional, 1936.

Ynsfran, Pablo Max, ed. *The Epic of the Chaco: Marshall Estigarriba's Memoirs of the Chaco War, 1932–1935*. Austin: University of Texas Institute of Latin American Studies, 1950.

Peru

de la Barra, Felipe. *Historiografía General y Militar Peruana y Archivos. Introducción al Catálogo del Archivo Histórico Militar del Perú*. Lima: Imprenta del Diet, 1962.

Basadre, Jorge. *Historia de la República del Perú*. Fifth edition; 10 vols. Lima: Editorial Historia, 1961.

Belaúnde, Victor Andrés. *La Vida Internacional del Perú*. Lima: Imprenta de Torres Aguirre, 1942.

Carey, James Charles. "United States Policy in Peru, 1919–1930." Ph.D. dissertation, University of Colorado, 1948.

Corpancho, Manuel Nicolás. *Perú y Ecuador. Cuestión Internacional . . .* Lima: Impreso por J. E. del Campo, 1861.

Gálvez, Juan I. *Conflictos Internacionales: El Perú contra Colombia, Ecuador y Chile*. Lima: Librería Orfeo, 1919.

García Salazar, Arturo. *Historia Diplomática del Perú: Chile, 1884–1922*. Lima: n.p., 1930.

García Sayan, Enrique. *Notas Sobre la Soberanía Marítima del Perú, Defensa de las 200 Millas de Mar Peruano ante las Recientes Transgresiones*. Lima: n.p., 1955.

Resumen de Historia Diplomática del Perú, 1820–1884. Lima: Talleres Gráficos Sanmartí y cía., 1928.

Mariátegui Oliva, Ricardo. *Nuestra Patria y sus Fronteras: Historia de los Límites del Perú*. Lima: n.p., 1961.

Moore, John Bassett. *Brazil and Peru: Boundary Question*. New York: Knickerbocker Press, 1904.

Pike, Frederick B. *The Modern History of Peru*. New York: Frederick A. Praeger, 1967.

Porras Barrenechea, Raúl. *Historia de los Límites del Perú*. Lima: Casa Historial E. Rosay, 1926.
Quell, Otto. "Iber-Amerikanisches Archiv." *Literaturbericht,* VIII (1934), 297–338, 381–417; IX (1936), 50–89, 133–50.

Trinidad and Tobago. See also British Commonwealth Caribbean

Carmichael, Gertrude. *The History of the Indian Islands of Trinidad and Tobago, 1498–1900*. London: n.p., 1961.

Uruguay

Fitzgibbon, Russell H. *Uruguay, Portrait of a Democracy*. New Brunswick, N.J.: Rutgers University Press, 1954.
Taylor, Philip B. *Government and Politics of Uruguay*. New Orleans: Tulane University Press, 1960.
Weil, Thomas E., *et al. Area Handbook for Uruguay*. Washington, D.C.: Foreign Areas Studies Division, The American University, 1971.

Venezuela

González Oropesa, Hermán, and Pablo Ojer Caligueta. "Informe que los Expertos Venezolanos para la Cuestión de Límites con Guayana Británica Presentan al Gobierno Nacional." *Revista "Sic,"* No. 284 (April, 1966), separate 16-page publication.
Jatar Dotti, Braúlio. "Las Divergencias de Venezuela en Cartagena sobre Integración Subregional." *Política* (Caracas), VIII (November, 1969), 11–28.
Landaeta Rosales, Manuel. *Invasiones de Colombia a Venezuela en 1901– 2–3*. Caracas: Imprenta Bolívar, 1903.
Ministerio de Relaciones Exteriores. *Informes que los Expertos Venezolanos para la Cuestión de Límites con Guyana Británica Presentan al Gobierno Nacional*. Caracas: Relaciones Exteriores, 1967.
————. *Reclamación de la Guyana Esequibo. Documents, 1962–66*. Caracas: Relaciones Exteriores, 1967.
————. *Anales Diplomáticos de Venezuela*. Caracas: Relaciones Exteriores, n.d.
Parra, Francisco J. *Doctrinas de la Cancillería Venezolana*. New York: Las Americas Publishing Co., 1956.
————. *Estudios de Derecho Venezolano*. New York: Las Americas Publishing Co., 1955.
Platt, D. C. M. "The Allied Coercion of Venezuela, 1902–1903: A Reassessment." *Inter-American Economic Affairs*, XV (1962), 3–28.

Ralston, Jackson H., ed. *Report of French-Venezuelan Mixed Claims Commission of 1902.* Washington, D.C.: Government Printing Office, 1906.
————. *Venezuelan Arbitrations of 1903.* Washington, D.C.: Government Printing Office, 1904.
Rojas, Armando, ed. *Los Creadores de la Diplomacia Venezolana.* Caracas: n.p., 1965.
Schoenrich, Otto. "The Venezuela–British Guiana Boundary Dispute." *American Journal of International Law*, XLIII (July, 1949), 523–30.
de Sola, René. *Guyana Esequibo y el Acuerdo de Ginebra.* Caracas: n.p., 1966.

Index